Feminist Designer

Feminist Designer ✳ ✳

→ On the
Personal ☺
and the
🌧 Political
in Design 🌐

**Edited by
Alison Place**

The MIT Press
Cambridge, Massachusetts
London, England

The MIT Press would like to thank the anonymous peer reviewers who provided comments on drafts of this book. The generous work of academic experts is essential for establishing the authority and quality of our publications. We acknowledge with gratitude the contributions of these otherwise uncredited readers.

Designed by Alison Place. This book was set in Bastardo Grotesk designed by Giulia Boggio, CoFo Sans designed by Maria Doreuli, and Fraunces designed by Phaedra Charles. Printed and bound in the United States of America.

Library of Congress Cataloging-in-Publication Data

Names: Place, Alison (Alison L.), editor.
Title: Feminist designer : on the personal and the political in design / edited by Alison Place.
Description: Cambridge, Massachusetts : The MIT Press, [2023] | Includes bibliographical references and index.
Identifiers: LCCN 2022049787 (print) | LCCN 2022049788 (ebook) | ISBN 9780262048422 (hardcover) | ISBN 9780262375894 (epub) | ISBN 9780262375900 (adobe pdf)
Subjects: LCSH: Design--Social aspects. | Feminist aesthetics.
Classification: LCC NK1520 .F46 2023 (print) | LCC NK1520 (ebook) | DDC 744--dc23/eng/20221116
LC record available at https://lccn.loc.gov/2022049787
LC ebook record available at https://lccn.loc.gov/2022049788

10 9 8 7 6 5 4 3 2 1

This book is dedicated to all the feminist teachers—past, present, and future.

Contents

Preface

In the feminist spirit of transparency, this preface offers an account of how this book came to be, by whom, through what means, and within what context. In many ways, writing, compiling, and editing *Feminist Designer* was a feminist project in itself.

I inhabit this world as both conspirator and judge. My positionality has undoubtedly played a role in the book's content and development. I am a white, cisgendered, able-bodied woman. I am a mother. I am educated with an advanced degree and hold a position of considerable power as a tenure-track professor at a research university and as the director of a design program. My educational background and professional experience are in the fields of graphic design and journalism. I have worked in both corporate design jobs and nonprofit institutions. I am not a feminist scholar in the traditional sense, but reading and learning feminist theory have profoundly shaped me as a person.

I came to feminism the same way many white millennial girls did who grew up in the 1990s in the United States—through the highly marketed narrative of "girl power." I was raised by parents who taught me I could be anything despite being a girl, and that's the takeaway I carried with me throughout my adolescence, despite some lingering feelings that something wasn't right. I learned about the women's movement in history class as a kind of relic of the past, and although I agreed with feminism in principle, I was under the impression it was no longer necessary to identify with the label. Upon entering adulthood, my politics evolved quickly and constantly as my eyes—and my body—met the real world: sexism in the workplace, abusive relationships with men, state politics that limited my bodily autonomy, as well as insidious discrimination and inequality in politics, the media, health care, and the economy. I arrived at a new understanding of feminism's role in my life just in time for the presidential election of 2016 and the most brazen display of systemic sexism and misogyny I had ever witnessed.

In the fall leading up to the election, while conducting research for my graduate thesis, I interviewed a white, male, distinguished professor who was involved in developing a policy that affected political speech on campus. The interview went horribly awry—he berated me, manipulated me, and denigrated my thesis work. He also made sure his sexist views were known about the first female presidential candidate in US history. It wasn't the sexism or even the abuse of his power that shocked me—it was how easily the encounter stumped me and prevented me from doing my job. I came away from that experience feeling exasperated but determined to better equip myself to do the work of feminism as a designer and researcher. Years later, I set out to write the book I needed in that moment.

Content for this book was gathered and developed through three different avenues. In 2021, I posted an open call for proposals, seeking case studies, essays, or other formats of work that demonstrated feminist ways of doing design.

I received 135 submissions in response to the open call; I selected 17 of them. I invited 16 additional contributions to round out the topics and perspectives represented. I wrote and developed all other content.

Many of the ideas shared in my writing are not new, and many of them are also not my own. This book was built on the shoulders of feminist giants—profoundly shaped and informed by philosophers, political scientists, social scientists, scholars, designers, and activists whose knowledge and inspiration saturate these pages. Citation is not just a feminist act but also feminist memory. In the words of Sara Ahmed, "Citations can be feminist bricks: they are the materials through which, from which, we create our dwellings."[1] If this book is a dwelling and the citations are bricks, the contributors are the walls, the roof, the floors, and the cozy furniture. They built upon the structure of the concept and brought it to life. I took my curatorial duties as an editor seriously and worked painstakingly to represent a wide range of disciplines, backgrounds, topics, and geographical locations in the book. This framework required me to reject many incredible submissions and actively to seek out contributors whose work might be less well known. All of the writing in this book was created *for* this book, with only a few exceptions, which are noted in the text. Each author engaged in a collaborative process with me to arrive at the final text and image selections. There was much deliberation, discussion, and editing throughout the process.

Finally, and most importantly, every single person whose work resides within these pages was compensated for their labor and their intellectual property. Each contributor was offered an honorarium of $250 (per author, not per contribution). I asked authors who are white, in well-supported academic positions, or are otherwise dominantly situated to consider forgoing their honoraria so that a larger pool of funds could be distributed to authors who are Black, Indigenous, people of color or nonwhite, are LGBTQIA+, are from the Global South, or identify with any other historically excluded group. About half the authors decided to forego their honoraria, which allowed me to pay those who identified as marginalized $500 per person. The honoraria were funded by a combination of sources: the advance I received from the publisher, an endowed fellowship award from the University of Arkansas, and annual research funds provided by my department. My research assistants, whose work was also invaluable to bringing this book to life, were compensated hourly for their labor.

The process of writing and editing this book took place during a particular moment in time both in the world and in my life, and this context inevitably shaped the content and tone. Although not originally the impetus for the book, an animating force while writing it was the complete and utter exhaustion I felt as a woman and a new mother existing in the United States amid a racist and sexist presidency, a global pandemic, and an ever-growing assault on human rights. Less than two weeks after I printed copies of my book proposal to share with publishers at a conference, COVID-19 shut down the world. When I signed my contract with the publisher, I was working from home full-time with my partner and a one-year-old, with no access to childcare. Over the next year and a half, time carved out of my schedule for writing was interrupted or abandoned many times by family quarantines and daycare classroom closures due to COVID outbreaks and staffing shortages. I wrote many pages of this book one-handed on my phone while nursing an infant. I wrote many more pages while that infant turned toddler watched *Daniel Tiger's Neighborhood* on the couch next to me, or on weekends in my office away from my family. The work continued, sporadically but earnestly, through an intense pre-tenure review, a new appointment as director of my program, the purchase of and moving into a house, several more COVID surges, and, in the six months leading up to my manuscript deadline, two miscarriages in a row. Two weeks after I turned in the manuscript, the Supreme Court ruling in *Dobbs v. Jackson Women's Health Organization* immediately overturned *Roe v. Wade* and stole the right to safe and legal abortion and maternal health care away from every person with a uterus in the United States. This book is a response, whether directly or indirectly, to these many ongoing and overlapping lived realities; it is an insistence upon the right to be heard, the right to care for one's self, and the right to be cared for by others.

When I started writing this book, I came across the words of author Toni Cade Bambara in an interview in *Black Women Writers at Work*: "I have no shrewd advice to offer developing writers about this business of snatching time and space to work," she said. "I do not have anything profound to offer mother-writers or worker-writers except that it will cost you something. Anything of value is going to cost you something."[2] These words stuck with me throughout the process, reminding me that struggle was inevitable, maybe even useful. She was right—it did cost me something. Any cause or effort we devote ourselves to will necessarily ask something of us. But struggle is not always virtuous, and I lived in the tension between my ambition and my need for self-preservation. The tumult of the past few years brought hardship, but it also brought clarity; I became more convinced than ever that this book needed to be in the world and more committed than ever to not harming myself while bringing it to life. The pandemic, the academic tenure track, and early motherhood were the crucible that morphed this book into being and in many ways morphed me into being as well.

1   Sara Ahmed, *Living a Feminist Life* (Durham, NC: Duke University Press, 2017), 16.

2   Toni Cade Bambara, "Toni Cade Bambara," interview in *Black Women Writers at Work*, ed. Claudia Tate (Continuum, New York 1983), 16.

When did feminism become a word that not only spoke to you, but spoke you, spoke of your existence, spoke you into existence? When did the sound of the word feminism become your sound?

Sara Ahmed

LIVING A FEMINIST LIFE

On the personal and the political in design

Alison Place

Design today is troubled—and troubling.

The role of design in our lives has exploded in recent decades to become nearly ubiquitous and almost entirely unavoidable. It mediates our relationships, our work, our communication, our health, our communities, our sense of self. Few if any aspects of our existence are untouched by the design of artifacts, spaces, systems, and technologies. Design is often touted as an intervention for improving or optimizing our lives, which obscures its role in reflecting and perpetuating deeply embedded power structures in society that oppress people, exploit labor, and deplete resources. We tend to overestimate how much of design's negative impact is due to individual designers' implicit bias, while overlooking how deeply entangled it is in complex power structures and deeply rooted systems of oppression. Occasionally, it is possible to draw a line directly from a decision made by a designer to an instance of blatant oppression, such as automated soap dispensers that don't recognize hands with dark skin or an airport scanning machine that allows bodies to be read only as male or female. But the ways in which design reinforces oppression are most often not so clear, webbed in systems and processes that are much more complex than one ignorant decision. When design is part of the solution, it is also inevitably part of the problem, too.

Design is an activity that humans have always done. It was only relatively recently professionalized as the discipline that we understand it as today. In *Design, When Everybody Designs*, Ezio Manzini writes that "in a world in rapid and profound transformation, we are all designers,"[1] including individuals, organizations, businesses, public entities, cities, and nation-states. However, as Sasha Constanza-Chock argues in *Design Justice,* inclusive visions of design as a universal human activity conflict with the political and economic realities of the discipline. "True, everyone designs," they write, "but only certain kinds of design work are acknowledged, valorized, remunerated and credited."[2] The discussion of design throughout this book aims to expand upon the traditional understanding of design in order to validate alternative ways of doing design, while simultaneously calling on professionalized designers to use their power within the systems they can access to enact much-needed change.

The existing frameworks we have for doing design equitably leave much to be desired. Design for good, design for social impact, and human-centered design are frames whose very existence demonstrate that dominant ways of doing design are neither good nor socially beneficial. Most designers say they want to improve people's lives, but good intentions are not enough. Even socially conscious frameworks leave a designer woefully ill equipped to address the complex and changing role that design plays in reinforcing power structures and reproducing inequality. In our increasingly globalized world—and our increasingly *designed* world—designers need to understand the complexities of power and be held accountable for the role they play in larger social, political, economic, and environmental systems.

In other words, designers should all be feminists.[3] Feminism is not just about gender; it is also about power. When viewed through a feminist lens, the trouble with design is not simply a matter of unintended consequences—it is a matter of ingrained power structures that influence design's methods and dictate its impact. Now more than ever, we need feminist ways of doing design, and we need ways of doing feminism through design. The purposes of engaging feminism within design are, first, to examine the ways in which designed artifacts and systems as well as design processes and methods either reinforce or undermine oppression at the intersection of gender, race, class, ability, and other situated identities and, second, to propose and make space for alternative ways of doing design otherwise. Feminism and design have more in common than you might think. As collective endeavors to shape human experiences, the two share mutually beneficial objectives; design provides a medium for putting feminist theory into action, and feminism provides a framework for making that action more equitable and beneficial to the lived experiences of real people. Design is still a rapidly evolving discipline, and it is reasonable to understand it as a project that is unfinished and possible to change. At its root, design is a way of thinking, learning, and engaging with the world. So is feminism.

What Is Feminism?

A plurality of evolving definitions, critiques, and objectives has been a hallmark of feminism since its inception. In the United States, the history of the feminist movement is often divided into "waves" marked by specific political and cultural contexts. (Many feminists, however, reject the notion of "waves," arguing that it obscures and devalues the impact of feminist action taking place between the waves and creates the illusion that feminism lies dormant at all other times.) A brief history of feminism in the United States will help us here.

"First-wave feminism" refers to the suffragette movement in the late nineteenth and early twentieth centuries, focusing on women's right to vote and participate in democratic government. It was led by white women who sought political equality with men and largely exploited and undermined the participation and interests of Black women, Indigenous women, and other women of color.

"Second-wave feminism" refers to the women's liberation movement in the 1960s and 1970s, which was concerned with the economic and social emancipation of women from patriarchal structures.[4] Taking place alongside the civil rights movement, it saw the establishment and rise of Black feminist thought. It was characterized by internal struggles between women of different races and classes, struggles that informed alliances and strategies moving forward.

"Third-wave feminism" began in the 1990s and confronted the second-wave position on femininity, exploring constructions of gender in the media, embodied performances of gender, and other gender norms. Some say we're still in the third wave, but most feminists believe the past decade has brought about a fourth wave, driven by the internet and women's abilities to share stories and call attention to abuse. It includes hashtag activism, such as #MeToo, and a focus on intersectionality, while calling for rights such as equal pay and bodily autonomy.

Today, in the early 2020s, the state of feminism is less clear. If it's true that feminist movements tend to come in waves, the fervor of the Women's March in 2017, the Kavanaugh Supreme Court confirmation hearings in 2018, and "nevertheless, she persisted" seem to have given way to a post-Trump, post-COVID, and—most devastatingly—post-*Roe* malaise. Women bore the brunt of the pandemic, working the most overtaxed and underprotected jobs (as teachers, nurses, caregivers of the elderly and the young), cutting their hours to take on additional care duties, or leaving the workforce altogether. The era of the #girlboss is decidedly over, but it's not yet clear if it's because we finally see through the deceptive scam of "leaning in" or if we're simply too exhausted to try. Perhaps it is inevitable that a movement that was at the height of fashion in the past decade would start to seem out of touch in the next. As the journalist Michelle Goldberg wrote in the *New York Times* in June 2022, "Feminism is particularly given to cycles of matricide; what is liberating to one generation is often mortifying to the next."[5]

This book stems largely from feminist histories, theories, and pedagogies that emerged in the United States, while aiming to highlight and amplify transnational feminisms. The struggle against patriarchy and male domination has always taken place in every corner of the globe. Because virtually all countries are structured by patriarchal mentalities, the global standard for being human is male, and women in nearly every culture and country are "othered"—a common condition that is both unique to each locality and context yet deeply familiar to every human who identifies as a woman. Feminist movements have emerged in countries around the world in response to issues such as abuse, war, unpaid labor, exclusion from the workforce, poor housing conditions, lack of access to education, limited economic opportunity, restricted bodily autonomy, ecological destruction, and more. In the introduction to *Sisterhood Is Global: The International Women's Movement Anthology*, Robin Morgan writes that "an indigenous feminism has been present in every culture in the world and in every period of history since the suppression of women began."[6] Although white women with class power have long declared ownership of the feminist movement, Black women, lower-class women, and other women of color have always done the work of feminism, with or without the label. The brand of feminism that has been exported from North America and Europe often connotes a neocolonial paternalism in which white women declare themselves "liberated" and thus are in the position to "liberate" their less fortunate sisters[7] (a theme explored in depth in Maryam Mustafa's essay in chapter 2). Discussions of feminism throughout this book aim to be vigilant in critique of white feminism and its allegiance to the ruling class within the white-supremacist capitalist patriarchy.

Feminism has been endlessly reinvented, repackaged, and revised over the past two hundred years. It has always been a shape-shifter, not because it can't decide what it should be but precisely because it *refuses* to decide what it should be. It contorts, bends, and crouches to fit into the spaces it needs to go. It morphs, evolves, and transforms to respond to what it's up against. Sara Ahmed says that "to live a feminist life is to make everything into something that is questionable."[8] Feminism is about questioning norms, power structures, and ideologies, including feminism itself. A major strength of the feminist movement throughout history has been its self-critical tendency, the willingness to change direction when needed. As feminist scholar and writer bell hooks put it, "Just as our lives are not fixed or static but are always changing, our theory must remain fluid, open, responsive, to new information."[9] Feminism does not give us meaning; we give meaning to it through our struggles.

Because of this continuous change through struggle, feminism defies a singular definition. Contemporary views on the values, objectives, and impacts of feminism vary widely. Today, feminism can range from a serious political agenda to a buzzword with a devotional gloss. Popular definitions, such as the Beyoncé brand of feminism,[10] tend toward meanings that focus on women's equality with men, a summary with which most feminist theorists would disagree. hooks promoted the widely influential definition that feminism is a "political movement to end sexism and sexist oppression,"[11] a definition we'll return to throughout this book. Others take a more expanded view, opting for a feminism that encompasses more than just the opposition to oppression based on sex (a thread explored in depth in chapter 4). hooks was outspoken in her insistence that each component of her definition was critical to advancing feminist causes. In 2016, she sharply criticized Beyoncé for invoking the term *feminist* while perpetuating what hooks viewed as the commodification of a movement.[12] The next year, 2017, *Merriam-Webster* named *feminism* the word of the year, and hooks again called for action. "We have to restore feminism as a political movement," she said in an interview with *BUST*. "The challenge to patriarchy is political, not a lifestyle or identity. We have to return to very basic education for critical consciousness around what visionary feminist politics really is about."[13]

Within academics, feminism is viewed as a domain of critical theory that examines "ways in which literature or other cultural reproductions reinforce or undermine the economic, political, social, and psychological oppression of women."[14] Such frameworks prove limiting for our current overlapping crises of wealth inequality, social injustice, and environmental collapse. Eschewing the need for a single definition, this book engages with feminism, first and foremost, as a critique and analysis of power. Within the pages that follow, you'll see this framework employed to resist power structures relating to gender, but often the effort goes well beyond gender. Owing to the concept of intersectionality and the key assertions of Black feminist thought (see chapter 1 on power), this book emphasizes that oppression based on gender is never just about gender. A simultaneous examination by means of race, class, sexual orientation, and other markers of identity is necessary to elucidate the overlapping oppressions most people face. Feminist critiques of power aim to connect individual experiences to the systems that oppress them. This book also explores critiques of power in design that consider impacts on more than just humans (see chapter 3 on care). Patriarchal domination manifests in all systems in all places, even within each of us.

Feminist perspectives in design are not new, and this book aims to expand and build on previous contributions to meet the demands of our current moment. Entanglements of feminism in design have perhaps seen their own "waves" of interest, responding to political and social contexts over time. Early perspectives connecting feminism and design came about with the second wave of feminism and the emergence of women's studies, calling attention to the ways in which women had been excluded as both designers and users. As various design professions began to examine women's experiences in designed environments, the examination brought into question the dichotomies public/private, city/suburb, work/home.[15] For the first time, women's diverse needs were considered. Most often, a feminist focus on design concerned itself with history, recovering women's contributions and intervening in the white, male-dominated canon. That was Cheryl Buckley's aim when she laid out a feminist agenda for design history in her essay "Made in Patriarchy" in 1986, stating that "a feminist approach is neither a side-issue nor a novel historical perspective—it is a central concern of contemporary design history." She called attention to the "cultural codes" and "rules of the game" that have obscured, ignored, or distorted women's role as producers or consumers of design.[16]

Over the past 50 years, feminist perspectives in design have grown in many areas of the discipline and even flourished in some, despite continuing to be marginalized. The design disciplines where feminist voices have arguably been most prolific are architecture and urban planning, forcing reexaminations of how women and families live and how spatial design privileges certain genders and bodies.[17] Industrial design and graphic design have also employed feminist perspectives as a way of analyzing the role of gender in the material culture of designed artifacts.[18]

Not surprisingly, feminist approaches to design have generally been concerned with the relationship between *women* and design—how they are affected by it and how their contributions to it are regarded. These two inquiries have been thoroughly investigated in existing literature. Historically, they tended to be based on universal accounts of women, which assumed a cisgender, white, heterosexual, able-bodied woman. Only recently has the work expanded to advance our understanding of the ways in which the impacts of design are felt at the intersections of gender and race, class, and other identities. Most feminist discourse in design seems to imply that the problems raised would not be problems if more designers were women and if their perspectives were valued. As a result, the feminist refrain within design for decades has been the repeated call for representation and inclusion of women in the field. This book, however, is a call for us to move beyond this narrow application of a feminist lens. Feminist design is not only about what designers do or who does it—it is about *how* we do design and *why*. More women in the design field and more designs made for women are not sufficient solutions to address the complex role design plays in perpetuating sexism and racism or the exploitation of labor and resources. This book instead calls in feminist critiques of power to reimagine all aspects of the design discipline—our tools, our methods, our relationships, our institutions, our culture, and our impact.

There is some historical precedent for feminist ways of doing design. Sheila de Bretteville was one of the first influential voices to promote feminist design as a methodology. From 1971 to 1974, she led the Feminist Design program at the California Institute of the Arts, where she aimed to nurture creativity by teaching women to value and express their unique capacities as women, such as creating relationships, working collectively, nurturing others, and providing comforting environments. Women in the program learned to bring feminist approaches to commercial design projects, to create nonthreatening living and working environments, and to utilize technology to build, rather than replace, human relationships. De Bretteville laid out key elements of feminist design, such as making women's experiences public and visible; encouraging strength, grace, and warmth; establishing a caring and responsible connection between people and things; and striving to transform the dominant, male-centered culture of design.[19]

> ✳ Feminist design is not just a thing
> you do; it's how you do every thing. ✳

Fifty years later, de Bretteville's methodological approach is echoed in the expansive ways that feminism is applied to design today. Contemporary approaches to feminist design are simultaneously well established and continually emerging. From graphic design to industrial design to design research, designers are questioning normative thinking and embracing design in the *otherwise*. They are rejecting design's entanglements with capitalism, confronting the patriarchal roots of the educational system, rethinking paternalistic ways of regarding "users," creating access for more voices and views, and reimagining a professional culture that centers collaboration and care. I would especially like to call attention to the work of the feminist technology and design scholars Shaowen Bardzell, Catherine d'Ignazio, and Sasha Costanza-Chock, whose work surrounding issues of equity and feminism in design has been deeply influential in the development of this book and blazed the trail for it to exist.

The rapidly expanding array of feminist design practices shows there are a need and a demand for a more equitable and just design discipline. Feminist designers are pushing the discipline forward with novel tactics and mindsets to meet the demands of our current political, social, and ecological challenges. In many ways, though, they are also softening the discipline—smoothing its sharp, arrogant edges and making it pliable, porous, and adaptable as we evolve toward an uncertain future. The voices within this book are just a few in the growing chorus of feminist designers working in every area of the discipline, in diverse ways, to enact change. They are an embodiment of the commitment that feminist design is not just a thing you do; it's how you do every thing.

What's in This Book

First, a few words on what this book is not.

This book is not about women designers or what it's like to be a woman in design, although you will find perspectives and stories of many designers who identify as womxn.[20] It is not about doing design for feminist causes, although it presents many feminist issues raised and addressed through design. It is not about the history of feminist design or about feminist retellings of design history, although historical perspectives of both feminism and design undergird many of the concepts and discussions throughout the book. It is not a catalog of selected designers who should be idolized as founders or leaders of feminist design, although you will find many inspiring examples of leadership within these pages.

This book is about doing design in feminist ways, with an emphasis on tools, methods, and frameworks and how they inform what we do and the impact we have. The ideas are relayed through the personal experiences of feminist designers, sharing what it's like to be a person who operates design through a feminist lens. It features the voices of 43 contributors representing 16 different countries on six continents and addressing more than a dozen areas of design, including graphic design, interior design, exhibition design, artificial intelligence, product design, disability design, and design education. The contributors are practitioners, theorists, researchers, educators, and activists, and their diverse—sometimes contradictory—perspectives represent a mix of styles, methods, and conventions. They arrive at feminism from many different places, bringing to it unique values that reflect their background and positionality and thus allowing for greater plurality of lived experience.

This book does not aim to offer an account of what feminism prescribes that we do as designers. As Sara Ahmed writes in *Living a Feminist Life*, feminism does not implore us to adopt a set of ideals or norms of conduct. To present an instruction manual for feminist design would demand the creation of new norms and therefore a new hegemonic system. Ahmed instead offers that feminism might mean asking questions about "how to live better in an unjust and unequal world, how to create relationships with others that are more equal, how to find ways to support those who are not supported or are less supported by social systems."[21] Drawing on Ahmed's words, this book proposes that being a feminist designer is about asking questions—how to do design ethically under capitalism, how to design with people in equitable ways, how to demonstrate care through design, how to teach respectfully, how to collaborate to transform the discipline. It is an invitation to question what design is and to imagine design otherwise.

The content is organized into chapters based on six key themes of feminism, but each theme is fluid and appears throughout the book, not just in a single chapter. Each chapter contains an introduction, case studies, essays, and dialogues that explore the theme from diverse and sometimes conflicting perspectives. Chapter 1, "Power," addresses how power works and the ways in which design is entangled in power structures of domination. Chapter 2, "Knowledge," explores the role that knowledge plays in the design process and the role that design plays in shaping knowledge. Chapter 3, "Care," considers care as an animating force in designing for and with others. Chapter 4, "Plurality," explores what it means to design in a world where many worlds fit. Chapter 5, "Liberation," addresses liberation as both an end goal and a process in feminism and in design. Finally, chapter 6, "Community," considers how we work together to enact change through design. At the end of the book, there is a recommended reading list for each chapter that I and the other authors compiled for further exploration of the concepts within the chapter. The texts in each chapter are entitled similarly—beginning with the word *on* followed by the topic addressed (with one exception)—to convey that neither are these texts authoritative, nor are they the definitive perspective on the subject matter. Each author reflects on a topic through a first-persons lens, from the standpoint of their own situated knowledge, while connecting that topic to wider struggles in feminism and design. As the book's subtitle indicates, the personal is not just political—the personal can also be universal. The more particular we are with our stories, the more people can relate to them. The more space we hold for ourselves, the more space we create for others.

My hope is that this book will create a space for you, dear reader. A space where you feel seen and heard, a space where you find a feminism that speaks to you—not because of what the book brings to you but because of what you bring to it. I also hope that by seeing yourself within these pages, you will find solidarity in the work to be done. Feminism is not just work; feminism is homework. Sara Ahmed says that to become a feminist is to stay a student. "If feminism is an assignment, it is a self-assignment. We give ourselves this task."[22] Our task is to stay vigilant, stay open, and stay curious. To be a feminist designer is to see the world as it is and to continually imagine it otherwise—to willfully occupy the space between epistemological despair and radical hope.

1   Ezio Manzini, *Design, When Everybody Designs: An Introduction to Design for Social Innovation* (Cambridge, MA: MIT Press, 2015), 1.

2   Sasha Costanza-Chock, *Design Justice: Community-Led Practices to Build the Worlds We Need* (Cambridge, MA: MIT Press, 2020), 14.

3   This statement draws from Chimamanda Ngozi Adichie, *We Should All Be Feminists* (New York: Knopf Doubleday, 2014).

4   Betty Friedan, *The Feminine Mystique* (New York: Norton, 1963).

5   Michelle Goldberg, "The Future Isn't Female Anymore," *New York Times*, June 17, 2022, https://www.nytimes.com/2022/06/17/opinion/roe-dobbs-abortion-feminism.html.

6   Robin Morgan, "Planetary Feminism: Politics of the 21st Century," in *Sisterhood Is Global: The International Women's Movement Anthology*, ed. Robin Morgan (New York: Feminist Press, 1996), 5.

7   bell hooks, *Feminism Is for Everybody: Passionate Politics* (New York: Routledge, 2014).

8   Sara Ahmed, *Living a Feminist Life* (Durham, NC: Duke University Press, 2017), 2.

9   bell hooks, *Feminist Theory: From Margin to Center* (1984; repr., London: Routledge, 2000), xiv.

10   In her song "Flawless" (2013), Beyoncé spliced in spoken-word verses about how girls are raised compared to boys, including the line "Feminist: the person who believes in the social, political, and economic equality of the sexes," sparking a renewed interest in the term among young people.

11   hooks, *Feminist Theory*, 26.

12   bell hooks, "Beyoncé's *Lemonade* Is Capitalist Money-Making at Its Best," *Guardian*, May 11, 2016, https://www.theguardian.com/music/2016/may/11/capitalism-of-beyonce-lemonade-album.

13   Lux Alptraum, "bell hooks on the State of Feminism and How to Move Forward under Trump: BUST Interview," *BUST Magazine*, February–March 2017, https://bust.com/feminism/19119-the-road-ahead-bell-hooks.html.

14   Lois Tyson, *Using Critical Theory: How to Read and Write about Literature* (Milton Park, UK: Taylor & Francis, 2011), 83.

15   Joan Rothschild, ed., *Design and Feminism: Re-visioning Spaces, Places, and Everyday Things* (New Brunswick, NJ: Rutgers University Press, 1999).

16   Cheryl Buckley, "Made in Patriarchy: Toward a Feminist Analysis of Women and Design," *Design Issues* 3, no. 2 (1986): 4, doi:10.2307/1511480.

17   For contemporary feminist perspectives in architecture and urban planning, see Meike Schalk, Thérèse Kristiansson, and Ramia Mazé, eds., *Feminist Futures of Spatial Practice: Materialisms, Activisms, Dialogues, Pedagogies, Projections* (Bamberg, Germany: Spurbuchverlag, 2017).

18   Judy Attfield, *Wild Things: The Material Culture of Everyday Life* (Oxford: Berg, 2000).

19   Sheila de Bretteville, "Feminist Design," *Space and Society* 6, no. 22 (1983): 98–103.

20   *Womxn* is an intersectional term intended to signal the inclusion of those who have traditionally been excluded from white feminist discourse: Black women, women of color, trans women, as well as gender-nonconforming and nonbinary people. With the removal of *man* or *men* at the end of the term, *womxn* signals an alternative descriptor because it's not defined in relation to men.

21   Ahmed, *Living a Feminist Life*, 1.

22   Ahmed, *Living a Feminist Life*, 7.

Power

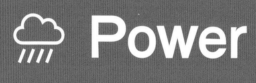

Systems of oppression, inequality, and inequity are by design. Therefore, they can be redesigned.

Antionette Carroll

TWITTER, JUNE 24, 2020

On power

Alison Place

For far too long the design discipline has projected itself as neutral. The stereotypical designer conjures notions of a skilled service provider situated as an impartial channel between client and user. Beginning with their education, professional designers are taught to serve as neutral actors and universal problem solvers. The origins of design's professed neutrality can be traced back to Western-centric pedagogies rooted in modernism, a cultural movement that embraced simplicity and rejected tradition—a framework that still dominates design education today. Modernist design was bolstered by a "fight against ugliness"[1] that rejected traditional aesthetics. This paternalistic perspective prized cleanliness, the absence of clutter, the stripping away of all cultural and social context, and the flattening of character to appear universal. Modernist dogma positioned the designer "above the audience," tasked with "educating the masses,"[2] like a missionary doing the aesthetic work of god. Carried out almost entirely by white men of European origin, successful modern design divorced content from form and context from practitioner. Within this prescriptive structure, design was proclaimed neutral, able to communicate any message and embody any human experience.

Critiques of neutrality in design are not new, but discourse has failed to advance past the subject of neutrality to address design as a social and cultural practice that is deeply interwoven with inequitable power structures. As a discipline, design is woefully late to the discussion about power that has been happening in other disciplines for decades. Understanding the political nature of our actions as well as the systems with which we are complicit is foundational for analyzing and reimagining design through a feminist lens. In an interview in *Eye on Design* magazine in 2019, the design educator Danah Abdulla said, "The choices we make as designers are intrinsically political: With every design choice we make, there's the potential to not just exclude but to oppress."[3] As with all mechanisms of oppression, design choices operate within larger structures of power. In their revelatory book *Design Justice*, Sasha Constanza-Chock asserts that design is an enterprise that reproduces inequalities structured by the *matrix of domination*, a term coined by the Black feminist scholar Patricia Hill Collins[4] to refer to the interlocking systems of white supremacy, heteropatriarchy, capitalism, and settler colonialism. These four structures provide a rich lens with which to understand design's relationship to power.

White Supremacy

Design is a tool that reflects the values and frameworks of dominant ideologies in society. Darin Buzon argues that modernism's (and thus design's) tendency to center itself as the end-all, be-all approach to universal human aesthetics reveals it as a by-product of white supremacy, mirroring the latter's prescriptive superiority complex. "After all," Buzon writes, "what is modernism if not the cultural weapon to erase nonwhite aesthetics?"[5] A discipline dominated by modernist thinking and 71 percent white[6] easily functions as a tool for the erasure of margins and the elimination of difference through symbolic violence. Jen Wang writes that when designers are demographically homogenous, one perspective dominates the discourse on what constitutes "good" design and who creates it. Because whiteness is projected as the default, any so-called neutral tool or method serves whiteness. By creating aesthetic standards of design and typography, modernism codified white supremacy into visual form.[7]

Heteropatriarchy

In addition to whiteness, design favors the straight, cisgender male as the norm and marginalizes or erases bodies that stray from that norm. Heteropatriarchy is a sociopolitical system where primarily cisgender and heterosexual males have authority over cisgender females and people with other sexual orientations and gender identities.[8] For example, body scanners in airport security lines force every body that walks through them to be labeled as "male" or "female," all but erasing trans bodies or any body that exists outside the gender binary. In her book *Invisible Women*, Caroline Criado Perez writes about a phenomenon she calls "one-size-fits-men,"[9] in which ostensibly gender-neutral objects are designed to fit the average proportions of men's bodies by default, making things such as smartphones, pianos, and personal protective equipment uncomfortable, impossible, or even dangerous for women to use.

Capitalism

Design as a professionalized activity was thrust into being by capitalism because it could be systematized and mass-produced, thus generating consumption and materialism. Capitalism is an economic system defined by the private ownership of the means of production and their operation for profit, which pits members of a society against one another. Capitalism, by definition, breeds inequality. It prizes ideals of individualism and competition while incentivizing the exploitation of labor, the depletion of natural resources, and the hoarding of wealth. Design is a cog in the machine of domination that enables the economic prosperity of the Global North through exploitative capitalism that relies heavily on cheap labor and natural resources from the Global South.

Settler Colonialism

Maggie Gram writes, "We attribute to design a kind of superior epistemology: a way of knowing, of 'solving,' that is better than any other method which differs."[10] Designers' self-appointed authority willfully expands their jurisdiction to the point that they may colonize anything as a "design problem" to be solved.[11] (Consider, for example, the self-aggrandizing power of the "how might we" question.) The Native feminist scholars Maile Arvin, Eve Tuck, and Angie Morrill define *settler colonialism* as a persistent social and political formation in which newcomers (colonizers or settlers) come to a place, claim it as their own, and do whatever it takes to disappear the Indigenous peoples, while exploiting the land and importing forced labor.[12] Design is a project of erasure and assimilation whose modernist roots are linked to the colonial rise in power. Our definition of "innovation" originates from countries and cultures that have acquired their dominance through global empires and the far-reaching colonization not only of land and natural resources but also of knowledge, bodies, gender, sexuality, cultural practices, and aesthetics.[13]

Design's complicity in these four structures of power is reflected not only in the design of artifacts, spaces, and technologies but also in the methods and tools designers use, from the white saviorism of design for social impact to the "bullshit"[14] of design thinking. Designers' claim of wanting to improve people's lives without openly contesting established hierarchies or power structures has created a dissonance that we can no longer ignore. A feminist critique of power calls into question many of our ways of doing design.

Although definitions of feminism vary widely, most feminist theory is undeniably concerned with power—critiquing gender subordination, analyzing its intersections with other forms of subordination such as racism and class oppression, and envisioning prospects for individual and collective resistance and emancipation.[15] For women, power is often sold to us through illusory narratives such as "girl power" or—its grown-up equivalent—"empowerment." But power is not gained through experiences that simply make us feel good. Power is influence. Power is agency. Power is the ability to self-actualize and shape the world around you.

The gender scholar Naila Kabeer says that one way of thinking about power is in terms of the ability to make choices; to be disempowered means to be denied choice.[16] Another way we often hear power referred to is as a resource that is unequally and unjustly distributed and must be redistributed, also known as the "distributive model of power."[17] Some feminist theorists reject this definition, arguing that when we view domination as the concentration of power in the hands of a few, we fail to illuminate the broader social, institutional, and structural contexts that shape individual relations of power. If we aim solely for a change in the distribution of power, we risk leaving the power structure itself intact. Many assert instead that power is relational, as in "power-over," or the capacity to impose one's will on others.

Another relational way of analyzing power is through the lens of the "other." Simone de Beauvoir initiated this framing in *The Second Sex*: "She is defined and differentiated with reference to man and not he with reference to her; she is the incidental, the inessential as opposed to the essential. He is the Subject, he is the Absolute—she is the Other."[18] This dichotomy is echoed in the spatial metaphor of the margins versus the center, a foundational framework of the feminist writings of bell hooks[19] and many others. (The concept of the "margins" is explored further in chapter 2.)

Power can also be understood more abstractly. Many feminists have drawn on the concept of disciplinary power[20] to critically analyze normative femininity. The feminist philosopher Sandra Bartky analyzes the disciplinary practices that engender specifically feminine "docile bodies," such as dieting practices, limitations on gestures and mobility, and bodily ornamentation. Bartky observes that "it is women themselves who practice this discipline on and against their own bodies ... a self-policing subject."[21] This self-surveillance, she argues, is a form of obedience to patriarchal norms that are culturally produced within power structures. Design can also be said to hold disciplinary power, shaping behaviors and norms that perpetuate self-surveillance. If design is in the business of producing and upholding norms, feminism is in the business of rejecting norms.

Because power is most often understood from the position of the socially dominant, and domination is implicitly masculine, many feminists prefer to reconceptualize the idea of power from a specifically feminist standpoint, defining it instead through a lens of capacity or ability, as in the capacity to produce change or to transform oneself and others. Nancy Hartsock refers to the feminist understanding of power as "energy and competence rather than dominance."[22] Jean Baker Miller argues that "women may want to be powerful in ways that simultaneously enhance, rather than diminish, the power of others."[23]

> ✳ Deeply rooted power structures are not a conundrum we can "diversity-equity-and-inclusion" our way out of. ✳

Undeniably, the most influential feminist conception of power is intersectionality, which highlights the complex, interconnected, and cross-cutting relationships between diverse modes of domination, including (but not limited to) sexism, racism, class oppression, ableism, and heterosexism.[24] Intersectionality is a concept that grew out of centuries of Black feminism but was coined by the law professor Kimberlé Crenshaw [25] to connect sexism and racism as systems of oppression that work together and mutually reinforce one another, presenting unique problems for Black women who experience them both simultaneously and differently than white women and/or Black men. The Combahee River Collective, a Black feminist organization in Boston in the 1970s, defined this combination as "interlocking systems of oppression."[26] Within intersectionality, power is distinctly relational; people are either dominantly or nondominantly situated in relation to others based on various aspects of their identity and in different contexts. This framework reveals the nuance and complexity of social power inequities at the intersection of multiple identities, which implores us to consider individual experiences rather than to lump social groups together. Intersectional feminism has become the focus of contemporary feminist culture, often used as a rhetorical device to indicate that women are not a monolith or to explicitly reject feminisms that center whiteness by default. An emphasis on power differentials rooted in white supremacy remains key to the application of intersectionality, or, in the words of Flavia Dzodan, feminism will be intersectional, or "it will be bullshit."[27]

When analyzed through various feminist understandings of power, design's relationship to power cannot simply be a tally of who benefits and who is harmed.

Deeply rooted power structures are not a conundrum we can "diversity-equity-and-inclusion" our way out of. Multiple lenses are necessary, as are constant questioning and unlearning. By acknowledging and embracing the complexity of oppression and the myriad shapes it might take, we create space for new ways of navigating, critiquing, redistributing, and dismantling power through design.

Professional designers are invariably in positions of power, whether of the coercive or empowering variety. As discussed in the introduction, the myth that designers are neutral is dangerous because it assumes that the designer is fundamentally well intentioned and unencumbered by cultural or social context. As experience designer Isabelle Yisak says, "The notion that our work calls upon our 'professional' selves and not our 'personal' selves is a problematic one."[28] Designers are humans with viewpoints and situated knowledges, which is not a bad thing. Acknowledging your positionality as a person and a designer is a step toward revealing hidden power structures in the design process. So is identifying your own implicit bias(es) and internalized oppression.

Design that addresses power inequities also requires us to shift our roles and methods. Rather than centering ourselves as experts and handing down solutions to others, our task is to support and enhance the power of people and communities to solve their own problems. This calls for collaborating and codesigning with reduced hierarchies. Rich Hollant, founder of the design studio CO:LAB, asserts that "design is secondary to building relationships and being in communities."[29] However, it must be noted that "socially engaged" design is easily co-opted as a tool for capital rather than collective community work. Design that is powerful in the transformative sense must address the unique individual experiences of marginalized people while remaining critically attuned to broader systems and the roots of problems.

In this chapter, designers, theorists, and educators consider the role of power in design, from branding to pedagogy to cultural aesthetics. They explore themes such as intersectionality, identity, and authority, while posing questions about their own roles within oppressive systems. If design mediates our relationships to established power structures—whether they be familial, institutional, historical, economic, political, cultural, or social—then every design decision either reinforces or subverts a power dynamic. The essays, discussions, and case studies in this chapter demonstrate that feminist ways of designing are not just about critiquing power but also about creating it. The power of designers is the power to enable opportunities for more choices, more agency, more freedom, and more capacity to transform.

1   The Italian modernist designer Massimo Vignelli famously said, "The life of a designer is a life of fight, fight against ugliness."
2   Darin Buzon, "Design Thinking Is a Rebrand for White Supremacy," *Medium*, March 1, 2020, https://dabuzon.medium.com/design-thinking-is-a-rebrand-for-white-supremacy-b3d31aa55831.
3   Anoushka Khandwala, "What Does It Mean to Decolonize Design?," *Eye on Design*, June 5, 2019, https://eyeondesign.aiga.org/what-does-it-mean-to-decolonize-design/.
4   Patricia Hill Collins, *Black Feminist Thought: Knowledge, Consciousness, and the Politics of Empowerment* (New York: Routledge, 2000).
5   Buzon, "Design Thinking Is a Rebrand for White Supremacy."
6   American Institute of Geographic Arts (AIGA), "AIGA Design Census," 2019, https://designcensus.org/data/2019DesignCensus.pdf.
7   Jen Wang, "Now You See It: Helvetica, Modernism and the Status Quo of Design," *Medium*, December 8, 2016, https://medium.com/@earth.terminal/now-you-see-it-110b77fd13db.
8   Francisco Valdes, "Unpacking Hetero-patriarchy: Tracing the Conflation of Sex, Gender & Sexual Orientation to Its Origins," *Yale Journal of Law and the Humanities* 8, no. 1 (1996): 161–211.
9   Caroline Criado Perez, *Invisible Women: Data Bias in a World Designed for Men* (New York: Abrams Press, 2019), 157.
10   Maggie Gram, "On Design Thinking," *N plus One Magazine* 35 (Fall 2019), https://www.nplusonemag.com/issue-35/reviews/on-design-thinking/.
11   Buzon, "Design Thinking Is a Rebrand for White Supremacy."
12   Maile Arvin, Eve Tuck, and Angie Morrill, "Decolonizing Feminism: Challenging Connections between Settler Colonialism and Heteropatriarchy," *Feminist Formations* 25, no. 1 (2013): 8–34, doi:10.1353/ff.2013.0006.
13   Claudia Mareis and Nina Paim, "Design Struggles: An Attempt to Imagine Design Otherwise," in *Design Struggles: Intersecting Histories, Pedagogies, and Perspectives*, ed. Claudia Mareis and Nina Paim (Amsterdam: Valiz, 2021), 11–22.
14   Tricia Wang, "The Most Popular Design Thinking Strategy Is BS," *Fast Company*, June 28, 2021, https://www.fastcompany.com/90649969/the-most-popular-design-thinking-strategy-is-bs.
15   Amy Allen, "Feminist Perspectives on Power," in *Stanford Encyclopedia of Philosophy*, ed. Edward N. Zalta (Stanford, CA: Stanford University Press, 2005), https://plato.stanford.edu/entries/feminist-power/.
16   Naila Kabeer, *Gender Mainstreaming in Poverty Eradication and the Millennium Development Goals: A Handbook for Policy-Makers and Other Stakeholders* (London: Commonwealth Secretariat, 2003).
17   Iris Marion Young, *Justice and the Politics of Difference* (Princeton, NJ: Princeton University Press, 1990).
18   Simone de Beauvoir, *The Second Sex*, trans. Constance Borde and Sheila Malovany-Chevallier (London: Random House, 2009), 6.
19   See bell hooks, *Feminist Theory: From Margin to Center* (1984; repr., London: Routledge, 2000).
20   Disciplinary power is a concept developed by the philosopher Michel Foucault, who analyzes the disciplinary practices developed in prisons, schools, and factories in the eighteenth century—including minute regulations of bodily movements, obsessively detailed time schedules, and surveillance techniques—and how these practices shape the bodies of prisoners, students, and workers into docile bodies.
21   Sandra Bartky, *Femininity and Domination: Studies in the Phenomenology of Oppression* (New York: Routledge, 1990), 80.
22   Nancy Hartsock, *Money, Sex, and Power: Toward a Feminist Historical Materialism* (Boston: Northeastern University Press, 1983), 224.
23   Jean Baker Miller, "Women and Power," in *Rethinking Power*, ed. Thomas E. Wartenberg (Albany: State University of New York Press, 1992), 247–248.
24   Allen, "Feminist Perspectives on Power."
25   Kimberlé Crenshaw, "Demarginalizing the Intersection of Race and Sex: A Black Feminist Critique of Antidiscrimination Doctrine, Feminist Theory and Antiracist Politics," *University of Chicago Legal Forum* 1989, no. 1 (1989): 139–167.
26   Keeanga-Yamahtta Taylor, *How We Get Free: Black Feminism and the Combahee River Collective* (Chicago: Haymarket, 2017).
27   Flavia Dzodan, "My Feminism Will Be Intersectional or It Will Be Bullshit!," *Tiger Beatdown*, October 10, 2011, http://tigerbeatdown.com/2011/10/10/my-feminism-will-be-intersectional-or-it-will-be-bullshit/.
28   Antionette Carroll, "The Future of Educational Leadership" (PowerPoint presentation, Strategic Design Network, San Diego, CA, 2018).
29   Rich Hollant, "Rh_sharing_w/My Peeps," paper presented at the Design + Diversity Conference, Columbia College, Chicago, August 1–3, 2019, https://www.youtube.com/watch?v=6_OSXeY-drH4.

On calling yourself a designer

Who gets to call themselves a designer? Design studies scholar Claudia Marina questions the boundaries of what we call "design" and who gets to do it.

Claudia Marina

Designers are protective people. This self-preservation is a form of survival, perhaps, in the face contemporary design, which threatens to absorb disparate practices and call everything design. If everything is design, then I suppose nothing is. As I am writing this essay, I am also preparing to give a lecture on this topic, and I'm nervous because I don't know if I'll be able to deliver the message efficiently—a quality designers love but is rarely the reality of the mythologized "design process." I sit at my computer to write my script, and I begin thinking about whether I can call myself a designer. My instinct is to say no, and then I offer: I am a writer, a teacher, a theorist, but not a designer. Designers who hire me to teach classes, such as the one for which I am preparing the lecture, often like that I am not a designer because this position gives me an interdisciplinary perspective. But isn't design inherently interdisciplinary if it responds to human or ecological needs (or to the anxiety between the two)? Despite my field being design studies, I still feel as though I'm at an introduction with design. This feeling isn't an insecurity but rather an innate curiosity. I feel as if I have to say this not least because I am a woman, which seems to affect the voice of authority I have on the subject. (One anonymous online reviewer on Ratemyprofessors.com described me by writing, "She literally doesn't know what she's doing." To that person, I ask: Do you?)

At what point did you feel comfortable calling yourself a designer? Are you still negotiating this? If I can successfully convince others that I am, do the long-term implications of that acceptance destabilize the institution of design and render it meaningless? I cannot practice design without positioning myself as a woman who is white and Cuban American, from Miami, and born in 1993—which makes me a millennial. All these conditions might explain the propensity that institutions or industries have for initially not taking me seriously. Scholars encourage me to walk into a room and start off with this issue of positionality, which always feels a bit like lacking confidence—though I understand its academic reasoning. But I would like to be known for my ideas, not for the body that delivers them—naively. Perhaps it is my own form of self-preservation to evade criticism and allocate my stubbornness to, once again, being a writer, "not a designer," when I stand at the front of an auditorium and begin to speak.

To use a term designers love, my recent thinking on the relationship between design and feminism is that it is one of design's many *wicked problems*. This sort of thinking stems not only from my experience of being a woman in design but also from reading about design in general. Richard Buchanan considers the problem of understanding design itself to be wicked. "The flexibility of design often leads to popular misunderstanding and clouds efforts to understand its nature," he writes. He extends his idea to the positionality of the person writing that history: "*One could go further and say that the history of design history is a record of the design historians' views regarding what they conceive to be the subject matter of design.*"[1] In the questioning of the difference of design in various contexts, to ignore the actual body of the designer—and who gets to call themselves one—leaves out the visceral reality of design. How I experience it is not the same as how my neighbor does, and herein lies the difference in "what [you versus I] conceive to be the subject matter of design." In embracing the wickedness of design and the resulting confusion of who gets to practice it, a feminist design practice today necessitates a series of questions rather than definitive answers—some of which I invite you to think about with me.

In 1971, a decade before feminist design historians began to seriously question design's subject matter and construction of gender, Victor Papanek wrote that design is "cleaning and reorganizing a desk drawer, pulling an impacted tooth, baking an apple pie."[2] At a very surface level, I knew this was true, but why hadn't design historians seriously examined everyday life as an essential part of design rather than as an area that design serves? Why were consumers (historically imagined as women) not treated as designers, too?

Feminist design history has much more at stake than just writing women into the history books. To be a feminist designer is to be aware of difference as a basis for all interaction, which concerns more than just women. Culturally, design is so enmeshed with ideas of rationality, productivity, and problem solving that systemic issues stemming from design culture make their way into everyday conversations without so much as questioning how design has been appropriated by capitalism and, by extension, cisheteropatriarchy. For example, why did the interior designer Florence Knoll feel the need to distinguish herself from women in general when she told the *New York Times*, "I am not a decorator. The only place I decorate is my own house."[3] Knoll was referring to the right to be taken seriously, and she justified the holding of this right not because she is a human who is not biologically predisposed to domesticity or more "feminine" forms of space planning but because she received her design education from canonized male architects.

Because I have taught in an interior design program, I often encourage my students to seriously question whether decoration is a practice exclusive to the home. More pressingly, is Knoll's assertion rooted in design's internalized misogyny? Why is it that when men design at home—as in the story of Steve Jobs and Steve Wozniak designing the first Apple computer out of Jobs's family garage—their practice is recorded under the guise of "innovation"? In fact, Wozniak has said, "We did no designs there ... no prototyping, no planning of products."[4] Yet the prioritization of innovation over maintenance is so prevalent in American culture that the Apple garage has joined the HP garage ("the birthplace of Silicon Valley") as a protected historic landmark. Garages are more likely to be seen as spaces where we go to design something singular. The designing that happens in kitchens or bedrooms, by contrast, is rarely recognized perhaps because its practice is so enmeshed with the body. It does not subscribe to the creation myth but instead follows the quieter practice of adaptation, maintenance, and care. Why is it that the construction of gendered spaces continues to influence what we value? How is design complicit?

In my mind, what Florence Knoll seemed to be saying is somewhat the occupational equivalent of "I'm not like other girls"—the kind of thinking that seeks acceptance and respect from people in power by relating and identifying closer to them than to those who exist as "other" by comparison. In Knoll's case, the latter would be women who designed through informal networks of craft or were educated by means of home décor magazines throughout modern history. They practiced design where they could, in spaces where they were not excluded from developing expertise (i.e., the home). As Cheryl Buckley argued in 1986, "If a feminist approach to design is to be articulated, it must cut across these exclusive definitions of design and craft to show that women used craft modes of production for specific reasons ... because they had access neither to the factories of the new industrial system nor to the training offered by the new design schools."[5] In 2020, revisiting her original questions from that earlier article, Buckley found, "That the small scale, domestic, intimate, and, perhaps, the transitory and incidental remain on the periphery of designers' interests is indicative that this [a feminist approach to design] has yet to be done."[6]

∗ As designers in a capitalist system, we identify ourselves by our occupation rather than by our role in communities. But who are designers when they step out of the studio and enter the space of consumption? ∗

As designers in a capitalist system, we identify ourselves by our occupation rather than by our role in communities. But who are designers when they step out of the studio and enter the space of consumption? Maintenance workers and manual laborers who are incorrectly perceived as participating only in the peripheries of design may be less likely to recognize their own role in design systems. With the prevalence of codesign rising to the occasion of trying to solve design's internal democracy issue, I wonder what participatory design would look like without the designer's participation. Such a provocation requires us to ask ourselves: What do we gain from exclusion? Sometimes I have no idea what design means, which is exactly what keeps me in it. This instability urges me to find a way to reconcile my belief in design as inherent to everyday life and its intricacies, even in the institutions that increasingly limit a sense of agency to participate.

My position—one in which I feel comfortable—is that of both an outsider and a designer. The questions that arise out of a feminist design practice are intrinsic to the types of questions that arise from considering design in relation to yourself and the institutions that affect the way you think about your ability to practice it seriously in everyday life. These questions ask who is allowed in a place, what kind of technology allows an object to materialize, and how many degrees a machine is removed from the mind. The gap widens between the sketch and the thing, between the idea and the building, between the verb and the noun. Do we even need the word *designer*?

Claudia Marina is a writer and educator who teaches design history and theory at Parsons School of Design in New York.

1 Richard Buchanan, "Wicked Problems in Design Thinking," *Design Issues* 8, no. 2 (1992): 19, emphasis in original.
2 Victor Papanek, *Design for the Real World: Human Ecology and Social Change* (New York: Pantheon, 1971), 3.
3 Quoted in Virginia Lee Warren, "Woman Who Led an Office Revolution Rules an Empire of Modern Design," *New York Times*, September 1, 1964.
4 Brandon Lisy, "Steve Wozniak on Apple, the Computer Revolution, and Working with Steve Jobs," *Bloomberg Businessweek*, December 4, 2014, https://www.bloomberg.com/news/articles/2014-12-04/apple-steve-wozniak-on-the-early-years-with-steve-jobs.
5 Cheryl Buckley, "Made in Patriarchy: Toward a Feminist Analysis of Women and Design," *Design Issues* 3, no. 2 (1986): 7, doi:10.2307/1511480.
6 Cheryl Buckley, "Made in Patriarchy II: Researching (or Re-searching) Women and Design," *Design Issues* 36, no. 1 (2020): 22, doi:10.1162/desi_a_00572.

On smuggling feminism into design institutions

Founder and head of the Design and Gender Studies Program at the University of Buenos Aires, Griselda Flesler discusses feminism as a curricular blueprint and the challenges of institutional change.

Dialogue with Griselda Flesler

Alison Place You have said you were born a feminist. What do you mean by that?

Griselda Flesler I come from a family of empowered and autonomous women. My grandmother went to college at a time when few women did and worked all her life. My mother taught me the value of being independent and a free thinker. My older sister had a sign on her apartment door that said, "Say no." For me, it was a mantra, to say "no" to a lot of things, like occupying the stereotypical place of the feminine, calm, and quiet girl. In other ways, though, paraphrasing Simone de Beauvoir, one is not born but rather becomes a feminist.[1] I have learned to be a feminist every day thanks to the enriching exchange of my feminist colleagues, teachers, friends. When I started teaching in design history, the absence of women in the narrative was clear, especially the absence of Latin American designers, despite [my] being an Argentine design faculty. It became the subject of my first postgraduate thesis. I studied Judith Butler, Teresa de Lauretis, and Eve Kosofsky Sedgwick, which caused a shift from a women's focus to a gender and diversity focus, and that was the seed for the creation of the Design and Gender Studies Program.

AP The Design and Gender Studies Program is the first of its kind. What is the objective of the program?

GF The objective was to start the conversation about the intersection between gender and design, something that was not systematized or formalized in my university. In classes, we integrate theoretical and methodological tools from the field of gender studies to reflect on the processes of production, circulation, and consumption of design. We especially aim to denaturalize the idea that "gender studies" is limited to issues related to women; there are many identities that intersect with gender to affect someone's place in society. It is essential to think in feminist pedagogies because our statements teach, confirm, and reinforce meanings and values, while they block and restrict others.

AP Describe the context in which the program was created. Were feminist issues visible on campus or in Argentina?

GF Since 2003, I had been teaching a single class on gender and design while continually "knocking on doors" to create more space for these topics. Finally, the opportunity arose in 2013 with a postgraduate course called "Design, Feminist Theory, and Gender Studies: A Theoretical and Critical Perspective of Contemporary Design," which was the seed that would later become the program. At that time, it was a different climate from the one that exists today in Argentina. Although the feminist movement has been organized in

Figure 1.2.1 Graffiti next to the main entrance of the Faculty of Architecture, Design, and Urbanism reading "Feminismo es revolución." Photograph by Maya Ober.

Argentina for decades, in fields such as architecture and design they were not present in a systematic way. In my college, feminist issues were looked at from the side. Feminist issues in Argentina gained greater visibility in 2015 with the first mobilization of the Ni Una Menos[2] collective and the public drafting of a "feminist agenda." Only five brave people signed up for the first class in 2013, but in 2020 the course had more than 80 enrollees from all over the world.

AP What does it mean to incorporate a gender perspective into design, from a curricular perspective as well as a student-centered perspective?

GF In Argentina, 80 percent of undergraduate students attend public universities, which are free for everyone, regardless of nationality. It is the greatest social equalizer we have. It makes the public university a dynamic site crossed by politics and social problems and therefore connected with the main demands of society. It is essential to think of design as well as of education as tools for access to citizenship. When we talk about citizenship, we are necessarily defining a limit, a border that defines what citizenship is. Design can be a transformative force, but it can also be at the service of the reaffirmation and fixation of an exclusive and selective system. Incorporating a gender perspective is a way to locate design as a tool to create more space for diversity and equality. What we have observed is that students in our program become very critical students in other programs, too. They incorporate concepts that they later transfer to their jobs as architects or designers because it [our program] is not only about theoretical content on gender studies but about how to incorporate them into the design process.

AP The program draws direct influence from the discipline of gender studies. What can design learn from gender studies?

GF In universities, the demand for education with a gender perspective has spread, particularly in the field of social and human sciences but also in the design disciplines. This demand conveys a critique of higher education, programs, curricula, and the teaching body as well as [of] the allegedly neutral status of university knowledge. It also fosters a critique of universalism and a review of existing pedagogical devices. Mainstream design reaffirms the idea of a universal subject, and our challenge through gender studies is to disarm that. An example of how this theoretical framework is applied in the program is the final project, which is based on local and national laws that challenge design from a gender perspective. In recent years, Argentina passed laws that recognize issues such as violence against women, adolescents, and girls; breastfeeding awareness; the right to abortion; and sexual education as a human right. More than 200 students participate in this class, working in interdisciplinary groups to develop a design project that addresses one of these laws through various thematic axes of the course, such as feminist critique of universalism, fallacy of neutrality, identity as narration and not as essence, critiques of

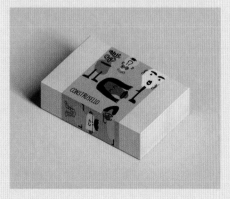

Figure 1.2.2 *Construsellos* is a playful tool that allows children to explore identity construction and the existence of non-hegemonic and non-binary bodies. Design by students Maria Belen Bugallo, Mora Dellatorre, Maria Molina, and Estefania Soledad Rojas. Courtesy of @dyeg.fadu.

Figure 1.2.3 Urban furniture designed to challenge the barrier between the public and the private, fostering the appropriation of public space as a form of resistance by women and pregnant bodies. Design by students Vargas Siles, Luis Alberto, Martín Almirón, Silvia Burastero, Sofía Pironio, and Florencia Vázquez. Courtesy of @dyeg.fadu.

heteronormativity, queer approaches, and rejecting binaries. (See figures 1.2.2 and 1.2.3.)

AP The program also incorporates queer theory. Can you describe how queer perspectives relate to feminist design in the classroom?

GF The queer signifier has traveled far beyond its local origins and as a consequence has shifted meanings in significant ways. In the Design and Gender Studies Program, we consider current tensions concerning what queer design means, while critically analyzing the notion of design with a "universal gender perspective" on which mainstream design politics is based. Queer perspectives allow us to think about a feminism that is not concerned with fixed definitions and clear rules in design. Instead, we embrace doubt, deviation, even the idea of failure. It is a perspective that inquires about the political power of the failure of a "productive" life in heteronormative terms. Working with a conceptual framework based on Sarah Ahmed's concept of "queer use,"[3] we also question "functional" design and the

solutionist perspective with which we often teach design. I believe this perspective is fundamental to avoid a self-proclaimed feminism that ends up generating new fixed "feminist rules."

AP What are some feminist ways of teaching that the program explores?

GF From the beginning, it was important to me to establish some axes around feminist ways of working. First, power is distributed. The teaching team is formed as a cooperative where we distribute the salary of each person based on their responsibilities and not based on the institution's criteria. Second, our goal is to create a good work environment, sensitive to the particularities of students. As bell hooks taught, we try not to leave out eros and eroticism in the pedagogical process because "a pedagogy that dares to subvert the mind/body split allows us to be whole in the classroom."[4] Lastly, we have an open-door policy. We have lectures by different invited specialists who enter and leave the program to generate dynamism so that no one settles too much in their place of privilege.

AP You describe your work as "infecting" and "smuggling" feminism into androcentric institutions. What does that mean?

GF When we think of the term *infect*, we think of diseases like viruses. In fact, fifteen years ago, when I talked about feminism and design in my school, colleagues and students looked at me as if I were going to infect them with some disease. The term *infect* is also useful in that it prompts you to think about what is considered abnormal or dangerous at a given time in a specific society and how it is culturally constructed and deconstructed. As Judith Butler explains, the existence of "the normal" is always and necessarily contingent upon the existence of the abnormal.[5] There is always a system that regulates which side you are on and defines and defends that border. That system is hegemonic, which means it is dominant in society; therefore, we are all part of its production and reproduction, whether on a small or large scale. The other term that I have used is *to smuggle*, which has to do with material or symbolic actions that challenge and crack the borders.

AP What are the obstacles to being a feminist and doing feminist work within an institution?

GF The obstacles within institutions are many, and the institutional inertia is vast. It is expressed in resistance and fear, in entrenched sexist practices, and [in] the underestimation of the gender agenda in a context of inequity and scarcity of resources. Still, the advancement of the feminist agenda is taking place across all the academic units of the university in a heterogeneous way and with different rhythms, characteristics, and agents that mobilize it in each one of them. The bond that we are weaving between different generations, disciplines, management spaces, chairs, teacher networks, unions, student bodies, and nonteachers interested in a more egalitarian university, free of violence, is a project that is gaining more and more strength, and it is only possible if it is a chorus, all singing together.

AP What advice do you have for students, teachers, or members of other universities who conspire to "smuggle" feminism into their institutions?

GF Make allies. Weave networks. Share as much as possible, and do not seek to agree on everything. The networks you weave must include people who are outside your institution and can give you an unaffected look at what is happening. Learn to regulate urgency and patience. Build microstructures that constantly crack the patriarchal rock. Changes in institutions are slow. Don't underestimate the need to take care of yourself. It is urgent to ask: Who cares for those who care in academic institutions? Do not think you are indispensable, and, at the same time, build spaces that become indispensable for the institution.

This conversation took place over email in March 2022. It has been edited for clarity and length.

Griselda Flesler is a graphic designer, investigator, and associate professor of design and gender studies in the Faculty of Architecture, Design, and Urbanism at the Universidad de Buenos Aires (UBA). She holds an MA in design theory, and she is also a PhD student in the Faculty of Social Sciences at UBA.

1 Simone de Beauvoir, *The Second Sex*, trans. Constance Borde and Sheila Malovany-Chevallier (London: Random House, 2009).
2 Ni Una Meno's, Spanish for "Not one [woman] less" is a Latin American fourth-wave grassroots feminist movement that started in Argentina.
3 Sara Ahmed, *What's the Use? On the Uses of Use* (Durham, NC: Duke University Press, 2019).

4 bell hooks, "Eros, Eroticism and the Pedagogical Process," *Cultural Studies* 7, no. 1 (January 1993): 58, doi:10.1080/09502389300490051.

5 Judith Butler, *Gender Trouble: Feminism and the Subversion of Identity* (London: Routledge, 1990).

On the contradictions of feminist branding

Is feminist branding possible? The graphic designer and educator Aggie Toppins considers branding through an intersectional feminist lens based on historical insights and a case study.

Aggie Toppins

Feminist, antiracist, and decolonial scholars have laid the theoretical groundwork addressing design's complicity with white supremacy and capitalist patriarchy. Design stands charged to make a profound transition from a service industry to a *field of knowledge* that recognizes multiple perspectives and commits to long-term visions of equitable, sustainable futures. Although it is important for radical theories to become transformative actions thoughtfully over time, the urgency of our global crises beckons designers to reform practices now.

But how? As is the case for many designers, my training has been so inter-twined with capitalism that I struggle to imagine emancipatory theories in practice. Capitalism is proficient at absorbing and foreclosing what challenges it. It's worth debating if feminist branding is possible; here, however, I accept the ambivalence of designing under capitalism and seek to neutralize its harms.[1] Here, I reconsider branding through an intersectional feminist lens, point to historical insights and the recent "femvertising" trend, and exemplify my analysis with a case study from my own studio.

Groundwork

Designer critiques of power are not new. In the 1970s, Victor Papanek challenged designers to awaken to the negative impacts of consumerism on people and the climate.[2] A decade later, Cheryl Miller highlighted design's racial exclusions,[3] while Cheryl Buckley examined gender bias.[4] In the 1990s, Martha Scotford expanded feminist research in a hard-hitting essay that identified multiple blind spots.[5] Collectives such as *Futuress* and Decolonising Design now carry the mantle, imploring designers to move away from the singularity of Western, patriarchal thought. Claudia Mareis and Nina Paim show that design is still confronting its "modernist and postwar heritage, which rests on colonialist and imperialist foun-dations."[6] Design has long mythologized itself as rational and objective, concealing the subjective imperatives of dominant culture while upholding universalist claims.

Feminism rejects the universal, recognizing instead that knowledge is *situated*; it is historically contextual and culturally specific, and it reflects the experience of the knowing subject. This essay comes from my experience as well as from principles of intersectionality, a framework developed by Kimberlé Crenshaw for examining inequality through coexistent social factors such as race, gender, and class. Although my privileges as a white American are real, so are the vulnerabilities I know through class struggle and gender. I was raised by a single mother in a family whose income barely rose above the poverty line. Today, I work in a petite-bourgeois field where there are many women designers but few women leaders. My life informs my arguments as much as my research does.

Challenges

Branding is fundamentally antifeminist. It's connected to private interests and wealth accumulation: profit over people. Even if their goals are not financial, brands operate within a paradigm of competition and remain linked to symbolic capital. Capitalism regulates economic activities and all social relations.[7] In a market society, everything is branded: multinational corporations, grassroots community initiatives, and social media "influencers" alike. To be sure, brand-design values are almost always capitalist values. Yet the potential of feminist branding need not be dismissed because it operates within this system.

✳ So long as capitalism structures people's lives,
the end of branding is nowhere on the horizon.
It is worth imagining how to resist the system
provisionally from within. ✳

Branding is historically linked to violence and coercion. It originated centuries ago in acts of identifying property (by burning the flesh of enslaved people and livestock), distinguishing groups (as in medieval warfare), and authenticating (state) communications. Corporate identities emerged when modern companies began differentiating their products and services. Corporations eventually shifted from making compelling products to issuing charismatic brands. Today, branding does not simply identify goods. It fuels desire. Brands influence lifestyles and mediate relationships. Brands surveil us. So long as capitalism structures people's lives, the end of branding is nowhere on the horizon. It is worth imagining how to resist the system provisionally from within.

Feminist Design Principles

In the mid–twentieth century, the task of the corporate-identity designer was to translate business qualities into clear, distinctive forms. The beacon of the modernist brand was the absolute trademark. Minimal but memorable trademarks were thought to be enduring symbols that could represent everyone in the organization. By the 1970s, feminist designers began rejecting modernism by creating mutable trademarks.[8] It is now mainstream for brands to deploy "open systems" with many trademark states. Mutable trademarks seem to overcome brand absolutism, but they also reinforce it by repositioning the trademark from absolute symbol to assimilating structure.

Some brand identities de-emphasize trademarks and rely on memorable graphic languages composed of color, pattern, and typography. Compared to the rigidity of modernist identities, these adaptive systems make brands seem inclusive in their contextual specificity. Perhaps by swapping the trademark for an extensive kit of parts that can be arranged in myriad ways, brand identities can visually communicate the feminist value of pluralism.

Form is only part of the puzzle. Methodology is another. Branding projects differ, but they traditionally unfold in some variation of investigation, creation, and implementation phases. Design teams commonly do research that involves listening to stakeholders or studying the sector before creating assets. The process excludes most of the people who will use the brand. The final design is often unspecific, impersonal, and bureaucratically imposed on constituents. Dorothy E. Smith gives this process a name: "ruling relations" are institutional ways of generalizing "interpretations of people's local experiences, constructing new and standardized forms of subjectivity coordinated with the demands of empire and capital."[9] In other words, brand-design teams translate real people's stories into criteria and then use those criteria to shape reductive representational systems capable of generating capital. "Femvertising" is another ruling relation. Dove's "Real Beauty" and Pantene's "Don't Be Sorry, Shine Strong" campaigns manipulate women's self-conscious conditioning in order to sell beauty products. The term *femvertising* sounds like *feminist advertising*, but it is often paternalistic, lacks intersectional differentiation, and trivializes women's issues as something commodities can solve. Corporations can appeal to socially minded consumers through femvertising even while maintaining inequitable policies. For Smith, a feminist standpoint recognizes actual people without essentializing them or organizing them into capitalist agents.

Feminism endorses collective processes. A feminist designer acts as a facilitator who acknowledges that everyone brings expertise and is capable of designing in some sense. The Design Justice Network's community-centered process embodies this principle by building genuine relationships, co-creating, and ensuring longevity through community ownership.[10] This may seem impractical for corporations, but even there designers and organizations can collaborate as intentional teams that enact feminism in form and method.

Case Study

I began considering the possibilities of feminist branding when I started working with the Women's Group on Race Relations (WGRR), a network of women in St. Louis who foster intersectional relationships and facilitate conversations about race and racism. I collaborated with six founding leaders to create an identity that would help members identify one another in public, bring communications into an identifiable visual language, and attract new audiences with a fresh, energetic presence.

At first, I worried that branding presented insurmountable contradictions to WGRR's cause. I was concerned about the futility of using "the master's tools," in Audre Lorde's metaphor, to "dismantle the master's house."[11] Yet Sara Ahmed reminds us that to be a feminist at work means to challenge everyday sexism.[12] We can create feminist tools and build a new house. In considering what those tools might be, I spent time listening to WGRR's leadership. We established a foundation of mutual trust and respect. The leaders' telling of their own life experiences,

Women's Group on Race Relations

Figure 1.3.1 WGRR's signature trademark features a detachable symbol. Courtesy of Aggie Toppins and Camryn Cogshell.

previous projects, and vision for the group shaped criteria and provided content while remaining local and specific. WGRR's signature trademark features a detachable symbol, which Camryn Cogshell, a student at Washington University in St. Louis, drafted and I later refined (figure 1.3.1). The symbol consists of a series of overlapping rings, which appealed to WGRR because it represented different worlds intertwining. We chose to honor this contribution, refine the symbol, and bridge it to color and typography. The challenge then became one of applying feminist principles to the use of a trademark.

To build flexibility into WGRR's brand, I created numerous compositions that integrated the symbol in various ways (figure 1.3.2). Then, to balance the trademark's prominence, I selected a robust suite of typefaces (figure 1.3.3). Since the font industry is dominated by white men, I proposed to WGRR that we license typefaces designed by women and nonwhite designers. This choice embodies WGRR's mission while addressing a representational disparity in the font industry. It also allows the WGRR brand to continue evolving with the addition of new typefaces in the future. The resulting identity is an elastic language that encourages customization rather than standardization. It is timely, not timeless.

Figure 1.3.2 WGRR communications incorporate the symbol in different ways. Courtesy of Aggie Toppins and Camryn Cogshell.

Figure 1.3.3 WGRR's brand identity includes a robust suite of typefaces created by women and nonwhite designers. Courtesy of Aggie Toppins and Camryn Cogshell.

WGRR's brand identity resulted from a collectively shaped process, and although the form is flexible, adaptable, and apropos of the women involved, it does not fall outside the conventions of brand-identity design. Some feminists strive for disobedient forms, taking the position of visual nonconformity. This approach has merits, but it is not always useful for clients. Feminist interventions cannot rest solely in form. Form is not unimportant, but it is also not enough.

Feminist branding is a capitalist contradiction as well as a provisional possibility. The paradox emerges from feminism's refusal of reductive, universal solutions and coercive tactics. Yet feminism also encourages us to challenge oppression where we work. Because capitalism co-opts dissent, feminist alternatives to branding must be receptive to feedback and capable of shifting. Feminist branding will not dismantle capitalism, but its forms and processes can subvert branding's patriarchal tenets and neutralize some of capitalism's harms.

A previous version of this essay was published in [ ] With Design: Reinventing Design Modes, Proceedings of the 9th Congress of the International Association of Societies of Design Research, *ed. Gerhard Bruyns and Huaxin Wei (Singapore: Springer, 2022).*

Aggie Toppins (she/her) is associate professor and chair of Design in the Sam Fox School of Design & Visual Arts at Washington University in St. Louis.

1 Erik Olin Wright, *How to Be an Anticapitalist in the 21st Century* (London: Verso Books, 2019), 53–60.
2 Victor Papanek, *Design for the Real World: Human Ecology and Social Change* (New York: Pantheon, 1971).
3 Cheryl D. Miller, "Black Designers: Missing in Action," *Print*, September–October 1987, 58–65, 136–138.
4 Cheryl Buckley, "Made in Patriarchy: Toward a Feminist Analysis of Women and Design," *Design Issues* 3, no. 2 (Autumn 1986): 3–14.
5 Martha Scotford, "Messy History vs. Neat History: Toward an Expanded View of Women in Graphic Design," *Visible Language* 28, no. 4 (October 1994): 367–387.
6 Claudia Mareis and Nina Paim, "Design Struggles: An Attempt to Imagine Design Otherwise," in *Design Struggles: Intersecting Histories, Pedagogies, and Perspectives*, ed. Claudia Mareis and Nina Paim (Amsterdam: Valiz, 2021), 15.
7 Ellen Meiksins Wood, *The Origins of Capitalism: A Longer View* (London: Verso, 2017), 7.
8 Ellen Lupton, "Graphic Design in the Urban Landscape," in *Design and Feminism: Re-visioning Spaces, Places, and Everyday Things*, ed. Joan Rothschild (New Brunswick, NJ: Rutgers University Press, 1999), 57–65.
9 Dorothy E. Smith, "From the Margins: Women's Standpoint as a Method of Inquiry in the Social Sciences," *Gender, Technology and Development* 1, no. 1 (March 1997): 116–119, doi:10.1080/09718524.1997.11909845.
10 Design Justice Network, *Design Justice Zine #2: Design Justice: An Exhibit of Emerging Design Practices* (Detroit: Design Justice Network, 2016).
11 Audre Lorde, "The Master's Tools Will Never Dismantle the Master's House," in *Feminist Postcolonial Theory: A Reader*, ed. Reina Lewis and Sara Mills (Edinburgh: Edinburgh University Press, 2003), 25–28.
12 Sara Ahmed, *Living a Feminist Life* (Durham, NC: Duke University Press, 2017), 14.

On fighting the typatriarchy

The type designer Aasawari Kulkarni discusses the origins of her feminist typeface, Nari, and the patriarchal underpinnings of the type design industry.

Dialogue with Aasawari Kulkarni

Alison Place What brought you to design, and what was your design education like?

Aasawari Kulkarni I was a creative kid. Growing up in India, there were not many options for creative careers. I went to the National Institute of Fashion Technology, where I focused on different things like fashion journalism, fashion photography, and graphic design, which led me to type design. After I graduated, I worked at the Indian Type Foundry, where I designed my first Devanagari typeface called "Suhas." I knew this was something I wanted to do, but I felt like I needed more education, so I went to graduate school at the Maryland Institute College of Art. That was the first time I realized design can be about more than just selling things; it can be about cultural criticism, cultural theory, and bringing that aspect of yourself and your journey into it. It changed the way I approached design.

AP What sparked a feminist approach to your design practice?

AK The first time I really thought about the patriarchy is when I read *The Palace of Illusions* by Chitra Banerjee Divakaruni, which was a retelling of the oldest classic mythologies from India, the Mahabharata, from the shero's perspective. It got me thinking about the nature of patriarchal storytelling in India. When I got a chance to do a project on self-inquiry during grad school, I revisited one of my favorite stories from childhood that my grandmother used to tell me, the Ramayana. It's the epic tale of the abduction of King Ram's wife, Sita, by Ravana, the demon king of Lanka. King Ram has been worshipped on a pedestal equal to God, as being the most perfect human to have walked the planet. However, I found the ending of this story later: he abandoned his wife to keep the royal throne stain free because she was kidnapped by another man. It disturbed me that we have been praying to a man without considering the role, perspectives, and strength of the woman, Sita. I decided to retell the story in a way that focuses on her journey and perspectives in order to show that the god we have been praying to is not so perfect. I realized I am a storyteller. As designers, we all are.

AP When did you begin to integrate feminism as a method or a process in your work?

AK When I was researching for my thesis, I learned about variable fonts, and my mind was blown. I saw so many possibilities because of the breadth of choice and fluidity that variable fonts gave you. That summer I was reading about feminist theory and how to integrate it in design. Something clicked, and I asked myself, "How might I make a font that is feminist? How could I make a tool that is feminist as opposed to just making a stand-alone project?" When I was working on this, I was also working on a project with an organization called Feminism in India

It might be assumed that feminism travels from West to East. It might be assumed that feminism is what the West gives to the East. That assumption is a traveling, assumption, one that tells a feminist story in a certain way, a story that is much repeated; a history of how feminism acquired utility as an imperial gift. That is not my story.

SARAH AHMED
LIVING A FEMINIST LIFE

Figure 1.4.1 [top, bottom right] Nari Variable Specimen book.

Figure 1.4.2 [bottom left] Quote from Sara Ahmed's book *Living a Feminist Life* typeset in Nari Variable.

All images courtesy of Aasawari Kulkarni.

[that was] about how gender-based violence is portrayed in media and how usually the victim is shown in a very vulnerable position. We made illustrations where the victim wasn't shown as weak and where the oppressor wasn't shown as a monster because oppressors aren't usually monsters; they're regular people. The illustrations became a part of a media tool kit of open-source imagery that feminism in India has been asking

media outlets in India to use instead of using pictures that depict women as weak. I liked the idea of making a "tool" that anyone could use and add to.

AP You've written about what you call "typatriarchy." What is that, and how did it inform the making of a feminist typeface?

AK When I started this project, I was trying to understand what feminism is. I came across the definition by bell hooks that it's not just about equality, but it's a movement to end sexism and sexist oppression. I tried to write a definition of feminism for myself—the fight against patriarchal systems that deny choice, expression, and opportunity to a person on

* The qualities I chose represent the women I looked up to [while] growing up, who were soft but strong, loud with a purpose. In Indian society, women assume different roles at different points in their life. *

the basis of their gender—then I made an analogy of that to design. There are only a selected few fonts that have always sat on the pedestal of "good" design (i.e., patriarchal systems). Expressionist typefaces are always on the edges (i.e., denied choice/opportunity).

They never get mainstream attention like grotesque typefaces. The patriarchal system in this case is the constant use of these typefaces, not the typefaces themselves, so I coined the term *typatriarchy*. Initially, I wasn't thinking about the fact that when I am designing this typeface, I'm also bringing in my identity and my experiences as a designer, as a woman. I know that the identity of the people who make things matters and that representation matters, but [they're] also not the only thing[s] that matter. Feminist design is not just about the identity of who makes things—it's a constant struggle of integrating feminist ways of designing and thinking. Through the term *typatriarchy*, I was analyzing the positioning and hierarchy of typefaces in design.

AP Why do you think that designers need more expressive typefaces in their toolbox?

Figure 1.4.3 A conversation between the East and the West. Courtesy of Aasawari Kulkarni.

Figure 1.4.4 [left] Nari in use. *BIOFILIE*, solo exhibition of the work of Giulia Tomasello, exploring female intimate care through wearable technology and biohacking. Design by Tauras Stalnionis. Photograph by Giulia Tomasello.

Figure 1.4.5 [below] Nari in use. Animal species that have gender-expansive biology or behavior dance around queer-affirming statements. Images courtesy of Biodiversity Heritage Library. Design by Shoshana Schultz.

AK Freedom of expression is very important in design. We've been extremely limited by what is assumed to be "good design." Type is about the literal meaning of what you're designing but also the visual meaning. Choosing a typeface speaks a lot about your design—Who designed it? Why was it designed? Does it convey the meaning of the words that you're using? There is a deeper layer of meaning to all your design choices because you invite someone else into your design by doing so.

AP How do gender stereotypes underscore the "othering" of expressive typefaces?

AK Gender stereotypes happen in type just like they do in the real world. Swiss, bold fonts are considered more masculine or neutral. High-contrast fonts are considered more feminine, more delicate. Who decided that? Instead of thinking about the gender of fonts, we could think about the greater meaning of what they stand for and what [a font] makes you feel. Is it a strong typeface? Is it an emotional typeface? Is it an angry typeface? That's where the need for fluidity comes in.

AP Can you describe your Nari typeface and how it incorporates fluidity?

AK *Nari* means "woman" in Hindi. While making [the typeface], I was thinking about what you feel when you select a typeface. Can a typeface be an extension of what you're feeling? Instead of naming the different weights, like regular and bold, I named them with qualities, like soft, flexible, assertive, neutral, loud, or hostile, and you can move fluidly between them (figures 1.4.1 and 1.4.2). Variable fonts work on axes, and Nari's axes are *voice* (weight), which moves from soft to loud; *mindset* (width), which moves from narrow to broad minded; and *fight* (contrast), which moves from assertive to aggressive. I was thinking about the idea of soft revolutions. The qualities I chose represent the women I looked up to [while] growing up, who were soft but strong, loud with a purpose. In Indian society, women assume different roles at different points in their life. Nari is fluid. Instead of being labeled as one extreme, you can be anywhere on that whole spectrum. I want designers to pause and think about the meaning behind the choices they're making with type, and perhaps that thoughtfulness will extend to other design choices they're making.

AP You're also an educator. How do you integrate feminist theory into your teaching?

AK I think about what was missing from my design education and what I wanted more of. One thing that has helped me grow into a feminist designer is being introduced to pluralistic points of view. There isn't just one way of designing, and it's so important to be introduced to different voices in the classroom. When we expand our minds, feminist design becomes more of a habit and a practice as opposed to just a stand-alone project. I teach about applying feminist theories of collaboration, citation, and mentorship to practice.

AP Feminism in the United States tends to be positioned as the only way to do feminism, which often erases other feminisms in other parts of the world. Is there tension in the way you show up as a feminist in the United States versus in India?

AK The feminist movements in India and the United States are so different. Living here, I feel like being a feminist is normalized. But in India, yes, there is a lot of tension talking to my relatives, both old and young. It's still a big challenge to normalize being a feminist in the Indian household. *Feminism* is still a word that might be frowned upon. There's a long way to go, but intersectional feminism is very, very important in India because there are so many different communities of people living together. Even though I am a minority in the United States, I come from a privileged background in India, and I recognize that. I have no authority to define the feminist movements of India from the narrowness of my own experience. That's why I relied on research for the Nari Specimen, a conversation between the East and the West, which was a dialogue between the two different cultures (figure 1.4.3). Sara Ahmed talks about how feminist movements have not come from the West to the East (figure 1.4.2).[1] It's [the specimen] a collective sample of the many voices from India, brought into this society that likes to center movements around itself.

This conversation took place over Zoom in July 2021. It has been edited for clarity and length.

Aasawari Kulkarni is a designer, educator, and writer from India. She holds an MFA in graphic design from the Maryland Institute College of Art and runs an independent design practice while teaching full-time at George Washington University in Washington, DC.

1 Sara Ahmed, *Living a Feminist Life* (Durham, NC: Duke University Press, 2017).

50 questions for every designer

The feminist entrepreneur Jennifer Armbrust implores designers to confront what they do and, more importantly, how and why they do it.[1]

Jennifer Armbrust

1. What are you selling?
2. Is it a product, service, or idea?
3. Where did you get your creative concept?
4. Are you borrowing revolutionary language to build a brand?
5. Are you appropriating someone's culture, art, struggle, or sacred spiritual ideals?
6. Are you using tropes of dominance or violence to create the illusion of authority?
7. Do you think about representations of race and gender?
8. Have you contemplated your role as a designer within capitalism?
9. Are you creating needs, wants, or longings?
10. Are you telling a story?
11. Is telling a story different than telling the truth?
12. Are you solving a problem?
13. What problem are you solving?
14. Is there a way in which your work might be creating or contributing to other problems?
15. Who benefits from your creative work?
16. Who profits?
17. Have you considered the ethics of the companies you sell your creative power to?
18. Do you respect the people you work with and for?
19. What about the earth?
20. These products you are selling, what are they made of—the raw materials?
21. The tools you use to make your work, where did they come from?
22. Do you think about how long these things will last?
23. And where they will go when we're done with them?
24. Do you think about the garbage?

25. Do you consider the people who make these products and tools?

26. How do they spend their days?

27. What are their working conditions?

28. How much money do they make?

29. Do they have a sense of personal agency in their work?

30. Do you have a sense of personal agency in your work?

31. Do you and your colleagues grapple with these complicated questions together?

32. Do you contemplate the social impact of what you're creating?

33. Is it okay to be a designer without weighing the larger implications of your work?

34. Or is being a designer "just a job"?

35. How do you use the money you make?

36. What are you working for?

37. What I mean to say is, *Why do you do what you do?*

38. Why do you get up every day and make work?

39. Do you believe in what you're creating?

40. Do you believe in what you're selling?

41. What are your core values, your own deeply held beliefs?

42. Is your work in alignment with these values?

43. Do you believe that you must compromise your values in order to survive?

44. What would it look like to honor your interconnection to the earth, the plants, and all living beings?

45. What would it look like to thrive financially, while living and working with integrity?

46. How would that *feel*?

47. Would that change the way you work?

48. Would that change the way you live?

49. Can you create the world you want to live in?

50. How can you start today?

Jennifer Armbrust (she/her) is a leader in the field of feminist entrepreneurship and the founder of Sister and Feminist Business School. Armbrust holds a degree in critical theory and political economy from the Evergreen State College.

1 Volume editor's note: This section does not follow the same titling convention as the rest of the section titles in the book, which may seem like a mistake, even an annoying one, to many detail-oriented designers. Consider it a feminist "swerve." In *The Poethical Wager*, Joan Retallack writes about "the swerve" as the feminine intervention to masculine logic. Masculinity loves tidy, linear structures. The feminine disrupts this hegemonic logic when it deviates, or "swerves." See Joan Retallack, *The Poethical Wager* (Berkeley: University of California Press, 2003).

✳ Knowledge

When we women offer our experience as our truth, as human truth, all the maps change. There are new mountains.

Ursula K. Le Guin

URSULA K. LE GUIN: THE LAST INTERVIEW AND OTHER CONVERSATIONS

On knowledge

Alison Place

In January 2021, the first vaccines against the COVID-19 virus began to roll out in the United States. As more and more people got their first and second shots, reports began to pop up from women who stated that the vaccine had caused changes to their periods.[1] Collectively flummoxed, people with uteruses asked science: How does the vaccine affect menstruation? And science replied: ¯_(ツ)_/¯.

Clinical trials for the vaccines didn't track menstrual changes as a possible side effect of the vaccine. In fact, there are currently no data linking any vaccines to changes in menstruation because there are hardly any data about menstruation to begin with. This data gap is part of a long history of medicine treating women's bodies like anomalies and just one of myriad examples of the erasure of women's knowledge by the scientific establishment. For much of modern medical history, women were completely excluded from medical trials because of menstruation or because they might be pregnant. Investigators worried that fluctuating hormones would add too many variables and thus confound their studies. In essence, they viewed the female body as needlessly complex and thought it would ruin their research. So the male body became the default site for knowledge production about the human body, obscuring women's health as extraneous and irrelevant. This power differential echoes throughout our society, including design. For example, it took five years after Apple's Health app was developed to include tracking features for menstruation. When design is made for a default user, it means women are left out.

The familiar phrase "knowledge is power" plainly conveys why knowledge is a feminist issue and thus is the primary concern of many feminist theories about social relations. We all produce knowledge through our experiences as we move through the world. As knowers, we experience the world through our bodies, our emotions, our values, our worldviews, our roles, and our relationships to others. For instance, one's social location affects one's access to certain types of information or one's ability to convey information to others. In research, knowledge is produced through inquiry about people's experiences and generalized to draw conclusions. However, mainstream research, like mainstream knowledge in general, tends to assume the position of privileged groups, helping to naturalize and sustain their privilege in the process.[2] Feminist theories of knowledge, or feminist epistemologies, call attention to the ways in which dominant conceptions and practices of knowledge systematically disadvantage women and other subordinated groups—for instance, by excluding them from inquiry or denying their authority as knowers. These theories aim to elucidate the ways in which structures of power obfuscate, erase, or reveal certain types of knowledge and how they influence what we believe to be true about the world. Feminist epistemologies are predicated on the distinction between dominant forms of knowledge, which are considered more salient and upheld as truth, and subjugated forms of knowledge, which are marginalized, undermined, or erased altogether.

A key contribution to feminist epistemology is feminist standpoint theory, which asserts that all knowledge and attempts at knowing are socially situated and calls attention to the ways in which gender and other social locations situate a knowing subject.[3] If knowledge is socially situated, then knowledge production is inevitably enmeshed in the power structures of patriarchal society. Because women and other marginalized identities are limited to certain roles in society, they hold and produce types of knowledge that are different from those produced by their white, male, or otherwise dominant counterparts. Standpoint theory holds that these different types of knowledge should be recognized and utilized as a resource rather than marginalized. A key strategy of feminist epistemologies is to destabilize normative conventions by investigating or even nurturing what lies in the margin, where alternative ways of knowing and doing are most visible.[4] By focusing on marginal perspectives of knowledge, feminist researchers expose the unexamined assumptions of dominant epistemological paradigms, avoid distorted or one-sided accounts of social life, and generate new and critical questions.[5]

Feminist standpoint theory also critiques Western scientific epistemology, which has dominated scientific discourse so completely that its specific way of connecting beliefs about knowledge with research practices appears seamless.[6] Although science presents itself as natural, universal, and objective, it is merely a one-sided story that is shaped by bias and reinforces the status quo. Objectivity in particular is a contested notion within feminism. According to feminist epistemology, Western cultural narratives about objectivity are grounded in positivist views of knowledge, which both perpetuate masculine notions of domination and subjugation and assert that researchers can find absolute truth and have the self-appointed authority to do so (sound familiar?). According to the feminist scholar Donna Haraway, objectivity, or transcendence of situatedness, is like "being from nowhere while claiming to see comprehensively."[7] Knowledge attempts that claim objectivity are merely power moves rather than moves toward truth. Feminist epistemologists reject objectivity in order to acknowledge the ways in which the values and assumptions of an inquirer inevitably shape knowledge production. Rather than lament the latter fact, feminist researchers urge us to embrace it. They opt for treating value biases as "epistemic resources" that help us see the world with and from new perspectives rather than as obstacles in the search for absolute truth.[8]

Feminist perspectives on knowledge call on us to insist on a better account of the world. Especially as designers, we have the power to bring to light knowledge that has been previously marginalized or erased, but omnipotence should not be our goal. We do not need the ability to know and theorize everything; we need instead the ability to translate knowledge among very different and power-differentiated communities. As Haraway argues, feminist objectivity means pursuing situated knowledges, which are marked by perspectives that are partial rather than universal and that are embodied rather than neutral. She critiques the "god trick" of objectivity as an allegory of the same ideology that governs notions of the separation of mind and body, of distance and responsibility. Situated knowledges call for a "view from a body, always a complex, contradictory, structuring and structured body, versus the view from above, from nowhere, from simplicity."[9]

Designing *with* and *from* embodied and situated knowledges is a direct confrontation to the "neutrality" of design. Many of the standard ways of doing design are strongly aligned with Western, positivist views of knowledge, from designers' claims of objectivity to their self-appointed authority to know what people need. Critically, designers fail to recognize that much of what they do is research and therefore carries with it assumptions about knowledge. A commitment to disembodied objectivity prevents us from seeing how deeply our identities, views, and methodological choices shape how knowledge is uncovered and utilized in the design process. Attempts to achieve "neutrality" and "objectivity" separate researchers from their subjects—and designers from their users—by abstracting their experiences into data, removing critical contextual information, and preventing a deep understanding.[10]

The disability studies scholar and designer Aimi Hamraie draws connections between knowing and making, characterizing knowledge as a site of engagement and transformation. "Knowledge is social, relational, material and spatially situated. Knowing both reflects and shapes the world. Knowledge, in other words, is a kind of design."[11] It's not just designers' knowledge and experiences that shape what they create, but also more often their *lack* of knowledge and experience. Incredulously, design is still operated as an intuitive process that centers the designer as the primary knower. In this regard, according to Hamraie, knowing is a gateway to making, because designers' knowledge is based on the assumption of a certain kind of user. The extent to which our design choices can meet someone's needs, then, depends on our ability to gather knowledge about someone else's experience that is authentic, robust, and contextualized. (For more on this topic, see the dialogue with Hamraie in this chapter.)

Knowledge is a key component in every decision we make as designers. Just as dominant research paradigms have long assumed the universality of a white, male-centered experience and have used it as the yardstick of unbiased research,[12] design suffers from the problem of the "default user"; even when a particular audience is targeted, design outcomes are created with a default user in mind, and in Western society the "default" identity is white, cisgender, and male. At the same time, marginalized people are treated as "edge cases" in the design process;[13] their experiences are perceived to be infrequent and less significant compared to the "default" experience, so their needs are not considered important enough to address. By applying feminist understandings of knowledge to design, the feminist human–computer interaction researcher Shaowen Bardzell introduces a new domain of user research: the "marginal user," which complicates notions of universal design and implies a new set of strategies and methods needed for user research.[14]

Placing our awareness on the knowledge at the margins is key to feminist ways of designing. The feminist activist and writer bell hooks called the margins a space of potential for change, "a space where there is unlimited access to the pleasure and power of knowing, where transformation is possible."[15] The civic design scholar Ceasar McDowell promotes the importance of designing at the margins as an act in opposition to universal design. He likens the dichotomy to the tension between the claim "Black Lives Matter" and the counterclaim that "all lives matter" in that centering the needs of those who are most vulnerable does not negate the needs of others, and designing to meet their needs does not prevent others' needs from being met. Echoing feminist strategies, McDowell asserts the "underlying structures that continue to reproduce inequality are only brought to life when those marginalized by society are put at the center."[16]

✳ Designers fail to recognize that much of what they do is research and therefore carries with it assumptions about knowledge. ✳

What does it mean to design at the margins? It requires us to shift—literally and figuratively—our vision, our priorities, and our perception of what is possible and to develop new methods of design. Feminist research methodologies prove instructive in the task of conducting research otherwise. A methodology is simply the combination of a researcher's methods and epistemology—or, simply, *how* and *why* they do their research. It is the terrain where philosophy and action meet.[17] When a designer asks someone to fill out a survey or observes someone testing a prototype, they are not only making explicit choices about how to gather knowledge (method) but also making implicit choices about where they believe knowledge to be situated and how they believe it to be "discoverable" (epistemology).

Developed and debated over many decades in the social sciences, feminist research methodologies are interventions that problematize traditional ways of doing research. Unlike positivist research, feminist research assumes an explicit agenda; according to the feminist scholar Sandra Harding, the goal is to understand how oppression works and to produce knowledge that will help fight against it.[18] Feminist research should raise questions about the relationship between authority and power as well as about the relationship between researchers and the researched.[19] Feminist methodologies emphasize acknowledging the researcher's positionality, reducing power hierarchies between the researcher and the subject, and rethinking traditional research methods. Feminist research methods are diverse, unconventional, and occasionally controversial. In *Feminist Methods for Social Research*, the feminist social scientist Shulamit Reinharz proposes nontraditional methods to reveal knowledge that is otherwise obscured—such as unstructured interviews, the researcher's self-disclosure, and "nurturing as a field method."

She encourages researchers to devise new quantitative or qualitative methods "because the knowledge we seek requires it."[20]

If feminist design is a methodology, it calls on us to reflect on our design methods and our beliefs about knowledge in the design process. It prompts a reimagining of our roles in relation to people, communities, and society as well as, more importantly, a reimagining of the role that other people play in the design process. The application of feminist epistemologies to design reveals many opportunities for more just and equitable ways of designing. To summarize just a few:

* Start at the margins. Design for the edge cases, not the default. As Sasha Costanza-Chock points out in *Design Justice*, "The people who are most adversely affected by design decisions ... tend to have the least influence on those decisions and how they are made."[21] Seek and elevate knowledge that has been structurally hidden or erased.

* Place greater value on qualitative data than on quantitative data[22] and emphasize context. We have been culturally conditioned to presume that numbers are neutral and objective and therefore more trustworthy, but quantitative data tend to conceal bias and reinforce stereotypes. Qualitative methods are more likely to capture human diversity and the nuance of lived experiences. "Consider context," a key principle in *Data Feminism* by Catherine D'Ignazio and Laura F. Klein, is a reminder that no data hold meaning in and of themselves without the story surrounding them.[23]

* Do not speak for others. Donna Haraway warns against the danger of romanticizing and/or appropriating the vision of the less powerful while claiming to see from their positions. Our understanding of the world should be marked by elaborate specificity and the "loving care to learn how to see faithfully from another's point of view."[24] Let other people tell their own stories and never try to be an expert on someone else's experience.

* Design *alongside* for the *long haul*. We all have heard the adage "design with, not for." But designing with marginalized people and communities requires investment over time as well, to avoid acting out a creative-savior complex.[25] The designer and educator Terry Irwin likens working with communities to a relay race: "Outside consultants—like any of us disciplinary experts—are never going to be the ones that will stay with that system. The people in the system need to be the ones to create the continuity. ... You're going to hand the baton off to somebody else, but the thread of continuity has to remain within the system itself."[26]

* Design processes should be community led. A key principle of disability justice, a movement for the rights of disabled people, is "leadership of the most impacted." This principle reflects the understanding that marginalized people live within the context of historical and interlocking systems of oppression; thus, leadership must come from those who best know those systems.[27] The role of the designer, then, is not to instruct or to prescribe but to gather resources and amplify.[28]

The essays, case studies, and dialogues within this chapter demonstrate the power of knowledge in design by placing knowledge at the center of their processes and utilizing unconventional methods to uncover it. Speaking from the standpoint of their own situated knowledge, the authors share work that centers communities of people who are typically excluded and erased from the design process—women in Pakistan, women entrepreneurs in rural Costa Rica, Black mothers in the United States, disabled people—and the methods they have employed to "nurture" the margins. They explore resonant themes such as reducing power hierarchies, codesigning, and questioning the dominant assumptions about marginalized populations. Most importantly, these authors don't just use design to reveal knowledge that has been hidden or erased—they use it to create opportunities for empowerment, justice, and self-actualization. When we critically question *how* we do things and *why* we choose to do them that way, we create space for knowing, doing, and imagining design otherwise.

1 Alice Lu-Culligan and Randi Hutter Epstein, "No, We Don't Know If Vaccines Change Your Period," *New York Times*, April 20, 2021, https://www.nytimes.com/2021/04/20/opinion/coronavirus-vaccines-menstruation-periods.html.
2 Joey Sprague, *Feminist Methodologies for Critical Researchers: Bridging Differences* (Lanham, MD: Rowman & Littlefield, 2016).
3 Sandra G. Harding, ed., *The Feminist Standpoint Theory Reader: Intellectual and Political Controversies* (New York: Routledge, 2004).
4 Shaowen Bardzell, "Feminist HCI: Taking Stock and Outlining an Agenda for Design," in *CHI '10: CHI Conference on Human Factors in Computing Systems* (New York: Association for Computing Machinery, 2010), 1301–1310.
5 Linda Martín Alcoff, *Visible Identities: Race, Gender, and the Self* (New York: Oxford University Press, 2006).
6 Sprague, *Feminist Methodologies for Critical Researchers*.
7 Donna J. Haraway, "Situated Knowledges: The Science Question in Feminism and the Privilege of Partial Perspective," *Feminist Studies*

14, no. 3 (1988): 584, doi:10.2307/3178066.
8 Elizabeth Anderson, "Feminist Epistemology and Philosophy of Science," in *Stanford Encyclopedia of Philosophy*, ed. Edward N. Zalta (Stanford, CA: Stanford University Press, 2015), https://plato.stanford.edu/entries/feminism-epistemology/.
9 Haraway, "Situated Knowledges," 584.
10 Sprague, *Feminist Methodologies for Critical Researchers*.
11 Aimi Hamraie, *Building Access: Universal Design and the Politics of Disability* (Minneapolis: University of Minnesota Press, 2017), 10.
12 Katharine Sarikakis et al., "Feminist Theory and Research," in *An Integrated Approach to Communication Theory and Research*, ed. Don W. Stacks and Michael B. Salwen (New York: Taylor & Francis, 2008), 504–523.
13 Sara Wachter-Boettcher, *Technically Wrong: Sexist Apps, Biased Algorithms, and Other Threats of Toxic Tech* (New York: Norton, 2018).
14 Bardzell, "Feminist HCI."
15 bell hooks, "Choosing the Margin as a Space of Radical Openness," *Journal of Cinema and Media* 36 (1989): 15–23.
16 Ceasar McDowell,

"Design for the Margins," TEDx Indiana University, June 9, 2016.
17 Harding, *The Feminist Standpoint Theory Reader*.
18 Harding, *The Feminist Standpoint Theory Reader*.
19 Shulamit Reinharz, with the assistance of Lynn Davidman, *Feminist Methods in Social Research* (New York: Oxford University Press, 1992).
20 Reinharz, *Feminist Methods in Social Research*, 67.
21 Sasha Costanza-Chock, *Design Justice: Community-Led Practices to Build the Worlds We Need* (Cambridge, MA: MIT Press, 2020), 6.
22 The topic "quantitative versus qualitative data" has been debated and explored in depth in feminist research. See Nicole Westmarland, "The Quantitative/Qualitative Debate and Feminist Research: A Subjective View of Objectivity," *Forum: Qualitative Social Research* 2, no. 1 (2001): art. 13.
23 The topic of data ethics is explored in depth in Catherine D'Ignazio and Lauren F. Klein, *Data Feminism* (Cambridge, MA: MIT Press, 2020).
24 Haraway, "Situated Knowledges," 584.
25 Omayeli Arenyeka, "How to Think Differently about

Doing Good as a Creative Person," *Creative Independent*, December 14, 2018, https://thecreativeindependent.com/guides/how-to-think-differently-about-doing-good-as-a-creative-person/.
26 Liz Stinson, "Terry Irwin on Navigating a Mid-career Crisis and Solving Big Problems through Design," *Eye on Design*, August 16, 2021, https://eyeondesign.aiga.org/terry-irwin-on-navigating-a-mid-career-crisis-and-solving-big-problems-through-design/.
27 Patricia Berne et al., "Ten Principles of Disability Justice," *WSQ: Women's Studies Quarterly* 46, no. 1 (2018): 227–230, doi:10.1353/wsq.2018.0003.
28 Christina Harrington explores equity-based participatory design in depth. See, for example, Christina Harrington, Sheena Erete, and Anne Marie Piper, "Deconstructing Community-Based Collaborative Design," *Proceedings of the ACM on Human–Computer Interaction* 3, no. CSCW (November 7, 2019): art. 216, 1–25, doi.org/10.1145/3359318.

On feminist design that is beyond WEIRD

Not all feminisms are created equal. The human–computer interaction designer Maryam Mustafa demonstrates the critical role of situated knowledge in designing for women's empowerment.

Maryam Mustafa

Feminist thought is a natural ally to the design of technologies because of its central commitments to agency, fulfillment, identity, equity, empowerment, and social justice.[1] However, terms such as *agency* and *empowerment*, central to any discourse on feminist thought and design, are often understood by designers only within WEIRD ways of being and doing: Western, educated, industrialized, rich, and democratic. As design researchers, practitioners, and technologists strive to understand and explore what feminist design might look like and how to create equitable and just technologies, it is imperative we also explore what feminism, agency, and empowerment mean in diverse, non-WEIRD contexts.

Much of my work has been situated in Pakistan, which ranks 151 out of 153 countries on the Global Gender Gap Index published by the World Economic Forum.[2] It is a patriarchal, religious context where women have restricted mobility in public spaces, have monitored and limited access to the internet and social networking sites, and are constantly negotiating and renegotiating the space they occupy.[3] It is within this context that much of my work as a human–computer interaction researcher and designer has been situated. Most of my education and learning has taken place in Western contexts. I came to designing technologies in developing contexts *for* women from a place of assuming I understood what agency looked like. Much of what I thought I knew I have had to unlearn in working in Pakistan *with* women from diverse socioeconomic backgrounds. I did not understand or appreciate the implicit, subtle forms of resistance enacted by women in order to claim public spaces, such as the significance of loitering, hanging out with no purpose, as a form of defiance in a male-dominated society.[4]

One of my earliest studies in Pakistan was on the possibilities of digital financial services to provide banking services to the unbanked. Over the past decade, a great deal of funding has focused on financial inclusion and mobile banking as a one-stop solution to financial inclusion, particularly for women. The rationale is simple: having access to mobile wallets on your phone bypasses traditional constraints of mobility and documentation required to open bank accounts for women. Providing women with the ability to access financial services using online banking through their phones seems like a viable solution. Access to financial services is a particularly challenging problem in Pakistan; it is one of seven countries that in economic terms constitutes half of the unbanked population around the world. Less than 5 percent of women in Pakistan are included in the formal financial sector, compared to South Asia's average of 37 percent.[5] Closing this gap is vital because lack of access to financial services reduces women's ability to engage in productive economic activity and increases their likelihood of living in poverty. To explore the potential of mobile money for women in Pakistan, I spent time talking to women who might perhaps be at the tipping point of adopting mobile-money technologies. They all were microentrepreneurs who had taken small loans from microfinance institutions to set up microenterprises such as tailoring, saloonkeeping, and the preparation of frozen ready-made foods, which were businesses that they typically ran from their homes.

Our data revealed that most of the women in Pakistan save using three primary methods. First, they use rotating and savings credit associations (ROSCAs), which are borrowing and lending circles of women who know each other well and meet once a month to pool together a set amount of money; one person each month gets the pot (there is usually a predecided order). Second, they use money guards, usually older women who act as "banks" and hold on to money deposited by other women in the neighborhood. Last, many women use disposable income at the end of the month to buy gold, unstitched fabric, or other tangible goods that hold value. A vital element of all these saving mechanisms is the potential for secrecy and hidden transactions. The women we spoke to used ROSCAs and money guards to save secretly without their husbands' or their in-laws' knowledge, which allowed them more financial independence, autonomy, and control over their own assets.

The women we spoke to were aware of but unwilling to use the existing mobile-wallet services provided by different telecom operators because they did not see them as useful. For example, one participant, an older woman who runs a small home-based business, was aware of digital financial services for managing money but had never had enough disposable income to "save" in the sense of "putting it in an account and forgetting about it." Putting money into a digital account would not enable her to pay her vendors, contribute to her ROSCA (her primary method for saving), help her save for her daughter's dowry or pay her child's school fee. She did not see how the mobile wallet could meet her needs. In contrast, ROSCAs are powerful in that they allow women control over when to start saving, how much to put in, and how long to put in money, and they are inherently social in nature, leveraging women's existing social circles and trust within these circles.

Digitizing these women's financials without understanding the mechanisms they have created to circumnavigate their constraints and gain control over their own finances would strip them of their agency and disempower them. Most existing mobile-wallet technologies have not been designed with a localized understanding of how women navigate their financial independence and do not leverage the existing complex mechanisms women have established to exert their agency and autonomy, such as hidden savings. Therefore, a standard mobile-wallet application to manage money would make visible the financial transactions that the women have painstakingly crafted mechanisms to hide.

To cater specifically to women's aspirations, it is also important to consider the complexity of privacy norms and the gendered way in which they are performed. Most, if not all, current smartphone technologies and interventions work from a Western-centric framework of privacy, with the assumption that one phone is for one person, who can lock the device. However, this is not the typical model of phone usage for much of the Global South, especially for women. Women in South Asian countries such as Pakistan have access to mobile phones and the internet only as shared or monitored resources, which means they have access to a male family member's phone for a short time during the day. In this context, privacy is not established or maintained within an individualistic framework but is understood as a collective—preserving the family's (not the individual person's) privacy, honor, and dignity and upholding social norms. As a consequence, users associate privacy with scandal because if you have done nothing wrong, you have nothing to hide. This is particularly true for women, who, even when they have their own personal devices, share passwords with family members and actively work to give the impression of an "open" device and digital space that their family is free to monitor and see. It is important to think about privacy design as allowing women to enact specific boundaries while at the same time keeping these boundaries invisible and untraceable. It must allow women to be seen as upholding expected digital social norms but also include affordances to circumvent these norms. Current privacy design does not allow for this kind of invisible privacy. For example, although WhatsApp allows you to delete messages, it also leaves behind a trace of that deletion.

✳ Empowerment inherently demands a process
of change and the ability to make strategic life
choices, which necessarily implies the possibility of
alternatives or the ability to choose otherwise. ✳

Empowerment is a *process*. The social economist Naila Kabeer defines empowerment as a "process by which those who have been denied the ability to make strategic life choices acquire that ability" by accessing material, information, and ideological resources, which in turn allows them to redistribute power in their societies.[6] Empowerment inherently demands a process of change and the ability to make strategic life choices, which necessarily implies the possibility of alternatives or the ability to choose otherwise. Thoughtful, localized technology design has a great role to play in this process, more perhaps than anything else in a context such as the Global South, where women's mobility, access to social networks, finances, and work opportunities are so limited. Critically safe, contextualized digital spaces provide women with access to alternate ways of being and doing as well as access to choices and agency. Although agency often tends to be understood as decision-making, it can take on varied shapes and forms, such as bargaining and negotiation, duplicity and manipulation. It can be understood also as "power to"—the power to define your own life choices and pursue your own goals. Women in the Global South are prolifically co-opting platforms such as Facebook, Instagram, and TikTok to explore their identities, to push back against patriarchal boundaries, and to amplify their resistance by making available alternatives at the discursive level. Such platforms facilitate the imagining of different choices and realities, which is vital to the development of a questioning consciousness that allows women to move from uncritical acceptance of a social order to a critical perspective on it. Although these digital spaces are not easily available to women, women have co-opted them for their own purposes and to enact their own resistance, just as they have always figured out mechanisms to subvert the patriarchal order in their own way.

The key to empowering women is *contextualized*, *thoughtful*, *sensitive* design that considers what agency means to them in their context and does not further limit their choices. I leave you with a particularly powerful and insightful way of thinking about feminisms and empowerment by the South Asian feminist activist Kamla Bhasin: "Feminism is like water. It's everywhere, but it takes the shape of the container into which it is poured. My feminism is different … because I live in India, because my patriarchy is different, my technology is different."[7]

Maryam Mustafa is assistant professor at the Lahore University of Management Sciences. She has a PhD in computer science from the Technical University of Braunschweig, Germany, and is a Fulbright scholar with a master's degree from Cornell University.

1 Shaowen Bardzell, "Feminist HCI: Taking Stock and Outlining an Agenda for Design," in *CHI '10: CHI Conference on Human Factors in Computing Systems* (New York: Association for Computing Machinery, 2010), 1301–1310.
2 World Economic Forum, *Global Gender Gap Report 2020* (Geneva: World Economic Forum, 2020).
3 Sehrish Mushtaq and Fawad Baig, "Reclaiming Public and Digital Spaces: The Conundrum of Acceptance for the Feminist Movement in Pakistan," in *The Routledge Handbook of Religion, Gender and Society*, ed. Emma Tomalin and Caroline Starkey (New York: Routledge, 2022), 103–118.
4 Shilpa Phadke, Sameera Khan, and Shilpa Ranade, *Why Loiter? Women and Risk on Mumbai Streets* (New Delhi: Penguin, 2011).
5 Financial Inclusion Insights, "Pakistan Wave 5 Report: Fifth Annual FII Tracker Survey," 2018, http://finclusion.org/uploads/file/pakistan-wave-5-quicksites_final.pdf.
6 Naila Kabeer, "Resources, Agency, Achievements: Reflections on the Measurement of Women's Empowerment," *Development and Change* 30, no. 3 (1999): 1, doi:10.1111/1467-7660.00125.
7 Kamla Bhasin and Lilinaz Evans, "Women on the Edge of Time," interview by Hannah Pool, *New Internationalist*, July 2, 2014, https://newint.org/features/2014/07/01/feminism-women-edge-of-time.

On mother centered design

Design's impact is not just in its outcomes but in its processes as well. Designer Elizabeth Pérez proposes a framework that centers the knowledge of Black mothers.

Elizabeth Pérez

What if we trusted Black mothers to create the world we desperately need? What if we gave them the tools and resources they and their children deserve so that their lives would be about innovation instead of survival? What if we sought the expertise of those most vulnerable, with the most to lose, to design a shared reality that benefits everyone?

These questions were brewing within my practice when I began supporting pregnant people and new families as a birth and postpartum doula in 2013. I did so from a deep desire to feel and believe that how I utilized my time was committed to improving our collective reality. I was enthralled by the possibility of it all: a growing body, a baby that would eventually come out of that body, and the new family that would also be born. I attended support and advocacy trainings, expanded my network of childbirth professionals, and quickly developed a successful practice. Each time I was called into someone's labor, I would spring into action. Beginnings, no matter how hard, are magical, and witnessing someone in theirs was a deep honor for me.

What I didn't expect was how permanent things would feel when it was my turn. Behind the excitement of my pregnancy was a deep fear of death, of losing myself and my baby. Many of the lifesaving procedures used in obstetrics and gynecology today exist only because of the violent experimentation that enslaved Black women experienced, often without pain medication.[1] Today, Black women in the United States are 234 percent more likely than white women to die from childbirth-related causes,[2] a crisis that is especially prevalent in the South. In 2022, Republican senator Bill Cassidy said that Louisiana's maternal mortality rates weren't that bad if you don't count a third of the state's population—the third that is Black.[3] The disregard for Black women—for Black mothers—is ever present. As we navigate a post–*Roe v. Wade* reality, Black people giving birth are right to question whether their lives and their children's lives will be protected.

My labor was induced due to intrauterine growth restriction, which disproportionately affects Black women. The subsequent depression, anxiety, and post-traumatic stress disorder I experienced led me to rethink the ways I could support families and my immediate community without sacrificing my well-being and creativity. I knew that if I continued to work as a childbirth professional, my physical and mental health would deteriorate, which would negatively affect how I mothered my own son. In 2019, I decided to enroll in a graduate program that

Figure 2.2.1 The Mother Centered Design crest. Courtesy of Elizabeth Pérez.

explored art, design, and technology. This meant becoming a traditional student again, an adult learner, while still working as a childbirth professional and navigating my new role, that of mother.

In the essay "Motherhood, Media, and Building a 21st Century Movement," Malkia A. Cyril questions how it is possible for a household, a community, or a nation to be "effectively governed when women are held disproportionately responsible for its future yet are disproportionately neglected, abused, excluded, isolated and invisible."[4] The concurrence of my first year in a master's program and a pandemic ran me into the ground. Traveling from place to place, appointment to appointment, class to preschool pick-up all around New York City was wearing my spirit thin. The expectation to mother as if I had no other work and to work (and, in my case, to study and create) as if I had no other responsibilities was especially cruel. I often thought to myself, "If mothers are the vehicles for the future, why am I the only mother-student enrolled in a graduate program that serves as an incubator for designers and technologists?"

I found myself recalling the work of the Combahee River Collective, a radical Black feminist organization formed in Boston in 1974. Their introduction of the terms *interlocking oppression* and *identity politics* into our lexicon still give many of us the words we need to describe the weight of the oppressions we experience simultaneously. What would it look like for Black mother-designers to unravel themselves in the safety formed by one another's presence? For my master's thesis project, I set out to rethink how design processes can give Black mothers the opportunity to assess the conditions in which they are required to mother and, as a result, to assert the boundaries and possibilities that they envision for themselves and their children. I wanted to design an experience that brought us together and out of isolation into a relatable, creative space during a global pandemic where little hope and support existed for women like us.

This led me to design a series of world-building workshops that centered on Black mother-designers with support from Whitney Robinson of the Renée, a startup that crafted spaces and products to improve Black maternal experiences. Our goal was not to "solve" the challenges Black mothers face but instead to harness our collective wisdom and desire to see a better version of our lived realities. The workshops spanned three days, with modules that explored design methods, such as identifying pain points and joy points and developing "how might we" questions. The result was an evolving set of design principles paired with a manifesto. I invite anyone who works or engages with Black mothers to re-create this workshop, and I invite mothers of other oppressed and marginalized identities to use this workshop opportunity as a tool for their own liberation.[5]

✳ As we navigate a post–*Roe v. Wade* reality, Black people giving birth are right to question whether their lives and their children's lives will be protected. ✳

As designers, we have accepted the methodology of design as a way to "solve," but what we are ultimately doing is perpetuating a system of buying and selling. In response, the Mother Centered Design (MCD) framework aims to heal. It is an anticapitalist, antiracist, and antipatriarchal design pedagogy and practice. MCD calls into question current design practices, which are inherently capitalist frameworks that prioritize production and profit over resource sharing and relationships. The driving force behind the MCD principles is to uplift and center the

Principles of Mother Centered Design

Elizabeth Pérez

---

❶ We love Black women, uplift Black women, and value the genius that is the Black woman.

❷ We trust the authentic manifestations of our mothering; we look to each other for validation, not to the systems that stifle our creativity.

❸ We make space for generative and regenerative processes focused on healing and leaving a better-cared-for Mother Earth. We consider long-term impact.

❹ We create new visions and versions of ourselves that are relatable, adaptable, innovative, and flexible.

❺ We speak the name of our ancestors and honor their wisdom by preparing ourselves to be great ancestors ourselves. Afrofuturism is now.

❻ We work with community members to reduce the things that pull on us so that we have the energy to show up for ourselves and our children.

❼ We allow for joy and discovery and grace and empathy. We recognize we do not have all the answers—we learn as we go and trust the process.

Black mother, the original world builder and designer, in order to enact the change needed within our communities and society. When Black mothers have what they need to exist as whole human beings and not to worry about the safety and longevity of their lives and their children's lives, we will see the most fruitful and abundant harvest of social innovation. Through this careful planting, we use design thinking instead as a methodology that addresses existing inequities in everything and how they affect the needs and creativity of the Black mother, who has experienced the most harm from all systems. Through the liberation and uplifting of the Black mother, everyone else will be free, too.

Elizabeth Pérez (she/her) is a mother, multidisciplinary designer, and educator interested in the confluence of motherhood, world building, and the possibilities of design. She has taught at Parsons School of Design and completed a postdoctoral fellowship in the Interactive Telecommunications Program at New York University, where she received her graduate degree. She works as a user-experience writer at Deloitte Consulting and lives in Brooklyn, New York, with her son and coparent.

1   Shanker Vedantam, "Remembering Anarcha, Lucy, and Betsey: The Mothers of Modern Gynecology," NPR, February 7, 2017, https://www.npr.org/2017/02/07/513764158/remembering-anarcha-lucy-and-betsey-the-mothers-of-modern-gynecology.
2   Nina Martin, "Black Mothers Keep Dying after Giving Birth. Shalon Irving's Story Explains Why," NPR, December 7, 2017, https://www.npr.org/2017/12/07/568948782/black-mothers-keep-dying-after-giving-birth-shalon-irvings-story-explains-why.
3   Sarah Owermohle, "Why Louisiana's Maternal Mortality Rates Are so High," *Politico*, May 19, 2022, https://www.politico.com/news/2022/05/19/why-louisianas-maternal-mortality-rates-are-so-high-00033832.
4   Malkia A. Cyril, "Motherhood, Media, and Building a 21st Century Movement," in *Revolutionary Mothering: Love on the Front Lines*, ed. Alexis Pauline Gumbs, China Martens, and Ma'a Williams (Oakland, CA: PM Press, 2016), 32.
5   A workshop guide can be found at https://mothercentered.design.

On critical feminist frameworks for disability design

The disability studies scholar and designer Aimi Hamraie discusses access as a feminist issue and the deeply rooted ableism of design.

Dialogue with Aimi Hamraie

Alison Place Much of your work takes place at the intersection of feminism and disability studies as well as of feminism and disability justice. Where do those distinct terrains intersect, and in what ways do they differ?

Aimi Hamraie Disability studies is an academic field, while disability justice is a social movement, but they do intersect in important ways with feminist theory. The disability justice movement stems from the activism of disabled people of color and queer disabled people and places a huge emphasis on the Black feminist concept of intersectionality.

The field of disability studies historically has been concerned with the body as something that gets known and the consequences for how bodies get known. Similarly, since the 1960s feminist theory has critiqued biomedical ways of knowing the body, with an emphasis on the body as a locus of identity and knowledge. One of the questions that both disability studies and feminist theory are concerned with is what it means to fit or not fit into the built environment and the designed world.

AP What is the Critical Design Lab, and what are some of the things you do there?

AH Critical Design Lab is a collaborative of disabled artists, designers, and researchers. It's not tied to a particular institution, and we have members in three countries. We use ideas and practices from disability culture to shape design methodologies and protocols. And we do all of our work remotely and online, even since before the pandemic, partially for accessibility reasons and partially for geographic ones.

AP How do you define critical design, and how does that shape your work with the Lab?

AH Critical design as a methodology is typically about producing discomfort and antagonism in a user in such a way that highlights what has been taken for granted about other forms of design. But most disabled people already have the experience of being that type of user, without someone doing some kind of fun, critical project that's trying to produce it. There's this assumption within the discourse of critical design that the user is already normate, and that is why they're having a disorienting experience. Conversely, doing design work from the perspective of disability culture is also critical design in the sense of disorienting normate perception, but it puts disability knowledge at the forefront in order to show the norms that are taken for granted in different realms. Our projects in the Lab focus on different areas where that happens or where it's possible to intervene.

AP Another design framework you use in the Lab is protocols.[1] Can you talk about what

59

those are and what role they play in the Lab's practices?

AH The aim of our protocols is to create an alternative to the standardized form of the accessibility checklist, which essentially lets people off the hook if they have, say, a wheelchair ramp or some Braille text. The checklist doesn't really teach you anything about how access is produced and maintained and why. For one of our protocols, we started holding accessibility mapathons, which are crowdsourcing events where a whole bunch of people come to a place to do accessibility mapping (figure 2.3.1). The surveys we give people ask really critical questions, not just if something is present but also "How do you describe it? Can you find the path? What would you do if this happened?" Through the process of going to a place and filling out the survey, they have a better sense of how difficult it is to say if something is accessible or not. It brings them to a more complex and critical theory of access than if I had, say, given a lecture on it.

AP What are some other things we are missing when we talk about accessibility in design?

AH The mainstream dialogue on accessibility is still pretty dominated by compliance with the law, but the Americans with Disabilities Act doesn't cover all disabilities. Frameworks like disability justice or radical access[2] include more disabilities, like chronic illness or chemical sensitivity and now long-haul COVID. That includes a lot of people. It's about making sure our conception of access is broad. Accessibility also often gets subjected to economic calculations, like "When is it worth it?" or "How can it yield more productive workers or good consumers?" With product design, for example, there is a discourse around disabled people as a market that must be taken advantage of so as not to miss out on so many consumers.

Figure 2.3.1 A campus map from the Mapping Access project. Screenshot of a map showing an aerial view of a university campus. The map is labeled "VU Mapping Access." It shows trees and buildings from above, and colored pins indicate different forms of accessibility. A pop-up shows a building entrance and provides information. Image courtesy of Critical Design Lab.

I understand strategically why that appeals to a manufacturing logic, but it's also just really politically fraught to base whether or not access should exist on profitability.

AP When we do address accessibility in design, it can often be framed as a binary where something is either accessible or it's not: a wheelchair ramp complies with the law, or it doesn't; an image has alt text, or it doesn't. That keeps us from seeing issues of access that are more complex or emerge over time. How can we reframe accessibility outside of a binary?

✳ Critical design is typically about producing discomfort in a user in such a way that highlights what has been taken for granted about other forms of design. But most disabled people already have the experience of being that type of user. ✳

AH In disability culture, we tend to describe accessibility as an unfinished and never-ending commitment. The reason that's important is it's about humility. It shows that just because I care about this thing today doesn't mean someone else later on can't be harmed by it or have a conflicting need. Knowing that there isn't a perfect solution commits us to being in the process. Recognizing access as emergent and flexible and being able to be critical of what yesterday we thought was good access keep us committed to doing better next time. That's a good way to be in the world, as people and as designers.

AP A key theme of your book [*Building Access: Universal Design and the Politics of Disability*] is the idea that "knowing is a gateway to making."[3] Knowledge is typically taken for granted in the design process, with dominant forms of knowledge centered by default.

What needs to be done to center disabled people's knowledge in the design process?

AH All design rests on certain forms of knowledge, so when nondisabled designers are designing without experience of a disability, what they're doing is nondisabled design because their knowledge shapes the practice, and [the design] will always be based on the assumption of a certain kind of user. Designing *for* disabled people has happened for a long time, but even when disability is included in the design process, [the process is] still shaped by other cultural norms and assumptions, like the assumption that all disabled people are white. Designing *with* disabled people is what Ray Lifchez and Barbara Winslow, two architects at UC Berkeley, did with their book *Design for Independent Living*,[4] where they brought disabled people from the community into the design studio and treated them as user experts. Many people advocate for that approach, but it can be tokenizing. Now there are more disabled students who are entering the design professions, and they're facing a lot of barriers, but it's changing the discourse because it gives more control to people who not only have the lived experience but also are part of the community. When people are immersed in disability culture, they're going to have a very different perspective than just one person designing on the basis of their own individual experience.

AP When the framework is about "including" disabled people in the design process, as you said, it can be tokenizing and inadequate. What can nondisabled designers do to better center the knowledge of disabled people in the design process?

AH A simple thing they can do is make sure that disabled people, not just one token person, are part of the process from the beginning and [that] they're compensated equally, if not more. The ground of design already presumes that designers are nondisabled people and [that] they're bringing in an expert as a one-off thing, but there are design firms run and populated by disabled people who can be hired to do that work instead. Make sure access is available in the process, too. I know so many people who have been hired to do access consulting, and they show up, and they can't get in because the space isn't accessible.

AP Designers often deal with data, but data-collection methods don't typically capture the problems that disabled people face properly. In what ways do we need to rethink how we're collecting and using data related to disabled people's experiences?

AH Data are an empirical approach to knowledge. Data have politics too, just like all knowledge has politics, in terms of how we decide who gets to know and what kind of information is valuable. Often when we're talking about data, we're talking about a lot of data points that get aggregated and generalized. For example, if you're trying to figure out what slope of a wheelchair ramp somebody can use without getting tired, you would test a whole bunch of people and come up with an average. But the ways we do statistical research on general populations tend to favor the average or the norm, even if it's within a marginal population. One data practice that researchers use instead is to value the ninety-fifth to one hundredth percentile or the zero to fifth percentile instead of the fiftieth percentile. If we're just designing for the average within a population of wheelchair users, for example, then we're favoring the people who may have fewer access barriers than others. It can be a political practice to change how we do sampling and what part of the bell curve we designate as the prototypical user.

AP Are there similar practices that can be implemented in qualitative research?

AH Making sure more disabled people are on design-research teams is really important. And if you can't access that, you can involve people who are affected in the process of the survey design. For example, the surveys in the Mapping Access project were based on focus groups we did with different folks on campus who are impacted by building accessibility, including but not limited to disabled people. This helps to make sure you get the language right and ask questions that are going to produce types of knowledge that would result in better design. And people should be compensated for that work.

AP Just as designers are presumed to be nondisabled, disabled people tend to be framed merely as users. In much of your work, you argue that disabled people are inherently designers and always have been because of the need to constantly hack their environments and challenge things around them. When we call what disabled people do "design," how does that problematize or expand what has been traditionally considered "design"?

AH There are definitely power struggles over the idea of "what is design." It's important to remember that the design professions were not professionalized until the early twentieth century, but humans in general have been doing things called design for a long time before that. The only difference is now we have institutional structures that require you to go to certain schools or to get licensure. Because we live in a capitalist society, that process, by definition, excludes people who are not able to access higher education and therefore excludes all different forms of vernacular design. In the case of disabled people in particular, designers shouldn't just approach them as users but also as makers who have valuable methodological knowledge. They must also cite and compensate them for the designs that get produced because one way appropriation happens is when the original people who did the thing are not considered valid knowers and makers. It's important to recognize expertise and simultaneously pay attention to how expertise gets produced in our fields and who are the gatekeepers of expertise and professionalization.

AP What suggestions or advice might you have for nondisabled designers to be better co-conspirators with disabled people?

AH Nondisabled designers can uplift the agendas of disabled people better by joining our projects that are already happening. It would be great to have nondisabled designers show up and offer their knowledge and their work toward something they really believe in; to me, that's how to be a co-conspirator. Figure out what resources you have access to and redirect them toward disability projects and disabled designers. And learn about disability culture and things like ableist language as much as possible. Do the work of allyship in the spaces you have access to.

This conversation took place over Zoom in January 2022. It has been edited for clarity and length.

Aimi Hamraie (they/them) is associate professor of medicine, health, and society and American studies at Vanderbilt University and director of the Critical Design Lab. Hamraie is author of *Building Access: Universal Design and the Politics of Disability* (2017).

1 Michelle Murphy describes "protocol feminism" as a set of practices through which techno-science is made "accessible, routinizable, and do-able" (*Seizing the Means of Reproduction: En-*tanglements of Feminism, Health and Technoscience* [Durham, NC: Duke University Press, 2012], 30). 2 A. J. Withers, *Disability Politics and Theory* (Winnipeg, Canada: Fernwood, 2019).

3 Aimi Hamraie, *Building Access: Universal Design and the Politics of Disability* (Minneapolis: University of Minnesota Press, 2017). 4 Barbara Winslow and Raymond Lifchez, *Design for Inde-*pendent Living: The Environment and Physically Disabled People* (New York: Whitney Library of Design, 1979).

On female entrepreneurship and visual storytelling

The graphic designer and educator Gaby Hernández explores the role of the designer as a storytelling facilitator through ethnographic research and codesign with women entrepreneurs in Costa Rica.

Gaby Hernández

Learning Femininity

Acknowledging my identity and positionality is a vulnerable but essential element for my design research and teaching. I am a woman of color, an immigrant, born and raised in an urban and low-income household in Costa Rica, now working in the United States. My multidisciplinary and bilingual practice studies the role of visual communication design in everyday life from the perspective of the minoritized and oppressed. My late mother, Margarita, was profoundly influential in my early femininity. She was born in the 1950s, and her gendered perceptions were informed by a traditional culture of machismo; thus, many of her behaviors helped perpetuate patriarchy and gender inequity. And yet she permeated my childhood with seeds of mental, physical, and financial independence (figure 2.4.1). Through extensive academic tutoring, she nurtured my interest in the arts and social sciences, encouraging discipline and resiliency. She wished for a feminist environment conducive to expanding my perspectives and identity despite pressing financial limitations and social inequity.

Later, as a graduate student, I collaborated with visionary Maya women on design and entrepreneurship projects in rural México. This formative interaction exposed me to gender culture within their context and, for the first time for me, outside of my familiar surroundings. Motivated by an ever-growing interest in femininity and design across cultures, in 2009 and 2010 I conducted my thesis project in Costa Rica on Chira Island, a remote community at the northern end of the Gulf of Nicoya in the Pacific (figure 2.4.2). With the Women's Association of Chira Island (WACI), made up of entrepreneurs who pioneered ecotourism in their region, I experienced the intersectionalities of rural feminism in my country and witnessed visual storytelling's impact on female independence.

Building Connection

Media reports of Chira's aqueduct inauguration, water contamination from fruit plantations, and unsustainable fish extraction in the Gulf of Nicoya first acquainted me with Chira. It also motivated my focus on storytelling—a critical aspect of the feminist design framework that "calls for unearthing inequities and changing systems so that male privilege no longer functions as a normative mode of operation."[1]

Figure 2.4.1 *¡Mujeres Domésticas No!*
Mixed-media collage exploring multiplicity
of female identities living in a traditionally
machista culture. Courtesy of Gaby Hernández.

Figure 2.4.2
Puerto Palito, Chira Island.
Photograph by Gaby
Hernández.

Chiran women's perspectives on ecological decay and inequitable access became a fundamental element of their story.

Developing my thesis project in Chira required design research and field-work on the island and beyond. Entities and individuals with the knowledge and social capital to work in Chira were critical in this process, facilitating historic documentation about Chira's entrepreneurship and a connection with WACI. This prefieldwork revealed:

* The relation between the environmental and economic decline in Chira and response to it in the form of women-led entrepreneurship. Nonprofit institutions and universities helped projects emerge in the late 1990s, but not all were successful, and many women entrepreneurs stepped down quickly, according to Lilliana Martínez, founding member of WACI.[2] Throughout rural Latin America, women overcame limitations by challenging traditional roles that restricted them and perpetuated their dependence on men.

* How the historical figure of the campesina (countryside woman)—"strong, healthy, frugal, but slow and superstitious, of childish intelligence and resigned"[3]—sustained the perception that women and men have different rights and duties. In the words of Martínez, "Entrepreneurial work makes us look lazy or negligent with the upkeep of our households."[4]

* That domestic violence and emotional abuse are common in Chira. Dora Medina, a WACI founding member, connects men's excessive drinking and domestic abuse with low self-esteem among women.[5] As a consequence, many Chiran women aren't urged to study or be employed. Patriarchy "hides and minimizes the legacy of women in all aspects of life and society,"[6] a vicious circle.

In Chira, I stayed at or close to WACI's lodge, facilitating interactions in the common areas and homes. I documented mutually shared stories, which I sup-plemented with island trips and testimonies of other individuals related to WACI, including domestic partners and other relatives.

Visualizing Women's Success

WACI results from mutuality and sisterhood informed by shared experiences of struggle, trauma, and exclusion. Our collaborative project was defined as a collection of visual-storytelling artifacts designed to support women in Chira and in similar rural contexts with information to start new projects and collectives. Through representation, we aimed WACI to motivate others and to become a reference for women-led ecotourism. The most important outcomes of the project were:

Map of Connections. Chira is full of contradictions. A sense of community is shadowed by violence and stigma. Its fishing tradition is often interrupted by pollution, which also affects Chira's mangroves, one of WACI's places of operation. Women's activities are halted by machismo fed at the local cantinas (figure 2.4.3).

Timeline. This design visualizes ten years of WACI's entrepreneurial history. It features facts about WACI's origin, its relations with other groups and associations, its media elements, and its activities since 2000, such as the construction of its lodge, collaborations with nonprofit organizations, grant funding, and first ecotourism conference in Guatemala (figure 2.4.4).

Testimonial Documentary. The video shows the faces of the story. Based exclusively on WACI's interviews, it addresses the association's beginnings, the work context for Chiran women, and advice for other rural women.

Final Thoughts

Storytelling is a focal part of any critical feminist work. Through storytelling, we understand the world based on our lived experiences and sociocultural context. The feminist scholar Kaisa Ilmonen writes: "As feminists, our stories tell something about us. When we analyze feminist narratives on intersectionality, intersectionality itself becomes contextualized anew, opening up novel ways of knowing."[7] As this case study explains, by sharing our unique experiences of vulnerability, heterogeneous groups of women (in this case, WACI's members and I, an outsider from

Figure 2.4.3 *Map of Connections* user-tested at WACI's lodge in Chira. Courtesy of Gaby Hernández.

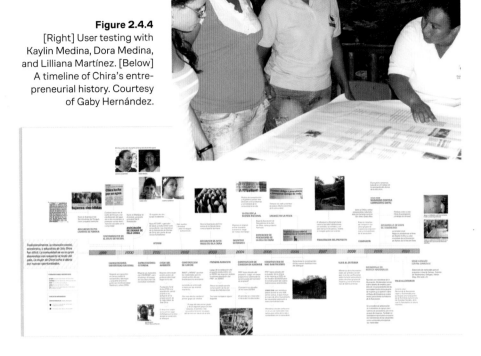

Figure 2.4.4
[Right] User testing with Kaylin Medina, Dora Medina, and Lilliana Martínez. [Below] A timeline of Chira's entrepreneurial history. Courtesy of Gaby Hernández.

urban Costa Rica) can work in a space of common understanding to formulate new ways to support others through their stories.

In communities with remaining machismo and gender-based exclusion, the visibility of female role models and their stories may constitute a turning point for marginalized women. Neha Kumar and her colleagues explain, "By engaging feminist solidarity and aligning on common differences, communities can learn to effectively leverage historical experiences of one context to illuminate research questions, design goals, and ideas for interventions in another."[8] This anecdotal solidarity benefits from every bit of shared feminist knowledge. As such, designers as external collaborators must avoid canonical hierarchies in achieving the goal to elevate women's untold stories.

Gaby Hernández (she, her, ella) is a Costa Rican designer, researcher, and Endowed Associate Professor of Graphic Design at the University of Arkansas. Her work on decoloniality, antiracism, equity, heritage, and identity has been internationally presented and published since 2012.

1   Sharra Vostral and Deana McDonagh, "How to Add Feminist Approaches into Design Courses," *Design Principles and Practices* 4, no. 4 (2010): 114, doi:10.18848/1833-1874/cgp/v04i04/37928.
2   Lilliana Martínez, founding member, WACI, in discussion with the author, July, 2009.
3   Juvenal, "La mujer costarricense: Su fisonomía moral y la influencia en la evolución de nuestra sociedad" [The Costa Rican woman: Her moral physiognomy and its influence on our society's evolution], in *Estudios de la mujer: Conocimiento y cambio* [Women's studies: Knowledge and change] (San José, Mexico: EDUCA, 1988), 27.
4   Martínez interview, 2009.
5   Dora Medina, founding member, WACI, in discussion with the author, July, 2009.
6   Marta E. Solano Arias, "A 90 años de la fundación de la Liga Feminista Costarricense: Los derechos políticos" [Ninety years after the foundation of the Costa Rican Feminist League: The political rights], *Revista derecho electoral del Tribunal Supremo de Elecciones de la República de Costa Rica*, no. 17 (Enero–Junio 2014): 358.
7   Kaisa Ilmonen, "Feminist Storytelling and Narratives of Intersectionality," *Signs: Journal of Women in Culture and Society* 45, no. 2 (December 2019): 347, doi:10.1086/704989.
8   Neha Kumar et al., "Engaging Feminist Solidarity for Comparative Research, Design, and Practice," *Proceedings of the ACM Human–Computer Interactions* 3, no. CSCW (November 7, 2019): article 167, 2, doi:10.1145/3359269.

On feminist technology for housing justice

Unlock NYC is a feminist technology and community-building collective that designs tools to fight discrimination while centering the experiences of those seeking safe, affordable housing.

Ashley K. Eberhart, Elizabeth Byrd, Madeline Avram Blount, Manon Vergerio, and Velvet A. Johnson Ross

Every time I call a listing, it was the same. The broker or owner would come up with an excuse to turn me down. I felt like I never had a fair chance to find housing for me and my kids.
—Elizabeth, Unlock NYC leader

I come from ... generation(s) of women ... from the school of hard knocks. Knocked around by unscrupulous landlords ... in neighborhoods that were food deserts, over-policed, [with] high unemployment, ethnic and racial segregation, overpopulation ... substandard housing not suitable for human dwelling, and degraded environmental quality.
—Fannielou Diane, Unlock NYC leader

What Keeps Low-Income New Yorkers from Finding a Safe and Affordable Home?

As researchers at Blue Ridge Labs, we interviewed dozens of people about their housing search, and we heard that discriminatory gatekeeping remains an unrelenting issue. We spoke to a mother in a homeless shelter who needed an apartment to keep custody of her children but who found realtors unresponsive whenever she mentioned her housing subsidy. Another woman showed us a notebook teeming with listings she had contacted during her multiyear search, only to still be looking.

We saw how tenants worked with advocates to record phone calls and send evidence of discrimination to the city. Many people had found housing because of that evidence and the city's subsequent intervention. With methods from community organizing and participatory design, we asked how we might make reporting discrimination efficient, affirming, and accessible. This work led to the founding of Unlock NYC: a women-led tech collective that designs free tools to report housing discrimination. People use our online chatbot to learn about their rights, to record phone calls, and to report unlawful treatment (figure 2.5.1). We send reports to a city agency responsible for enforcing antidiscrimination laws. Today, one-third of our users have had the chance to apply to lease an apartment after being initially turned away.

Figure 2.5.1
Reporting housing discrimination can be daunting. The Unlock NYC digital tools, codesigned with its users, provide a supportive, affirmative experience. Courtesy of Unlock NYC.

Unlock NYC is not only about getting keys. The reporting process affirms for users that what they face is not imagined, resolves lingering "feelings of craziness,"[1] and reinforces the fact that discrimination is not their fault. A large part of our work involves collecting data that reveal the scale of the problem and stories that show our users that they are not alone. We center the expertise of those who have navigated the complexities of searching for housing with a government voucher. We also forefront the intersecting identities that matter in this work: the designers who started Unlock NYC are white women without experience of housing discrimination, but the leaders who have joined are Black, multiracial, and Latinx women, some with decades of experience with the voucher system. In recognizing that we all speak from different places, with different "located lived experiences,"[2] we acknowledge an imbalance of personal encounters with oppression. We also celebrate the different bodies of knowledge each of us brings, and we walk together toward our goals in housing justice.

Unlock NYC as a Feminist Collective

Women experience the brunt of housing discrimination, do the bulk of reporting, and stand at the forefront of fighting for solutions. The struggle for fair housing has been particularly arduous for Black women, Indigenous women, and women of color. For many, the very concept of *home* evokes *woman*; for bell hooks, "houses belonged to women, were their special domain. ... [T]he folks who made this life possible ... were black women."[3] At the same time, for Black women in the city today, *home* can mean eviction, overcrowding, unhealthy conditions, and other harmful aspects of living in disinvested neighborhoods. This crisis is the product of decades of sexist and racist policies rooted in a white-supremacist property system.[4] As recently as 1970, women could not get a home loan without a male cosigner. As of 2016, 70 percent of heads of households in the New York City family homeless-shelter system were Black women.[5] If patriarchal forces "delegate … to females the task of creating and sustaining a home,"[6] women are also confronted with a rigged system where men hold the keys. All but one of New York City's top-20 worst evictors are white men.[7] Men also lead most of the public agencies where New Yorkers can report discrimination.[8]

How We Build Feminist Technologies

Unlock NYC is a nonhierarchical, consensus-driven collective (figure 2.5.3). We resist the male-dominated tech-world temptation of grandiose promises to instantly scale up our products and "disrupt" reality. Instead, we listen and learn from our community's wisdom and recognize that our localized efforts can be powerful forms of resistance. We honor the work of those closest to the problem rather than injecting new solutions from the outside. We know our tools are used by people experiencing trauma and disillusion, so we build with the compassion that we think every public service should provide. This caretaking also comes in the form of transparent, jargon-free consent and privacy policies as well as thoughtful encryption measures to keep user data safe. Finally, we make space for our own rest and well-being. We recognize the emotional labor we do for each other

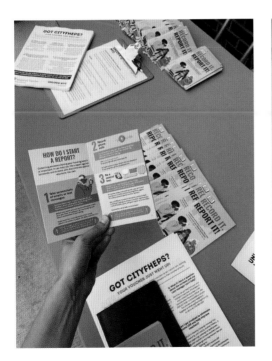

Figure 2.5.2 In 2021, we worked with Neighbors Together, the Center for Urban Pedagogy, and our users to design a pocket-size, illustrated "know your rights" guide called *Record It. Report It!* Courtesy of Unlock NYC.

Figure 2.5.3 During our fall 2021 annual retreat, we drew a collective timeline to visualize, reflect, and celebrate the previous year. Each of us highlighted moments that helped us grow or brought us joy. Courtesy of Unlock NYC.

rather than rendering it invisible. We commit to these principles, although current structures make it difficult to do so. In many ways, Unlock NYC is a world-making exercise: we create the world we want to see through how we work together. As the forces keeping people away from the home they deserve harness the power of new technologies, we will also build our own technologies of liberation and justice—and we will build them together.

Ashley K. Eberhart, MA, is a product designer, creative strategist, and social entrepreneur. Her writing appears in *Health Design Thinking* (MIT Press, 2020) and the journal *Public Health*.

Elizabeth Byrd is a mom of six kids with 16 years of experience living by means of a voucher in New York City. She advocates for her family by being on parenting leadership boards, social committees, and public panels.

Madeline Avram Blount is a technologist, researcher, and artist. She has worked as a software engineer, conducted ethnographic fieldwork on border systems and migration, and served as an organizer on political campaigns and movements.

Manon Vergerio is a critical urbanist with a background in participatory research, design, and community organizing. Based in Brooklyn, she is a longtime member of the Anti-Eviction Mapping Project.

Velvet A. Johnson Ross is a singer, actress, award-winning playwright, documentary producer, and historian. She has a BA from Brooklyn College in communications and an MA in women's history from Sarah Lawrence College.

1   "Black feminists often talk about their feelings of craziness before becoming conscious of the concepts of sexual politics, patriarchal rule" (Combahee River Collective, *The Combahee River Collective Statement*, April 1977, https://www.blackpast.org/african-american-history/combahee-river-collective-statement-1977/).
2   Linda Martin Alcoff, *Visible Identities: Race, Gender, and the Self* (New York: Oxford University Press, 2006), 42.
3   bell hooks, "Homeplace (a Site of Resistance)," in *Yearning: Race, Gender, and Cultural Politics* (Boston: South End Press, 1990), 41.
4   Cheryl I. Harris, "Whiteness as Property," *Harvard Law Review* 106, no. 8 (June 1993): 1707–1791, doi.org/10.2307/1341787.
5   New York City Department of Homeless Services, "NYC Department of Homeless Services Brings Women of Color Faith and Community Leaders Together for New, Targeted Homelessness Prevention Event," press release, June 24, 2016, https://www1.nyc.gov/site/dhs/about/press-releases/prevention-breakfast-press-release.page.
6   hooks, "Homeplace," 41.
7   Right to Counsel Coalition, JustFix.nyc, "NYC's Top 20 Worst Evictors in 2019," n.d., https://www.worstevictorsnyc.org/evictors-list/ citywide/.
8   David Brand, "NYC's 'Hollowed Out' Enforcement Units Struggle to Keep Pace on Housing Discrimination Cases," *City Limits Housing and Development*, June 1, 2021, https://citylimits.org/2021/06/01/nycs-hollowed-out-enforcement-units-struggle-to-keep-pace-on-housing-discrimination-cases/.

☺ Care

That visibility which makes us most vulnerable is that which also is the source of our greatest strength.

Audre Lorde
SISTER OUTSIDER

On care

Alison Place

Written in 2020, a year marked by a global pandemic and social justice uprisings, *The Care Manifesto* states that we are in a crisis of care.[1] Over the past few decades, ideas of social welfare and community have been pushed aside for individualized notions of resilience, wellness, and self-improvement, which has rendered people less able to provide care and less able to receive it. The concept of care has been mobilized in many fields within the social sciences, humanities, and urban planning, yet it remains largely unexplored and devalued in other areas of design. Designers' commitment to remaining neutral agents in market-focused, profit-driven enterprises persists, even while interest grows in frameworks such as design for social impact. In the title of an article published by *Futuress* in 2021, Cherry-Ann Davis and Nina Paim posed the question "Does design care?" Propelled by their exasperation at an industry that touts "inclusion" even while upholding the status quo, they problematized the notion of "care" as being co-opted and performed by designers while also being largely ignored and devalued. Care, they wrote, "has remained surprisingly and revealingly absent from design. In this strange field we claim our own, the prevailing idea is that 'care' is reserved for those who are unable to care for themselves."[2]

   It's not difficult to infer what a discipline cares most about when its reigning motto is "move fast and break things." As a tool for innovation, design has been integral to neoliberal capitalism's near-ubiquitous positioning of profit-making as the organizing principle of life. Any "care" that the industry can be purported to demonstrate is solely through the lens of profit; as described in *The Care Manifesto*, design undergirds a growing self-care and wellness industry, which relegates care to something we are supposed to buy for ourselves. It proliferates the expansion of platform-based markets for everyday care needs, thus undermining our communal-care resources and caring capacities by implanting market logics into traditional nonmarket realms. Meanwhile, powerful business actors promote themselves as "caring corporations" while actively undermining any kind of care offered outside their profit-making architecture[3] and disregarding care practices for workers, such as paid family leave and pay equity.

   Designers learn to prize an absence of care early on when they are conditioned to act as neutral agents who don't allow their identities or emotions to intervene in their work. What's worse, in their education design students are taught to wear suffering like a badge of honor as they endure violent critiques, pull all-nighters, and sacrifice their well-being to meet the demands of abusive programs. The culture of the industry reinforces this trauma through precarious working conditions, exploitation of unsalaried labor, lack of transparency and accountability, and the worshipping of "hustle culture." This way of living and working is inherently incompatible with the needs of marginalized people, such as those who are caretakers or are disabled, and thus leads to them being ousted from the industry early in their careers. It also pits designers against one another in constant competition, perpetuating cultures of toxic individuality and deteriorating systems for support or community building. In recent years, flattened by the pressures of living and working through a global pandemic, many designers have engaged the notion of care to raise concerns around the harmful culture of the discipline[4] and enact calls for better work–life balance.

I don't intend to insinuate that all designers are selfish people with no concern for others. On the contrary, most designers are well intentioned and want to improve people's lives through design, but the structures and methods we have come up with to achieve this goal are insufficient at best and harmful at worst. Two problematic frameworks designers turn to when designing with "care" are inclusion and empathy.

Inclusion is the buzzword favored by institutions and corporations for policies that provide access and resources to marginalized people and encourage belonging. In design, it often means adding extra features that make an artifact or space more usable for more people or seeking out underrepresented voices in research. It implies a corrective measure: to include those who have been previously excluded. When we analyze inclusion through a feminist lens, however, it is easily problematized by feminist understandings of domination and power. To "include" marginalized people is merely to invite them into a dominant power structure, while the power structure itself remains intact. As the designer and disability advocate Josh Halstead writes, "Somehow there is a class of designers and builders bestowing the right to be included on to the excluded."[5] Inclusive design and accessibility are often shaped by profit-driven mindsets that influence who is "included" in inclusion, which reinforces the power hierarchy between designers and users that treats marginalized people as "others." As feminism has taught us, rights gained can be easily taken away when power structures of domination remain in place.

Empathy is similarly problematized by notions of power. The term *empathy* refers to the process of experiencing the world as others do or at least as you think they do. In design, it tends to be a catch-all term for considering someone else's needs while designing for them. It's relegated to its own sacred step in the human-centered design and design-thinking processes, but it's often regarded more as due diligence than as emotional engagement, satisfied by a few interviews or observations. The human–computer interaction researchers Cynthia Bennett and Daniela Rosner write about where empathy goes wrong, noting that empathy, along with design thinking more generally, works as a means of "convincing designers that they have superior training and ethical tools to quickly assess and innovate on problems in domains they are unfamiliar with,"[6] an approach also known as the "design savior complex." Empathy can also carry bias; we are more likely to direct empathy toward people who look like us or share our background.[7]

Framed by good intentions, empathy places designers' attention on individual problems when structural or societal transformation is necessary.

In general, feminist perspectives understand empathy as formed within and through people's connections with others, placing it in historical context and implicating it in the uneven distribution of power. Many feminist scholars question the achievability of empathy, citing the "danger of a too-easy intimacy," wherein empathy upholds workings of colonialism and oppression.[8] The feminist cultural studies scholar Carolyn Pedwell argues that when empathy is understood as the experience of "co-feeling," not only does it invite "problematic appropriations or projections on the part of the privileged subjects, [but] it also risks obscuring their complicity in the wider relations of power in which marginalization, oppression, and suffering occur."[9]

When designers employ methods to produce empathy, they may mistake the *appropriation* of the experience of the person empathized with as their own. For example, an able-bodied designer donning a wheelchair in simulation exercises does little to reveal the nuance of a disabled person's experience. Empathy becomes a mechanism through which designers demonstrate their professional judgment by responding to their own personal reactions and, in turn, subverting the experiences they intended to uplift. Instead, Bennett and Rosner propose that designers shift understandings of empathy to one with accountability that foregrounds shared experiences over authoritative narratives.[10] Sara Ahmed agrees that empathy may sustain the very difference that it seeks to overcome, calling it a "wish feeling" more aligned with our imagination of what others feel than with reality. Ahmed suggests that instead of relying on the ability to "put oneself in the other's shoes," we feel empathy as a mode of being *with* but not *in*, which requires that we "take care, that we be careful."[11]

Whereas empathy may implore us to feel, care implores us to act. Many feminists insist that care is a radical and political act within white cisheterocapitalist patriarchy. Care is not just a "warm pleasant affection or moralistic feel-good attitude";[12] it is absolutely fundamental to our survival as a society. In "Sick Woman Theory," the disability justice activist Johanna Hedva asserts that the most anticapitalist protest is "to care for one another and to care for yourself[;] ... to take seriously each other's vulnerability and fragility and precarity, and to support it, honor it, empower it[;] ... to enact and practice community." Hedva calls for radical kinship through an interdependent society and a politics of care.[13]

Care can be understood as a feeling, an environment, an action or inaction. To care may mean to be charged with the protection, welfare, or maintenance of something or someone. It can be framed as a burden, as a responsibility, or as a privilege. It can feel good, or it can feel bad. It can do good, or it can oppress. According to *The Care Manifesto*, care is "a social capacity and activity involving the nurturing of all that is necessary for the welfare and flourishing of life," dependent upon "our individual and common ability to provide the political, social, material, and emotional conditions that allow the vast majority of people and living creatures on this planet to thrive, along with the planet itself."[14]

Feminist political scientists and philosophers often frame care as the historically feminized and therefore invisible practice of nursing, nurturing, or caring for others. Care is typically associated with women and the domestic space because the largest tasks of caring—those of tending to children and caring for the infirm and elderly—have been almost exclusively relegated to women.[15] Indeed, today two-thirds of paid and three-quarters of unpaid care work globally are performed by women.[16] However, many feminist scholars argue that the association between women and care is empirically and historically inaccurate because care was also traditionally the work of servants and enslaved peoples, and today members of unprivileged groups such as the working classes and people of color do disproportionate amounts of caring.[17] The undermining of care work has a long history intertwined with the rise of neoliberal capitalism and individualism, in which care work is seen as unproductive and therefore is consistently subject to less pay and social prestige. Our society is not designed to support care work, from the paltriness of family-leave policies to the constraints of the nine-to-five workday to the design of entire cities. Care, or the absence of it, can be structural. Neoliberal nation-states urge us to believe that the task of caring is for the individual, reinforcing the refusal to recognize our shared vulnerabilities and interconnectedness. However, the reality of our interconnectedness is undeniable; it calls on us to understand our own care needs within the larger context of those around us and the importance of mutual aid. Feminism is not just a practice of self-care but one of community care; it is caring for ourselves as a community.

> ✳ Whereas empathy implores us to feel,
> care implores us to act. ✳

Many feminists emphasize the notion of interdependence, framing care as being less about predetermined behaviors than about a situated, embodied way of responding to interdependence as it shifts across various contexts and temporalities.[18] In *Moral Boundaries*, the feminist political scientist Joan Tronto unpacks the political significance of care by extending it to "everything we do to maintain, continue and repair our world which we seek to interweave in a complex, life-sustaining web." According to Tronto, interdependency is the ontological state in which humans and other beings unavoidably live; thus, "care arises out of the fact that not all humans or others or objects in the world are equally able, at all times, to take care of themselves."[19]

Tronto also argues that care is not single actions but rather a habitual practice that can be refined over time. Seeing care as a practice is essential to avoid "over-idealizing care" or causing it to "reinforce patterns of subordination."[20] The feminist science and technology scholar María Puig de la Bellacasa echoes this argument by suggesting we look at design problems as speculative "matters of care" rather than as something we must care about. "The question is, then, not 'how can we care more?' but instead to ask what happens to our work when we pay attention to moments where the question of 'how to care?' is insistent but not easily answerable."[21] In this way, care is not a predetermined set of norms but rather an analytic or provocation that we explore as an ongoing practice.

An emphasis on care redirects our focus away from empathy and its unrealistic relational transference of emotion. Unlike empathy, care does not require emotional motivations or affections; it can be a conscious, deliberate, and reasoned choice. Care places accountability on designers to think more broadly about impact beyond the immediate audience or present moment, expanding their task from simply preventing harm to actually promoting healing. When designing with and for marginalized people who experience systemic oppression, a practice of care urges designers to consider the effects of intergenerational trauma, in which oppression and violence experienced by past generations are carried and embodied by younger generations. The Black feminist political scholar Deva Woodly describes the long-term trauma of Black women's oppression, which operates in the interlocking registers of gender, race, and class and is "both carried as a bodily and psychic memory and reinforced by daily experiences of devaluation, discrimination, domination, and exclusion."[22] Centering those who are in the margins must include addressing trauma, a topic that's explored throughout the essays, dialogues, and case studies in this chapter. To design for healing intergenerational trauma, our concerns must expand to include the past and the future, too.

Finally, care that sustains our survival as a society should not be relegated only to human relationships. Designing with care requires us to be attuned to fragile entanglements among the human and nonhuman others for and with whom we design. Amid the global climate crisis, the livelihoods and fates of all entities on the planet are unavoidably intertwined. Puig de la Bellacasa asserts that "care is a human trouble, but it does not make care a human-only matter," and argues for the significance of care required for thinking and living in more-than-human worlds, which include "nonhumans and other-than-humans such as things, objects, other animals, living beings, organisms, physical forces, and spiritual entities."[23] When considering the precarity of our climate and species, we must acknowledge that to practice care in design might sometimes mean not to design anything at all.

In this chapter, care is explored as an animating force for reconsidering methods, tools, and artifacts in design. Authors draw on their backgrounds as designers, social workers, and CEOs to call attention to a distinct lack of care in the discipline and ways that design can be used to understand care and facilitate healing. Although care might be a multinodal, ambiguous concept, the tensions between its various understandings are an incentive to continue "unsettling"[24] care in and through design. To embrace care as an organizing principle, we must do so collectively, a process in which care and care practices are understood as broadly as possible and marginalized voices are centered. Design as a practice of care should indeed be a practice that emphasizes the ongoing, responsive nature of listening, making mistakes, learning, and trying again. As the voices in this chapter demonstrate, we can disrupt the uncaring attitudes, environments, cultures, economies, and structures we inhabit, starting with ourselves and moving outward.

1 Care Collective et al., *The Care Manifesto: The Politics of Interdependence* (London: Verso, 2020).
2 Cherry-Ann Davis and Nina Paim, "Does Design Care?," *Futuress*, September 10, 2021, https://futuress. org/magazine/does-design-care/.
3 Care Collective et al., *The Care Manifesto*.
4 Davis and Paim, "Does Design Care?"
5 Quoted in Aaron Chu, "'Inclusive Design' Has Become so Widely Used That It's Meaningless. That Has to Change," *Fast Company*, November 29, 2021, https://www.fastcompany. com/90697288/inclusive-design-has-become-so-wide-ly-used-that-its-meaningless-that-has-to-change.
6 Cynthia Bennett and

Daniela Rosner, "The Promise of Empathy: Design, Disability, and Knowing the 'Other,'" in *CHI '19: Proceedings the 2019 CHI Conference on Human Factors in Computing Systems* (New York: Association for Computing Machinery, 2019), 3, doi:10.1145/329 0605.3300528.
7 Paul Bloom, *Against Empathy: The Case for Rational Compassion* (New York: HarperCollins, 2016).
8 See, for example, Saidiya V. Hartman, *Scenes of Subjection: Terror, Slavery, and Self-Making in Nineteenth-Century America* (Oxford: Oxford University Press, 1997).
9 Carolyn Pedwell, *Affective Relations: The Transnational Politics of Empathy* (London: Palgrave Macmillan, 2014), 10.

10 Bennett and Rosner, "The Promise of Empathy."
11 Sara Ahmed, "Becoming Unsympathetic," *Feminist-killjoys*, April 16, 2015, https://feministkilljoys. com/2015/04/16/becom-ing-unsympathetic/.
12 María Puig de la Bella-casa, *Matters of Care: Speculative Ethics in More Than Human Worlds* (Minneapolis: University of Minnesota Press, 2017), 2.
13 Johanna Hedva, "Sick Woman Theory," 2020, https://johannahedva.com/ SickWomanTheory_Hed-va_2020.pdf.
14 Care Collective et al., *The Care Manifesto*, 5.
15 Joan C. Tronto, *Moral Boundaries: A Political Argument for an Ethics of Care* (London: Routledge, 1993).
16 Care Collective et al., *The*

Care Manifesto, 17.
17 Tronto, *Moral Boundaries*.
18 Nel Noddings, *Caring: A Feminine Approach to Ethics & Moral Education* (Berkeley: University of California Press, 2013).
19 Tronto, *Moral Boundaries*, 103.
20 Tronto, *Moral Boundaries*, 116.
21 Puig de la Bellacasa, *Matters of Care*, 7.
22 Deva Woodly, "Black Feminist Visions and the Politics of Healing in the Movement for Black Lives," in *Women Mobilizing Memory*, ed. Ayşe Gül Altınay et al. (New York: Columbia University Press, 2019), 219.
23 Puig de la Bellacasa, *Matters of Care*, 2.
24 Puig de la Bellacasa, *Matters of Care*, 8.

On intergenerational maternal healing

Dialogue with Eden Laurin and Ellen Kellogg

Nyssa, a company founded by three mothers, designs for and starts conversations about the "unmentionables" in women's lives—postpartum recovery, menstruation, and menopause. Cofounders Eden Laurin and Ellen Kellogg discuss designing products with care and breaking the cycles of suffering in women's health.

Alison Place When I learned about Nyssa, I had just had my first baby, and the *Unmentionables* podcast was a powerful space for learning and connection at that time in my life. As a new mom, I was so hungry for that type of information and support, where women speak openly about the challenges of birth and postpartum. What specifically about your postpartum experience made you decide to start Nyssa?

Eden Laurin I gave birth at the University of Chicago, which is a lovely, science-driven hospital, and they took great care of me as a pregnant woman. But as soon as I gave birth, my child got taken to the NICU because he didn't take a breath right away, and everyone went with him, including my partner. It was just me and a nurse in the room, and she handed me what we all get—that stretchy mesh underwear, a plastic ice pack, and what looked like a puppy pee pad. She folded it like a sumo wrestler get-up, and she helped me put it on. I looked at her, and I said, "Are you serious?" And she said, "Congratulations, Mama." I couldn't believe how much money, time, and energy had gone into this birthing process, then here I am, alone with this diaper get-up. Our cofounder, Mia Clarke, had a child a few months after me, and we started to find the language to talk about what was so wrong with all of it. It only took a beat to realize we have been abandoned like this our whole lives, having to suffer on our own as women. That was the moment when Nyssa became something real for me.

Ellen Kellogg As women, we are so conditioned to suffer through. It's almost our culture. We suffer through our period, cramps; then we suffer through pregnancy and nausea. My big "aha" moment was when I realized that not only was I doing that, and my friends were doing it, and my family was doing it, but we were wearing it as a badge of honor. "How much did you tear in your pregnancy? And how many hours of labor did you go through?" I realized we'd been conditioned to revere our suffering rather than do something about it.

AP Because of that commitment to suffering, did you face hurdles in not just convincing women to buy a product but also in convincing them that they deserve to not suffer?

EK Absolutely. We've found it to be powerful and convincing to remind women: you do owe it to yourself, and you owe it to other women, particularly the next generation of women. I always think about my daughter—I want her to take care of herself, and if I don't model that behavior, she's never going to do it. I learned to suffer through because my mom suffered through—that's what women have always done—but I have to deliberately change my behavior to break the cycle. It's not selfish to stop your suffering. It's changing the game for ourselves and the generations of women to come.

EL In a postpartum state, there's a lot of searching for answers, but that's probably one of the steeper learning curves, that I as a woman and a consumer actually deserve to not suffer. The medical community is certainly not telling us that. Culturally, nothing's telling us to take care of our bodies in that way.

AP The products and knowledge that Nyssa shares are meant to help pregnant and birthing people heal during postpartum, which emphasizes physical healing, but there's also an aspect of emotional healing and intergenerational healing, too. As a new mother, I carried with me a lot of weight from the trauma that I felt from past generations of my mother and my grandmother, whether from stories I was told or the absence of stories in some cases. How do you see Nyssa addressing intergenerational healing?

EL When we have language to assign to these things, or we can say things out loud that we've hidden or felt ashamed about, there's so much healing that comes from it. My mom had a late miscarriage before she had me, and the doctor insinuated that it was her fault because she was cleaning behind the fridge. She only told a few people in her life when it happened, and they all then asked her, "Well, what were you doing when the miscarriage happened?" Her whole life, it was so steeped in guilt, shame, and discomfort. Then recently Mia did an *Unmentionables* podcast episode about miscarriage, and my mom called in. She finally found a space that was comfortable enough to share, and she found totally different language to work through those emotions over 30 years later.

EK My daughter is nine. I'm watching her mature, and she's on the cusp of puberty.

I feel so much more empowered to have those conversations with her, to open those lines of communication in a way that was never there for me. Healing is 100 percent at the core of what we do. Since very early on, Nyssa's mission has been about the unmentionables, not only in terms of the product we develop but [in] the conversation that we spark. I am blown away by what our audience shares with us because we are giving them an outlet to talk about things they could never talk about and to be part of a supportive community. Our mission is not the selling of our product; it's the healing that we're all doing together.

✳ When we have language to assign to these things, or we can say things out loud that we've hidden or felt ashamed about, there's so much healing that comes from it. ✳

AP The cultural shift is also critical, getting rid of the stigma around these issues and giving women and birthing people safe spaces to talk about them. What can designers do to contribute to that cultural shift?

EL It seems ludicrous that we even have to say this, but make sure that you're thinking of all bodies and all needs when you're designing. The story that you personally identify with is not the only story. At a bare minimum, it is our responsibility as designers to not put anything in the world that is not improving the lives of the people that are using it, and that takes work. We are constantly working to find fabric that's going to work with people's bodies, having it produced with the labor that we can stand behind, making sure it's packaged in a way that's recyclable, and still keep it at a price point that's accessible.

Figure 3.1.1 [right] Nyssa FourthWear Underwear is designed to securely hold ice or heat therapy between the legs, at the site of caesarean incision, and around the back, where postpartum recovering bodies need it most.

Figure 3.1.2 [top left] Nyssa Deluxe Postpartum Set includes FourthWear Underwear as well as the nursing and pumping-friendly FourthWear Postpartum Bralette designed with interior chest pockets to securely hold ice or heat packs over the breast for relief from engorgement and the discomfort associated with feeding, pumping, weaning, or lactation suppression.

Figure 3.1.3 [bottom] Nyssa VieVision Mirror is a hands-free mirror for between-legs viewing, designed to promote regular well-being checks, self-knowledge, and self-care.

All photographs by Marzena Abrahamik, courtesy of Nyssa.

It's a constant effort. We will be juggling that forever with every innovation.

EK There's so much that has been designed for an ideal way of being, an ideal way of looking. Focusing on a person's reality, first and foremost, will always land you in the right place. But it takes persistence, deep thought, and seeing beyond the surface. Innovation and design can get away from you if you try to move too fast or if you confine your design to the constraints of what's close at hand. And then comes trial and iteration—that's when the real needs and desires get revealed.

AP For the FourthWear postpartum underwear (figures 3.1.1 and 3.1.2), you've said the design process involved over a year of prototyping and included advisers like mothers, doctors, pediatricians, midwives, from all places. What are some takeaways from that process?

EL We didn't know we were going to design an apparel item. We thought it was going to be a spray because it seemed like an easy solution, and we had backgrounds in formulating those types of products. We did several focus groups and surveys, we met with doctors, and we brought on an adviser who was an ob-gyn surgeon. What everyone reacted to the most was the mesh underpants they give you and what an absurd solution it was. For instance, for people who have cesarean deliveries, they are told to cut the underpants to roll them down and not interfere with their scar. So we started looking at fabric as an innovation in and of itself, knowing it had to have its own functionality. Also, one of the biggest challenges was finding resources and building supplier relationships. We wasted a lot of time trying to explain to men why this product was necessary, but when we worked with women, they understood immediately.

We realized we could get further faster with shared empathy.

EK For us, as much time and effort go into uncovering the problem as [into] the solution. Because women have been taught to suffer silently, it's not obvious what the problems are. Many products available to women in the market today are "solutions" that aren't really solving a problem. In the process of designing all of our products, we leverage our network of professionals across an array of industries, whether it's health care [professionals], medical [professionals], aestheticians, or yoga instructors, as well as our consumer network to uncover the root of the problem. That can require as much time and effort as finding the solution, but it's necessary.

AP The knowledge that women and birthing people hold about their bodies is highly situated, and they've often been conditioned to hide it. How do you uncover knowledge that is socially and culturally situated or hidden?

EL It's as much about watching what people do as it is about listening to what they say. Often, we've had to observe a behavioral barrier rather than wait for someone to tell us about it. Don't make assumptions. Prioritize diversity in who you're talking to. You can start with your own network but continue to branch out. Keep asking questions. And just because you've got the product out, your job is not done. Continue to listen, continue to innovate, continue to learn and gather feedback. That's your responsibility as a designer.

EK Look for problems in moments of tension. Often in our research, we've been told by a medical professional that certain experiences are not common, but then we'll ask our community, and many will say they've experienced it. That tension tells us there's something that needs to be solved, not just by a product but by better listening and communication. There is a time and place to tap the medical expert community, but their insights are often conditioned by their training. In our process, we've learned to start with the consumer, then talk to the expert, then talk again to the consumer.

AP You describe Nyssa as a feminist corporation, but your work involves interacting with decidedly antifeminist sectors, like health care, investors, and suppliers. What does it take to work within systems that aren't working and try to change them from within?

EL A lot of people vilify that word, but it's true: we are a corporation. There are certain fundamentals that entails—like if we want to grow, we have to think about margins, cost of goods, and marketing freezes. We have to speak investors' language. We often feel the pressure to shift or change, especially as a women-led company, to meet others' expectations. It has taken a lot of growth, for me personally, to say we're going to be ourselves. We support work–life balance. We support having and growing a family. Our staff is all women. Over 90 percent of our vendors are women owned. We have to make certain concessions, like letting go of potential investors, but we feel proud we're shifting the paradigm of what people expect corporations to look like.

EK Early on in this company, we partnered with different groups to craft our brand story and messaging, and there was often this push to be angry—to blame men for our challenges, blame the health-care community, blame the patriarchy. That emotion wasn't authentic to us or the reason we created Nyssa. We had to have the confidence to do it our way, with elegance, truth, and a feminist mindset. I don't think we spend much time thinking about how to combat the established system. We trust that authenticity will prevail.

AP What is your advice for feminist designers entering the industry?

EL The work environment is very different from school. You might be in situations where you are the only one being the advocate for change. That can be a huge responsibility or a tremendous burden. Set boundaries but also try not to compromise. Even just calling things out and bringing attention to things you see can make a huge difference.

EK Think about your job being not just related to the tactics of your work but also related to evolving the culture at work. Think about the other people around you and their inherent biases or needs. Figure out the job to be done for what you're making but also think about the job to be done for your role as a feminist designer in the world. Being a feminist does not mean you have to be a woman or fulfill a certain role. For any person striving to affect change, you can only do it from a place of true authenticity.

This conversation took place over Zoom in August 2021. It has been edited for clarity and length.

Eden Laurin is cofounder and chief executive officer of Nyssa, creating innovations to solve for the unmentionables of womanhood. She specializes in product development and business management and is based in Chicago.

Ellen Kellogg is cofounder and chief strategy officer of Nyssa. She earned her MBA from the Kellogg School of Management at Northwestern University and is based in Chicago.

On designing with authenticity over perfection

The graphic designer and educator Rebecca Tegtmeyer reflects on what is lost and what is gained by hand-sewing analog data visualizations.

Rebecca Tegtmeyer

Threading a needle, aligning the stitch, looping up and down, repeating, reflecting, repeating, reflecting. Sewing is a way of making that relies on the cyclical, repetitive, and reflective process. With each stitch made, mistakes happen, requiring a quick negotiation to determine whether a fix is necessary or the mistake can go overlooked. Perfection loses out to authenticity; the uniqueness of the outcome is the reward to the sewer. It is in these qualities that I find the practice of sewing to be meditative and satisfying, fueling a long-term desire to connect sewing to my design practice. As simple as this desire seems, it has been a challenge for me to consider sewing as a legitimate and acceptable form of design making. Understanding sewing through the lens of cultural constructs, combined with the experience of being a working mother during the pandemic, motivated me to embrace sewing as a design practice.

Sewing as a Feminist Practice

Sewing is a historically embedded feminist practice tied to domestic household tasks and utilitarian "women's" work. Its importance and significance have shifted throughout history based on the tides of the economy and the needs of the family in which women were the caretakers. In the late 1700s and early 1800s, a woman who could sew was seen as a more desirable wife because she could meet the family's sewing needs with care and ease.[1] When the Industrial Revolution took hold, and the sewing machine was invented (by a man) for industrial purposes, "ready-to-wear" fashion became the ideal. Sewing shifted into a leisurely crafting hobby as it was no longer a necessary skill required to provide clothing and home needs.[2] During the Great Depression, sewing was once again a valued skill as women at home relied on their sewing abilities to efficiently reuse and repurpose fabrics for a variety of needs in the household.[3] Today, sewing is practiced for a variety of reasons and thus ranges from an art form to an act of resistance to a hobby. For me, it's a practice of making that provides the feelings of peace and satisfaction that making on the computer does not.

Expectations in Design

As a young design student in the late 1990s, I was expected to use the digital tools in graphic design production. This was during the time that analog methods in

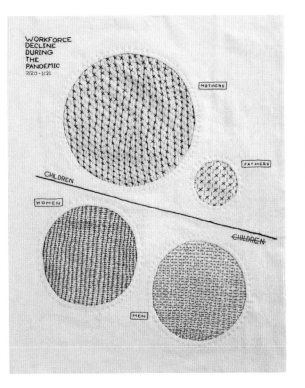

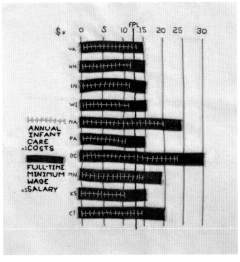

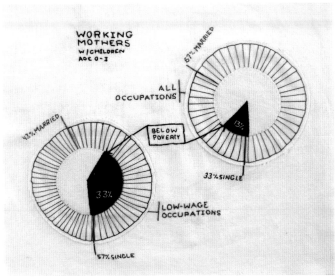

Figure 3.2.1 [top left] Workforce decline during the pandemic, Feb. 2020–Jan. 2021.

Figure 3.2.2 [top right] Annual infant care costs compared to full-time minimum-wage salary and the federal poverty line (FPL) in the 10 most "unaffordable" states.

Figure 3.2.3 [left] Working mothers with children ages 0–3, married and single, all occupations compared to low-wage occupations.

All images courtesy of Rebecca Tegtmeyer.

graphic design were being rejected in favor of design-software products (enter Adobe Systems). Designing on a computer was more cost effective, saved time, and created consistency for mass production—all qualities that are valued in a capitalist system focused on the bottom line. Through computer design, it was also simple for designers to create the perfect curves and clean lines prized in modernist design. A common understanding of "good design" hinged on how well a designer used digital software to make the end product look polished—in this scenario, authenticity loses out to perfection. This perspective was the mainstream frame-work in which graphic design was produced, a model that centers the lone, white, male designer.[4] The act of design was no longer about how communicative the artifact was or about the process, the tools, or the methods that went into making it.

The Pandemic as a Catalyst

These realizations, along with the experience of being a working mother during a pandemic, were pivotal in shifting my practice to include sewing. Pandemic life—although chaotic, disruptive, and deeply traumatic—served as the impetus for questioning my ways of working and, more broadly, the labor of mothers in the workforce. After the first year of the pandemic, data about women's participation in the labor force were revealed, indicating that more mothers than fathers had left the workforce.[5] This spurred further national discussions about the inequities of daycare costs from state to state,[6] women's salaries, and minimum wage. The data from the pandemic have revealed inequities and flaws in the US childcare systems that we've been living with and managing for decades. For these reasons, I felt compelled to make these realities visual through the creation of data visualizations (figures 3.2.1, 3.2.2, and 3.2.3).

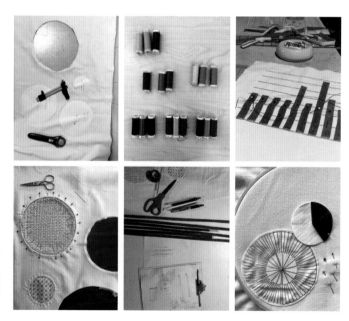

Figure 3.2.4
Materials, technique, and tools used in the process. Courtesy of Rebecca Tegtmeyer.

Figure 3.2.5
Sewing at the kitchen table with Elliot, my toddler. Courtesy of Rebecca Tegtmeyer.

Making Data Visual through Sewing

Visualizing data is my way of making sense of things for myself and crafting an argument. Rather than turn to the computer, I chose to hand-sew the analog visualizations. Like sewing, data visualization can be a feminist practice through the content presented and how it challenges power, through the form it takes by shifting the aesthetic choices, and through participation and inclusion in the process.[7] The sense of embodiment is characteristic of feminist data design and an outcome of the hand-sewn analog visualizations. Embodiment is embraced for me as the maker in that my decisions and actions of making are directly tied to the material and not mediated by technology. For the viewer, the piece is tangible and tactile, making it more relatable than data visualizations made through digital means.

The experience of hand-sewing the visualizations was quite different from working on the computer or even on the sewing machine (figure 3.2.4). Of course, those tools would have cut the time to produce the pieces down exponentially, but working slowly is part of the sewing practice. My decisions were more deliberate as I created each pattern and stitched each letterform. Unlike in making a digital artifact, mistakes were made but had to be embraced. Undoing wasn't an option—authenticity won over perfection.

To my surprise, sewing in front of my family is what had the biggest impact. Working in this way made me and my work more visible to my family because I wasn't isolated behind a screen or standing at a machine. My partner and kids were witnesses to the many hours that went into creating the unique patterns, line formations, shapes, and typography. If I had been designing on the computer, they would have had no idea what I was making or even care. They became actively engaged in my progress while I sewed on family road trips, on the living-room couch, or at the kitchen table (figure 3.2.5), asking questions and taking part in (some of) the design decisions.

Reflecting on the Embrace

For years, I didn't see sewing as a legitimate form of making in my design practice, despite the desire to do so. Understanding the contexts of why I thought working in this way was a challenge and not acceptable gave me the confidence to proceed. I had to look back at the history of cultural constructs and then question my positionality to them. Asking myself why I thought I had to do design in a certain way guided me in embracing sewing as a design practice.

Rebecca Tegtmeyer (she/her) is coauthor of *Collaboration in Design Education* (2020) as well as associate professor and associate chair in the Department of Art, Art History, and Design at Michigan State University.

1   Mary Beth Klatt, "Samplers Trace the History of Women and Their Families," *Chicago Tribune*, February 15, 1998, https://www.chicago-tribune.com/news/ct-xpm-1998-02-15-9802150435-story.html.
2   Rachel P. Maines, *Hedonizing Technologies: Paths to Pleasure in Hobbies and Leisure* (Baltimore: Johns Hopkins University Press, 2009), 9.
3   Sarah A. Gordon, *"Make It Yourself": Home Sewing, Gender, and Culture, 1890–1930* (New York: Columbia University Press, 2009), epilogue.
4   Martha Scotford, "Messy History vs. Neat History: Toward an Expanded View of Women in Graphic Design," *Visible Language* 28, no. 4 (1994): 367–387.
5   Jonathan Rothwell and Lydia Saad, "How Have US Working Women Fared during the Pandemic?," Gallup, March 8, 2021, https://news.gallup.com/poll/330533/working-women-fared-during-pandemic.aspx.
6   Economic Policy Institute, "Childcare Costs in the United States," last updated October 2020, https://www.epi.org/child-care-costs-in-the-united-states.
7   Catherine D'Ignazio and Lauren F. Klein, *Data Feminism* (Cambridge, MA: MIT Press, 2020), 17–18.

On embodying vulnerability through design

The designer and educator Jeff Kasper reflects on experience design to facilitate healing for queer survivors of trauma.

Jeff Kasper

wrestling embrace is a collection of conceptual objects and games, including exercise mats and playing cards, that facilitate contemplative and interactive exercises based on the measurable distances of intimate and personal space. The project features play objects fashioned after professional wrestling gear that foster active listening and gentle touch through guided contemplation and role play. Designed to be used by pairs of players, *wrestling embrace* provides a creative structure for navigating questions of consent, conflict, and care in interpersonal relationships. These creative tools for education, self-recovery, and community building were originally conceived with and for queer survivors of trauma who are working through experiences of anxiety and safety in relationships. As a consequence of the project's focus on both valuing and practicing emotional and physical vulnerability, the work is grounded in feminist theories of embodiment.

Project Development

The project began as a creative response to a personal traumatic event. In the months between the US Supreme Court's marriage equality ruling on June 26, 2015, and the mass shooting at Pulse, a gay nightclub in Orlando, Florida, on June 12, 2016, my former partner and I were the victim of violent homophobic aggression for holding hands in a popular New York City public space. Getting bombarded, ridiculed, and tousled on the street compounded past abuse in response to public intimacy. Reliving the event began to affect my adult relationships and made me fearful of close physical touch in public.

A friend encouraged me to join a confidential meet-up group for queer men and nonbinary folks with post-traumatic stress syndrome and working through abuse and gender-based violence. In 2016, I started writing conversation prompts and paper-prototyping "tools" to bring to the group. They included scores for making eye contact, listening, and gentle touch through hand holding. What I began to look for, as both designer and user, was a practice aid for being intimate with another person after so much fear of its repercussions.

Though it seemed simple, practicing vulnerability was something that many male and masculine-presenting members had limited experience with. As we grew up, holding hands with other boys or expressing our queer identities was never encouraged. Reconsidering the need for intimacy foregrounded a legacy of shame at being perceived as feminine and resurfaced internalized homophobia and ableism oriented around emotional sensitivity. Within what was originally conceived of as the limiting boundaries of masculine culture—defined by stoicism, antifemininity, and eschewal of the appearance of weakness—this project offered a softer spirit of play.

An Experiential Game for Practicing Vulnerability

The main play objects of *wrestling embrace* are eight interlocking, lightweight exercise mats for sitting, kneeling, and rolling (figures 3.3.1 and 3.3.2). The graphics merge the classic diagram for proxemic distances with the visual language of professional wrestling rings. The mats correspond topically to practices or questions offered on each card of the associated deck of 54 playing cards (figure 3.3.3). On the back of each card is one of sixteen knot illustrations that relate to one of the sixteen phrases that appear on the mats (figure 3.3.4). The card game prompts two players to enact unexpected situations that bring together the unpredictable nature of improvisation with the irresistible humor of relationship advice. The card

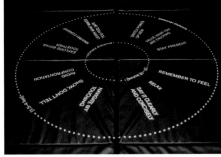

Figure 3.3.1 [above] Two players hold a spread of playing cards as they stand on the custom exercise mats in a lowly lit social space. Photograph by Manuel Martagon.

Figure 3.3.2 [top right] The padded mats create the boundaries of play featuring a circuitous design of concentric circles organized around two distances, personal space (1.5–4.0 feet) and intimate space (0–18 inches). Photograph by Yann Chashanovski.

Figure 3.3.3 [bottom] Close-up detail of a playing card in use. Photograph by Manuel Martagon.

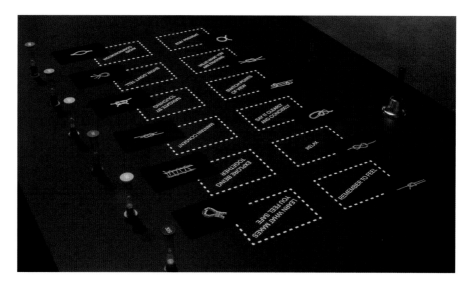

Figure 3.3.4 Details of various knot illustrations and their corresponding thematic category and text that appear on the exercise mats. The connection between the text and the knot illustration on the back of each card operates through a process of association akin to divination practices, as in tarot. Understanding is generated by the user in the context of their experience, memory, and association with the potential meaning of each knot. Photograph by Yann Chashanovski.

prompts were based on experiences in my own life and on anecdotes culled from support-group meetings. Each card explores the inner dynamics of giving and receiving care and what makes the user feel safe.

Embodying Soft Skills

Among many frameworks, such as trauma-sensitive pedagogy and harm reduction, the project centers feminist theories of embodiment, referring to the relationship of the lived body to thought, knowledge, and responsibility as well as taking leave of the idea that the mind does all the work in making meaning from experience. In the designing of *wrestling embrace*, it was critical to foster positive experiences of vulnerability that were as close to reality as possible while still being far enough from a triggering situation to be safe. The game does not prompt fictional scenarios but instead allows users to reconnect with bodily sensations and emotional states through mock social situations that happen in everyday life.

False divisions between mind and body have been consistently problematized in feminist discourse. Such divisions have been correlated with an opposition between male and female, wherein females are traditionally regarded as enmeshed in bodily existence in a way that makes attainment of rationality, a quality defined as distinctly male, questionable.[1] Locating this reality requires looking at the operation of bodily norms as well as at which bodies and their conduct are valued and which are not.[2] In traversing these dynamics, the design, prototyping, and use of *wrestling embrace* require users to engage with vulnerability in relation to the normative concepts of gender and ideals of dependency, strength, and autonomy.

Bodily vulnerability and consequently one's vulnerability to others are central to Judith Butler's later work. She describes how it is through the body that social beings become physically dependent on one another and vulnerable to material environments and to the violence that may be inflicted by others.[3] Social punishments and the threats of violence are usually aimed at those who fail to conform to social norms, including me, a queer male-identifying designer, and the survivor community whom I designed with and for.

Challenging such systems of meaning, the project builds on the understanding that traumatic events and norms are stored in the body rather than just in the mind; healing may come from working through the events experientially or somatically within a community context. *wrestling embrace* creatively makes tangible and playful the need for responsiveness in relationships—paying attention, listening, responding. The game exerts a feminist ethic that centers the premise that humans are inherently relational, responsive beings. In contrast to the sport of professional wrestling and the material culture of the wrestling ring utilized in the game's design, the project departs from the associated masculine concepts of aggression, competition, and domination. The use of the creative tools in the game subverts the association with prominent masculine culture by refocusing on practices that encourage emotional sensitivity.

Jeff Kasper (he/him/his) is an interdisciplinary artist, designer, writer, facilitator, organizer, and educator. He is assistant professor of design at the University of Massachusetts, Amherst, and the coeditor of *More Art in the Public Eye* (2020).

1 Kathleen Lennon, "Feminist Perspectives on the Body," in *Stanford Encyclopedia of Philosophy*, ed. Edward N. Zalta (Stanford, CA: Stanford University Press, 2019), https://plato.stanford.edu/entries/feminist-body/.

2 Elizabeth Grosz, *Volatile Bodies: Toward a Corporeal Feminism* (Bloomington: Indiana University Press, 1994), 14.

3 Judith Butler, *Undoing Gender* (New York: Routledge, 2004), 22.

On trauma-informed design

The social worker and designer Rachael Dietkus discusses what designers can learn from social workers and why designing with empathy is not enough.

Dialogue with Rachael Dietkus

Alison Place Your work takes place at the intersection of social work and design. What do the two disciplines have in common? Where do they diverge?

Rachael Dietkus The history of social work as a discipline is rooted in working with historically marginalized or vulnerable populations. In practice, it involves multiple moments of reacting to or proactively working toward some kind of human need. Macro social work, in which I'm trained, focuses more on understanding a person in their environment and how the systems and structures around them impact outcomes. That involves things like advocacy, policy, social change, administration, etc. My own trajectory has involved rights-based work, such as student activism and leadership development, social justice, human rights, and anti-death-penalty work. I also worked for Veterans Affairs with a program called Health Care for Homeless Veterans, where I started seeing the power of the intersection of design and social work. But as I looked deeper into the design aspect, I started noticing serious and complex issues, which were ostensibly also social work issues, being addressed from a design-centric way of problem solving [but] with no social workers involved. For instance, there are millions of dollars allocated to design-based projects to reform the foster-care system, with a number of projects minimally including social workers, emancipated foster youth, or other people systemically impacted or working within the system. Teams of designers are often paid handsomely to try to fix a system [but] with little to no involvement from people with lived experiences who have been advocating for solutions [and] with far fewer resources for decades. What's more, it's astounding how much federal money gets allocated for systems work but also how readily systems of oppression are maintained. This work requires a commitment to being antiracist; it has to be trauma informed; and it must be codesigned to foster cocreation and coproduction. That takes a completely new way of doing design that a lot of people do not know how to do, and it takes a long time to do it. At different times, I have been invited in as a social worker to learn what is happening and to address the ethical concerns.

AP Your most recent work has focused on defining and developing frameworks for trauma-informed and trauma-responsive design. Before we talk about those concepts, how do you define trauma?

RD I define trauma as a response to anything that happens too much, too fast, too soon, and/or for too long. A traumatic experience is also marked by a lack of protection or support, meaning that you don't have someone to assist or comfort you, either immediately or over time. Trauma lives in the body and can be stored as sensation, such

97

as pain, tension, or as a lack of sensation, like numbness. Additionally, trauma doesn't look the same for any two people; something that is a traumatic experience to me may not be a traumatic experience to you. Lastly, context is critical in how it shapes that experience both in the short-term and in the long-term as part of recovery. In social work, we learn a framework called the "principles of trauma-informed care,"[1] which explicitly targets health-care workers and first responders. My objective has been to take the pillars of those six principles as a foundation for understanding and adapting them in the context of design and design research.

AP What led you to create a design methodology around trauma?

RD While I was working on my MFA at the University of Illinois at Urbana-Champaign, I was immersed in design projects from both practice and pedagogical perspectives. The focus of the program is design for responsible innovation, which aligned closely with my personal and professional values as a practicing social worker–designer. However, what I was often seeing in practice—both in teams I was working closely with in higher education as well as [among] designers and teams worldwide—was an acute lack of understanding of the many harmful, unethical, unsafe, and manipulative ways we were conducting design research. I started creating a set of practices by focusing on the integration of social work values, design-research methods, and trauma-informed care principles. I've been pushing this further to include safety planning, the preconditions of care, and overall changes needed in design research.

AP You write about both trauma-informed and trauma-responsive design. How do you distinguish between the two?

RD They tend to be used interchangeably, but they are uniquely different. That's why the trauma river from Dr. Karen Treisman[2] resonates with me—because it illustrates the element of flow and movement within this work. You start by being sensitive to trauma; it might not change your behavior, but you're able to recognize it. After that, you start to build an awareness. Then with more knowledge, you become informed and understand the six principles. The last part of the river is responsiveness, which has an action component to it. You're informed, but you're consistently choosing to do something with it. It's the same reason I make a distinction between empathy and compassion in design; compassion is empathy plus action. A simple example of a trauma-responsive design choice is an informed-consent process that is flexible and adaptable to a participant's needs. In design research, there is no mandate or requirement to have consent procedures in place when you're doing human-subject research. There's an assumption that those rules don't apply to us as designers. Informed consent is an opportunity to be ethical, to be transparent, to establish safety procedures, to mitigate or reduce risk or harm, and to build authentic trust. Allow people to opt in or opt out, even after the interview is over. Treat them as partners in knowledge creation. There are authentic ways to demonstrate an immense amount of care for the people we are inviting into this process as well as for ourselves as designers. I see and hear incredible amounts of secondary and vicarious trauma in designers themselves, and I strongly believe that a source point for this is these exploitative and manipulative patterns in our practice.

AP Designers love to use the word *empathy* to describe their relationship with who

Trauma-Responsive Design Principles

Rachael Dietkus

---

❶ Building and Sustaining Trust with Meaningful Connections

Trust is the belief and confidence in the integrity, reliability, and fairness of a person, group, organization, community, or system. It is an essential human value that defines our relationships with others. We commit to trust through reciprocity—truly hearing and seeing people around us.

❷ Listening to Learn and Understand through Curiosity

The desire to learn, be understood, and understand the world around us is universal. With years of training and life experience with finely tuned observation and listening, we listen and talk with each other to deepen our shared understanding to empower and uplift one another's needs with equanimity.

❸ Establishing and Maintaining Ethical Rapport and Social Support

Rapport is a connection or relationship with someone else. We think of it as a state of harmonious understanding with another or group, a connection that must be continuously built through compassionate inquiry. However, rapport cannot be established when trust is nonexistent.

❹ Giving Authentically and Generously through Acknowledgment

Generosity is the act of being kind and giving to others, even when—and especially when—no one is watching. One's well-being greatly benefits from a consistent practice of generosity. We can build on this by amplifying best practices and creating new knowledge for the next practices throughout social work and design.

❺ Creating and Generating Access and Accessibility

We believe that when we have equity to access needed resources and mutual self-help and aid, we all benefit and can strive to contribute to what's fair and just in society. When we continuously strive for accessibility, adaptability, and acceptability, we are fluid and ready for multiple contexts.

❻ Perseverance and Consistent Care by Design

Perseverance and design care are the great levelers. When we design with care, we build up our capacity for steady courage in our daily convictions. Daily practice helps us shift despite obstacles, challenges, and barriers. We remain steadfast and mindful of care despite how hard or how long it takes us to reach our shared purpose.

---

they're designing for. How does being trauma responsive differ from practicing empathy?

RD There is some overlap in these concepts, although when I began bridging my values as a social worker with design, where I saw a connection was not with empathy. There's an approach from [the physician and author] Gabor Maté called "compassionate inquiry" that explores what it means to listen to someone with the goal of bringing in compassion, respect, acceptance, insight, healing, and connection to humanity. The approach requires building safety and trust so that when people share things with us in design research, we can acknowledge what has been shared in an ethical and responsible way. Trauma responsiveness is an intentional daily practice of how we show up every moment, not just in our work, but how we show up for ourselves, our peers and colleagues, and our friends and families. Becoming trauma responsive is transformational. Over time, you will start seeing the world differently.

AP Trauma-responsive design specifically addresses the power differential between a designer and a research participant, which is critical to a feminist design practice. Why else is trauma-responsive design a feminist issue?

RD There is significant power and inertia in trauma itself. It surrounds all of us at all times. Global research on trauma has shown that 70 percent of adults have experienced at least one significant traumatic event. I would imagine that we are closer to 100 percent now. Designers cannot ignore the significance of this. What makes this work a feminist issue are the impacts of safety and trust in how we "other" people. If we don't have safety measures in how we design, and if we don't have trust in our design systems, then we cannot create anything that will have lasting systemic or social change. We will simply be upholding an oppressive status quo. We have to go beyond just designing for "good enough for now." We have to be constantly assessing for and mitigating risk and have the foresight to anticipate whether anything we are doing could potentially cause harm later on.

AP It's astounding to consider the difference in oversight and accountability between social workers and designers, yet oftentimes they might be doing the exact same activities in their work, such as interviewing someone or addressing a community problem. In many ways, design is like the Wild West because it's a largely unregulated and undefined discipline. What needs to change in order for designers to be prepared to do work that is trauma informed?

RD To become a social worker, I had to earn a master of social work degree, complete 3,000 hours of supervised clinical experience, and pass a licensure exam. To maintain my licensure, I have to adhere to a code of ethics and complete 30 continuing-education

units every year. Aside from architecture, there is nothing equivalent for design practice. We are often relying on an individual designer's intrinsic motivation to seek out these kinds of responsible practices. I don't necessarily advocate for licensure for designers, but intrinsic motivation is not enough. It's far too individualistic, and it's not going to shift the way we do things collectively. There's a place for trauma-sensitive training in design education. In recent years, I've received several requests to speak in design classrooms, and it's because students are requesting it. I think it's coming from their own experience with trauma, and they are less hesitant to vocalize it. Design students in general are quite hungry for deeper immersion in social justice and social impact work. They have the passion, but they often lack understanding in systems thinking, radical participatory design, and transformative justice. This is such an institutional oversight on our part as we look at both social work and design futures. We also need to find opportunities for design students and social work students to be in classes and practice these skills together. I've seen the power of design-based methods in social work practice, and I know the inverse can add significant value for designers.

This conversation took place over Zoom in February 2022. It has been edited for clarity and length.

Rachael Dietkus (she/her) is a mom, social worker, design researcher, organizational strategist, and founder of Social Workers Who Design. She is educated and trained in both social work and design and practices being a designer who is trauma responsive. She is based in Illinois.

1 US Center for Preparedness and Response, "Infographic: 6 Guiding Principles to a Trauma Informed Approach," last reviewed September 17, 2020, https://www.cdc.gov/cpr/infographics/6_principles_trauma_info.htm. **2** Karen Treisman, *A Treasure Box for Creating Trauma-Informed Organizations: A Ready-to-Use Resource for Trauma, Adversity, and Culturally Informed, Infused and Responsive Systems* (London: Jessica Kingsley, 2021).

On the self-optimization of care

The design researcher Laura Devendorf reflects on design as witness to bodies and the self.

Laura Devendorf

Wear is a project that reflects on technologies for adaptation. It hyperbolically represents the pressure I feel to perform care using self-monitoring and self-optimizing technologies and my attempts to examine care through lived experience.

Wear takes the form of an "exoskeleton" to help me adapt to and find strength in my role as a mother. Specifically, it is a handmade house dress with handmade sensors embedded throughout the fabric that measure the various forces created by my body in encountering other bodies—children, chairs, and so on (figure 3.5.1). It records these interactions on a small memory card and plays them back as a heat map, revealing where, when, and how much pressure was collected over a given timespan. This project, commissioned by and exhibited at the Centre for Heritage, Arts and Textiles,[1] is accompanied by a video of the making process, highlighting how the garment came together through my labor in my home (figure 3.5.2). It was designed to aid in my personal reflection on my relationship to care as much as to be viewed by an audience.

Exoskeletons, most common in military and factory settings, are mechanical devices worn on the outer body to provide humans with increased ability. They form a genre of wearable technology that focuses on adapting human bodies to external or harsh environments and include garments from spacesuits

Figure 3.5.1
A photo of me in my exoskeleton/house-dress during the COVID lockdown in the winter of 2020. Courtesy of Laura Devendorf.

Figure 3.5.2 Stills from the creation of Wear, captured over six months via a GoPro head-mounted camera. Courtesy of Laura Devendorf.

to pregnancy corsets.[2] I became fascinated by the aesthetics of these systems because they at once aim to protect the wearer while also revealing that which the wearer needs protection from (or revealing what society expects us to perform as a space explorer, soldier, or fine lady). In taking up this form, I aimed to make a statement about biases enacted through technology and their effects on women's bodies. I wanted it to expose technological expectations of (self-)surveillance while reframing those technologies toward the honoring of a felt experience of care. This project, then, is not a refusal to perform optimization and adaptation but a desire to rearticulate these goals within alternative value systems.

As a design researcher, I study relationships formed between humans and machines. I'm curious about what we expect from these relationships and why. Why do we expect technology to make us better, faster, or stronger? What if it has made us slower, has made our experiences deeper, or has helped us disrupt our everyday routines in creative ways? These "what if" questions and imaginings of how things could be otherwise resonate with approaches to design such as critical technical practice,[3] feminist human–computer interaction,[4] and reflective design.[5] The key commitment in this work is using design as a way to generate and illuminate alternatives, to tell stories from the margins, and to create space for alternative ways of knowing and communicating.

These commitments to doing otherwise shape both the outcomes and processes of design. In the case of Wear, creating the dress involved responding to materials, weaving equipment, personal needs, and the experiences of close friends, Kristina Andersen and Aisling Kelliher, who collaborated on this project. We felt an expectation that women monitor and optimize their lives, bodies, and caregiving "intuitions" using technology. We attempted to balance this perspective with the need we felt at various points simply to surrender to a fundamental uncertainty and attend to our attachments, frailties, and vulnerabilities as sites of care, connection, and, ultimately, strength. Feminism in my design practice roots itself in a collective conversation. We create side by side, we tell stories of our lives, we make objects, and those objects become memoirs of our collective experience. In the words of Audre Lorde, "There are no new ideas, only new ways of making them felt."[6]

Even as Wear takes up the aesthetics of self-tracking and optimization through embedded technology and blinking status lights, it ultimately tracks moments where care is exchanged between bodies, specifically moments in which a physical force is exchanged between my body and another body. I wanted to capture the way my child sits on my hip, the way the wind presses against me as I ride my bike, the way my bed or a chair offers itself for my rest. I wanted to shift

Figure 3.5.3 Wear hung up and plugged in. Courtesy of Laura Devendorf.

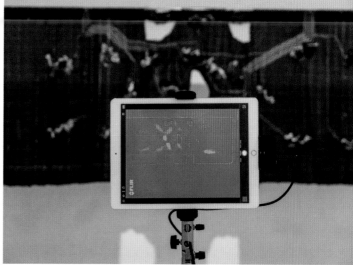

Figure 3.5.4 Wear installed at the Center for Heritage, Arts and Textile in Hong Kong. Looking at the fabric through the thermal camera reveals the areas that are heating based on how much force they received during 24 hours of wear. Courtesy of Laura Devendorf.

my intention from being better or stronger to simply honoring and respecting the care in my environment—the moments when the meeting of human and non-human agencies produces sensory experience. When taken off and hung, the garment transforms into a large rectangular map, inviting me and others to wander its surface and discover the evidence of care, the data of bodies touching bodies (figures 3.5.3 and 3.5.4). Using heat as the materiality through which care is represented attempts to simulate my body's experiences for someone else to touch, experience, and perhaps absorb. In the process of production, I tried to put as much of my body in the garment as possible through the hand-felting of the sensors, the hand-sewing of the electrical connections, the hand-weaving of circuitry traces through the garment, and the choosing of silk as the base material, hoping it would hold my scent and stain after I took it off.

Wear shows a possibility for doing technology otherwise. Framing care as relational and ongoing in our environments as well as designing from that perspective shift the focus from a future/better self to a present/enough self-in-the-world. I personally like to see the garment as a kind of photograph or memento that offers a space for being with or just being. Here it suggests *witnessing* as a design action, with and of equal importance to intervention. Today, the dress sits on a garment rack behind my desk, evidence of a performance of my own life. It serves as a record of a process, of a moment when I wanted to speak out. It gave me insights and pathways to continue to slip the beauty of care, collectivism, creativity, and chaos into technological systems.

Laura Devendorf (she/her) is a design researcher who has a fascination with the relationship between frustration and design. Through weaving practices, she reflects on the forces that shape humans and things and tells stories about design in the Anthropocene. She is based in Colorado.

1 Centre for Heritage, Arts and Textile (CHAT), *Interweaving Poetic Code*, exhibition catalog (Hong Kong: CHAT, 2021).
2 Michelle Millar Fisher, Amber Winick, and Alexandra Lange, *Designing Motherhood: Things That Make and Break Our Births* (Cambridge, MA: MIT Press, 2021).
3 Philip E. Agre, *Computation and Human Experience* (Cambridge: Cambridge University Press, 1997).
4 Shaowen Bardzell, "Feminist HCI: Taking Stock and Outlining an Agenda for Design," in *CHI '10: CHI Conference on Human Factors in Computing Systems* (New York: Association for Computing Machinery, 2010), 1301–1310.
5 Phoebe Sengers et al., "Reflective Design," in *Proceedings of the 4th Decennial Conference on Critical Computing: Between Sense and Sensibility* (New York: Association for Computing Machinery, 2005), 49–58, doi.org/10.1145/1094562.1094569.
6 Audre Lorde, "Poetry Is Not a Luxury," in *The Master's Tools Will Never Dismantle the Master's House* (1984; repr., London: Penguin, 2018), 5.

On health and healing in marginalized communities

Founder of *Womanly Magazine*, Attia Taylor creates media for those who are excluded from mainstream dialogues on well-being.

Attia Taylor

In 2017, I started *Womanly Magazine*: a small art publication that aims to educate women and nonbinary folks on preventive health care. *Womanly* began as a response to the lack of resources relating to health care that I, my family, and the Black and Brown women around me were experiencing. According to the US Centers for Disease Control and Prevention (CDC), one in four Americans does not have a primary-care provider or health center where they can receive regular medical services.[1] Furthermore, nearly nine out of ten adults have said they have difficulty using the everyday health information that is routinely available in health-care facilities, retail outlets, and media.[2] The CDC also reports that delays in health care can lead to poorer health and higher medical costs over time.[3] *Womanly* works to reverse these trends by creating content and programming to increase access for low-income communities, in particular communities of color, in Brooklyn, New York; Philadelphia, Pennsylvania; and Baltimore, Maryland.

It has been crucial for me as a creative producer, musician, and health advocate to create a platform that not only educates people on their risks but also informs deeper connections to and closes gaps within the health-care industry. My experience in health education began with a career at Planned Parenthood, a prominent provider of sexual and reproductive health care in the United States. While at Planned Parenthood, I noticed how responsive social media audiences were to health information on periods, sex, and birth control made into artwork via platforms such as Instagram and Tumblr. It was intriguing to see how people craved this content and where they found their lives intersecting with it. This realization led to building *Womanly* into a community where people could see themselves, learn, and find a place of intersection within their identity.

To understand the original design of *Womanly* is to also understand the relationship between magazines and their presence in my life thus far and what they represent for me in terms of race, economics, and accessibility. I created *Womanly* for Black and Brown women to see their faces in print—not on just one or two pages but again and again. Doctors' offices and waiting rooms in my North Philly neighborhood are often filled with *TV Guide*s and *US Weekly*s, magazines that showcase whiteness and thinness as health. By placing *Womanly* in waiting rooms,

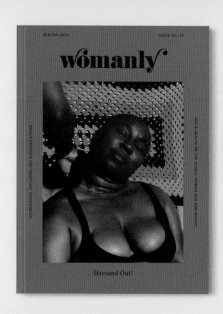

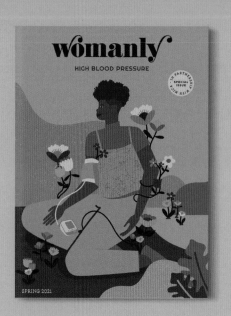

Figure 3.6.1 [top left] The food and nutrition issue offers hope through nutritional facts, community resources, recipes, personal narratives, and art for survival. Design by Jeremie Rose Wimbrow. Artwork by Singha Hon. Words by Yuri Lee. Photograph by Cara Elise Taylor.

Figure 3.6.2 [top right] The stress issue compiles stories, poetry, and art that remind us that we aren't alone in struggling with stress as well as tools and resources to help readers address stressors and lead a happier, healthier life. Design by Hannah Candelaria. Photograph by Cara Elise Taylor.

Figure 3.6.3 [bottom left and right] *Womanly* partnered with MFA in Illustration Practice at the Maryland Institute College of Art to focus on the topic of high blood pressure, also known as hypertension, in the city of Baltimore. Cover art by Meech Boakye. Design by Hannah Candelaria. Artwork by Singha Hon and Alexandra Folino. Words by Aarti Patel and Attia Taylor. Photographs by Ariana Mygatt.

we intervene in the crucial moment before someone visits with their doctor or connects with their community.

Designing a magazine about health and wellness with people of color in mind stemmed from my lived experience as well as from conversations with people young and old about what they wanted to see in the media regarding their lives and health. Our conversations demonstrated why seeing yourself represented is so important. As a team, we chose to build our health graphics and "how-to's" with those conversations in mind. In *Womanly*, we include a wider range of skin tones and different body types and design our issues for everyday folks with varying levels of education. We also curate stories and artwork in a way that flows to the reader. For example, you might read about someone's journey living with high blood pressure and then turn the page to learn about ways to prevent it.

To date, *Womanly* has created seven issues on the topics of sex education, heart health, aging, Black maternal health, nutrition, stress relief, and hypertension. Discussions on how to approach a magazine that is artful, educational, and accessible took a number of factors into account, including representation. For us to feel seen and visible in society, we must also see ourselves represented in the media we consume. Representation provides an outlet to feel safer and more accepted and increases our self-esteem as we move throughout the world. Magazines such as *Essence*, *Jet*, and *Ebony* were pioneers in creating space for Black women in print. Following in those footsteps, we designed a magazine that proudly expands on representation in race but also in gender identity, health, and age.

We donate a large portion of our print magazines to health clinics and community centers in low-income communities, and in that decision we began designing for people who may not seek out an art or health magazine online or in stores. We take into account color scheme, readability, illustration style, paper

Figure 3.6.4
Womanly provides magazines for free and for sale at events across the East Coast. Photograph by Marion Aguas.

types, and page count. All design efforts are led by our art director, Hannah Candelaria, and our lead graphic designer, Jeremie Wimbrow. Editorial efforts are led by our managing editor, Ariana Mygatt, and our editorial managers, Betty Fermin and Sarah Cuddie.

When we deliberate over potential topics for an issue, we often look to our communities to understand what health disparities they're experiencing. Early in the COVID-19 pandemic, our sixth issue covered food access and nutrition to highlight food apartheid in urban areas and to share resources for finding healthy food in a broken system that was damaged even more by crisis (figure 3.6.1). Design and content decisions considered what kinds of photography to include, how to make cultural connections, how to determine where racism affects what foods we eat, and how to educate people on nutrition without judging them. To ensure the issue could reach an audience as entertainment but also as a resource, our designers and editors were tasked with creating movement throughout the issue to ensure a flow that centered education, empathy, understanding, and inspiration.

We are intentional about how and where we show up for the communities we intend to serve. Whether it's through a magazine, billboard, social campaign, or event, our readers and audience feel drawn to our work because of a strong mission and brand identity. We have partnered with organizations such as Planned Parenthood of Greater New York, Ethel's Club, Brooklyn Arts Council, and other community-oriented institutions to make health information more accessible and creative.

As an all-volunteer project, *Womanly* has been able to reach thousands of people and have a lasting impact on their view of themselves and their health. One *Womanly* reader confided she was terrified about the maternal mortality rate for Black women in the United States and said, "You reached a first time Black mother, at a moment that couldn't be more perfect … in the doc's waiting room." To date, we have distributed more than 8,000 print issues of our magazines through clinics, community spaces, and museums as well as directly to individuals. As members of the communities we serve, we envision change enacted through grassroots collaborations not only with health-care practitioners, artists, and community leaders that advance the health and well-being of marginalized peoples but also with marginalized people themselves. In the long term, our work aims to rebuild trust and understanding between marginalized communities and the health-care system by designing our content for sustainability, inclusivity, and accessibility through the language of creativity.

Attia Taylor is a Brooklyn-based musician and creative producer and the founder of *Womanly Magazine*. She is passionate about building and cultivating communities through her projects and in support of the work of others.

1 US Centers for Disease Control and Prevention (CDC), "Healthy People 2020: Legal and Policy Resources Related to Access to Health Services," 2016, https://www.cdc.gov/phlp/publications/topic/hp2020/access.html.

2 New York University, "Health Literacy," 2020, https://www.nyu.edu/life/safety-health-wellness/live-well-nyu/priority-areas/health-literacy.html.

3 US CDC, "Access to Health Care," *CDC Vital Signs*, January 6, 2020, https://www.cdc.gov/vitalsigns/healthcareaccess/index.html.

On countermapping and codesigning with more-than-humans

The researchers Alexandra Crosby and Ilaria Vanni reflect on the creation of "planty maps," guides that facilitate dialogue between humans and their surroundings.

Alexandra Crosby and Ilaria Vanni

It has been several months since we officially completed The Planty Atlas of UTS; *however, we know that maps are never really finished. We had planned to distribute the printed maps to staff and students at the University of Technology Sydney at the start of the academic year, but due to the pandemic campus was closed through much of 2020 and 2021. Now that restrictions have eased, we meet at Central Station with copies of the map and a desire to reconnect with the civic ecologies of our workplace. There are still very few people around and lots of closed buildings, but we follow the plants, over weedy gutters, through overgrown nature strips, and into the scent of crushed gum leaves. As we take photos, chat, and scribble notes on the map, a sense of belonging begins to return.*

Planty maps guide people to care for place and connect to civic ecologies. They visually communicate walking routes that combine observational knowledge of place with historical and geographical research. Observations are made by paying attention to planty agencies—for example, the ways seeds travel throughout the city with bats and birds, then sprout along stormwater drains. *Marrickville Walks: Tropical Imaginaries of Abundance* was designed with the community space Front-yard Projects (where one of us was a janitor) as its starting point. *The Planty Atlas of UTS* (figure 3.7.1) was also designed around community walks, loosely based on permaculture principles of observation, interaction, and acceptance of feedback. *The Plantiness of Bankstown* (figure 3.7.2) was exhibited at the arts center and invited visitors to exit the gallery and get back out into the neighborhood. *The Planty Map of Green Square Civic Ecologies* (figures 3.7.3 and 3.7.4) presented points of interest collated during a climate action walk on Earth Day 2021.

In Alliance with Plants: A Feminist Methodology

Our Mapping Edges methodology has been adapted from two feminist research methods, countermapping and fabulation. In our work, countermapping is a way to follow plants, and fabulation is a way to design with plants.

In the creation, representation, and enforcement of territory, maps are deeply implicated in colonization. However, mapping as a redirective practice can also create powerful counterpoints to colonial and patriarchal assumptions about

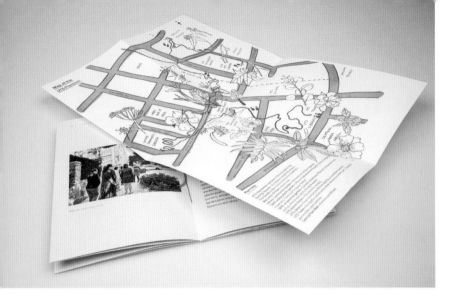

Figure 3.7.1
The Planty Atlas of UTS. A planty way to walk from the old library to the new library on the University of Technology Sydney campus. Graphic design and illustration by Megan Wong and Ella Cutler. Photograph by Karina Glasby.

the world. The sociologist Nancy Lee Peluso and many since her call this method "countermapping."[1] Countermaps can trace spatial injustices in cities and visualize civic ecologies that care for climate, soil, water, and other species. In settler-colonial societies, countermaps can resurface and amplify Indigenous relationships to environments. In Australia, where we are located, *country* is not a synonym of *land*; it is much more, and "it comprises ecologies of plants, animals, water, sky, air and every aspect of the 'natural' environment. Country is a spiritual entity: she is Mother."[2]

Our methodology begins with the premise that "re-mapping offers possibilities for conceptualizing space that is regional and relational, as opposed to state-sanctioned and static."[3] This approach also connects to the feminist philosopher Donna Haraway's concept of "situated knowledges," with which she challenges the god-trick vision of science—that is, "seeing everything from nowhere"—by acknowledging that our own position in the world is contingent and hence can produce knowledge with greater objectivity than if we claimed to be neutral observers.[4] The design researcher Linda Knight extends this argument to the practice of mapping and reclaims a form of "inefficient mapping" that does not aim to represent a whole but focuses on aspects and affects as a way "to notice some of what goes on without claiming to represent some kind of truthful or whole account of the time–place."[5] Inefficient mapping, she argues, allows the visual notation of the simultaneous, overlapping, and multiple movements of both human and nonhuman elements.

Similarly, planty maps intend to capture aspects and effects of urban ecologies so that people can follow plants, even if the process is inefficient. In other words, we posit that humans can communicate *with* plants—not in the sense of creating communication between humans and plants but in the sense of creating communication alongside plants and other ecological elements. Building on feminist approaches to interspecies relationality that show what plants can teach us through their encounters, we propose that plants and humans can also form design alliances, resulting in new visual stories of civic ecologies. For example, in making

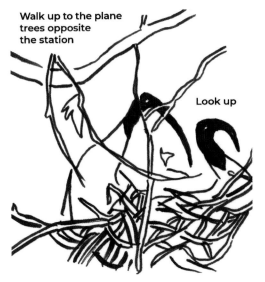

Walk up to the plane trees opposite the station

Look up

Who are the architects working on these trees?

Find two other non human architects

Figure 3.7.2 *The Plantiness of Bankstown*, detail, page 1. An Australian White Ibis, *Threskiornis molucca*, in a London plane tree, *Plantanius orientalis* (a symbol of colonial disturbance), creates a nest and recombinant ecologies. Graphic design and illustration by Ella Cutler.

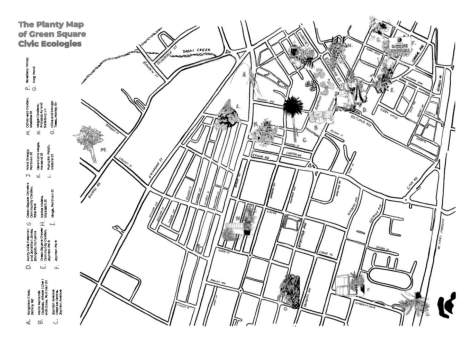

Figure 3.7.3 *The Planty Map of Green Square Civic Ecologies*. Graphic design and illustration by Ella Cutler.

Figure 3.7.4 Neighborhood walks at Green Square. Planty points of interest are noted to include on *The Planty Map of Green Square Civic Ecologies*, 2021. Photograph by Mapping Edges.

Marrickville Walks, we were enrolled by papaya, banana, and dragon fruit plants to follow paths and engage with their habitats and behavior patterns. We then created mapping devices that rely on these plants to communicate with other humans. By magnifying relationships between people and plants in urban settings, planty maps make more-than-human kin visible[6] and show alternatives to the power geometries regulating urban space.

This methodology also aligns with the work of the feminist design theorist Daniela Rosner, who is concerned with reworking and producing counterpoints to established patriarchal, heteronormative, and colonial design practices. Rosner joins a legacy of feminist scholars who write feminist histories to create feminist futures. She focuses on "fabulation" as a kind of storytelling practice that can help expand the prevailing methods of making things, technology, and worlds.[7] By tracing overlaps with other disciplines and dialogues, critical fabulation expands what it means to design.

Rosner also expands the possibilities of alternative design stories with a set of orienting tactics that include alliances, recuperations, interferences, and extensions. (These tactics replace what she outlines as the intellectual lineage of the four theoretical pillars of design: individualism, universalism, objectivism, and solutionism.) In making planty maps, we focus on these orienting tactics because they help us to destabilize the human-centeredness and sexism inherent in design discourse and to consider the role of plants in urban spaces. Alliances, according to Rosner, build "a composite of relations within a design setting rather than an aggregation of self-contained individuals."[8] Like planty relations, alliances are hybrid, collective, and entangled practices. As a way of creating interferences, planty maps disturb power relations and disrupt business-as-usual design by visualizing civic ecologies that show how the city might be designed and cared for differently. We interpret recuperations as a way to recognize absented narratives, such as the Aboriginal country on which our city is built. Finally, extensions stay with a design situation to create new circulations of content through transitions in form, such as the communication of knowledge shared while walking, then printed in a map, then extended to an online platform that grows over time.

In the design of planty maps and in our dialogue with feminist sociologists, geographers, and philosophers, we propose a powerful example of a feminist critical fabulation. As feminist designers in alliance with plants, we can stir up trouble in the city and enliven activist agendas both within and beyond the design disciplines.

Alexandra Crosby (she/her), University of Technology Sydney, is a transdisciplinary scholar and visual communicator researching design practice and theory. She works with Ilaria Vanni as Mapping Edges Research Studio.

Ilaria Vanni (she/her), University of Technology Sydney, is a writer, researcher, and educator. She is interested in how design and material culture shape the cultural, social, and political dimensions of urban environments. She works with Alexandra Crosby as Mapping Edges Research Studio.

1 Nancy Lee Peluso, "Whose Woods Are These? Counter-Mapping Forest Territories in Kalimantan, Indonesia," *Antipode* 27, no. 4 (October 1995): 383–406, doi:10.1111/j.1467-8330.1995.tb00286.x.
2 Shannon Foster, Joanne Paterson Kinniburgh, and Wann Country, "There's No Place Like (without) Country," in *Placemaking Fundamentals* for the Built Environment, ed. Cristina Hernandez-Santin (Singapore: Palgrave Macmillan, 2020), 68.
3 Stephanie Springgay and Sarah E. Truman, *Walking Methodologies in a More-Than-Human World: Walking Lab* (London: Routledge, 2018), 14.
4 Donna J. Haraway, "Situated Knowledges: The Science Question in Feminism and the Privilege of Partial Perspective," *Feminist Studies* 14, no. 3 (1988): 581, doi:10.2307/3178066.
5 Linda Knight, "Playing: Inefficiently Mapping Human and Inhuman Play in Urban Commonplaces" in *Feminist Research for 21st-Century Childhoods*, ed. B. Denise Hodgins (London: Bloomsbury Academic, 2019), 142.
6 Donna J. Haraway, *Staying with the Trouble: Making Kin in the Chthulucene* (Durham, NC: Duke University Press, 2016).
7 Daniela K. Rosner, *Critical Fabulations: Reworking the Methods and Margins of Design* (Cambridge, MA: MIT Press, 2020).
8 Rosner, *Critical Fabulations*, 81.

⁎ Plurality

No one way
works. It will
take all of
us shoving
at the thing
from all sides
to take it
down.

Diane Di Prima
REVOLUTIONARY LETTERS

On plurality

Alison Place

In her *TED Talk* in 2009, the novelist Chimamanda Ngozi Adichie spoke about the danger of the single story: show a people as one thing, as only one thing, again and again, and that is what they become. It robs them of possibility. "Stories are defined by how they are told and who tells them," she said. "Power is not just the ability to tell a story about another person, but to make it the definitive story of that person."[1]

The trouble with design is the single story. For far too long, designers have operated as though there is only one way of seeing people, one way of doing things, one way things should look, one solution to a problem. Dominant ideologies have enforced extremely narrow conceptions of what constitutes "good" design, clinging to modernist ideals of minimalism, universal solutions, and homogenous users. Designers' resistance to complexity—in their audiences, in their ways of working, in themselves—is palpable. It robs us of possibility.

The design process is traditionally one of simplification, aiming to reduce complicated problems down to a single manageable hurdle. Consider, for example, how the solving of deeply rooted social problems, such as gender discrimination in the workplace, has been attempted with a "tool kit." The design process is intended to result in one final, enshrined solution to a problem. This mindset is evident in the framework of "universal design," an absurdly masculine notion that designers' problem-solving abilities are all-knowing, all-seeing, and capable of meeting the needs of every human in the world. Disability studies scholars have thoroughly examined the limitations of universal design,[2] finding it to be generally unsuccessful and in many cases impossible. The feminist human–computer interaction researcher Shaowen Bardzell critiques the notion of Western universalism in technology and interaction design, especially in developing countries: "A timeless and universal stance in cross-cultural design is dangerous because it demotes cultural, social, regional, and national differences in user experiences and outlooks. It also quietly and usually unintentionally imposes ... Western technological norms and practices."[3] Designing for diverse populations across physical, social, and cultural differences requires the opposite of universalism: pluralism.

Plurality is simply the notion of more than one at once—more than one way of experiencing the world, more than one way of resisting oppression, more than one way of practicing feminism (hence the oft used term *feminisms*[4]). Feminist theory rejects the notion of a single way of doing or thinking. As discussed in chapter 2, a primary aim of feminist philosophers and researchers has been to pry open the "sovereign singular universal" by undoing the notion that human inquiry will eventually result in one epistemology or one ethics or one politics for all.[5]

Universalism can assert only similarities; therefore, it marginalizes what is seen as dissimilar. Feminism, in contrast, does not require the construction of a single story that represents one truth. Feminist ways of understanding the world elicit a plurality of negotiated meanings.[6] Although the question of feminism as pluralistic remains somewhat debated in feminist spheres—whether it is yet or not, whether it should be or not—design could do with a bit of plurality.

Though the philosopher Hannah Arendt was no feminist, she named plurality as one of the essential conditions of human existence, noting its "two-fold character" of equality and distinction. "We are all the same, that is, human, in such a way that nobody is ever the same as anyone else who ever lived, lives, or will live."[7] Arendt argued that human plurality is a matter not only of *whats* (types or groups of people) but also of *whos* (unique people living in ways that are not identical to other lives). The *whats* and *whos* are bound together because social groups are made up of unique human beings, and, conversely, each human being is unique because they live different lives within different groups. In other words, we all are plural.

Within feminism, plurality also connotes an element of contradiction or divergence—sometimes even disagreement or conflict—which feminists believe is not only inevitable but also vital to feminist struggle. Postmodernist feminists stress plurality rather than unity in the same way they reject conceptions of women as a homogenous group. They disavow "universalized and normalized accounts of women as a group on the basis that a feminism framed by such accounts becomes itself complicit in subordination."[8] Here we see ways in which plurality coincides with and reinforces the need for intersectionality. Viewing knowledge and people through a pluralistic lens opens up the possibility for many ways of knowing and doing as well as for many ways of existing and experiencing oppression. According to Donna Haraway, feminism is also characterized by a shifting plurality of perspectives in that people are not epistemically trapped inside their culture, their gender, or any other identity.[9] They can think from other perspectives. Thus, although we all have plural perspectives, their constitution is always shifting.

Most feminists embrace plurality as the foundational principle behind the rejection of the gender binary, the assertion that there are only two distinct and opposite genders: man and woman.[10] Much of feminist theory is predicated on the contention that the concept of gender is a social construct and that patriarchy is inherently the institutionalization and maintenance of the gender binary. The poet and author Alok Vaid-Menon argues that the problem of the patriarchy is not dominance of cisgender men over cisgender women but the violence of the gender binary itself, which not only erases and harms nonbinary and gender-nonconforming people but also damages gender-conforming people. In Vaid-Menon's words, "The future is not female. The future is free of racist and essentialist ideas of gender and sex."[11] Gender plurality also troubles notions of masculinity and femininity, which the exhibition designer Margaret Middleton explores in depth in their essay in this chapter.

Plurality is a characteristic embraced by another oppositional framework to patriarchy: the matriarchy. As a cultural construct, patriarchy goes well beyond the exploitation of women. It is characterized by actions and emotions that value competition, war, hierarchies, power, growth, the domination of others, the appropriation of resources, and a rational justification of it all in the name of truth. Matriarchy, in contrast, is not defined by the predominance of women over men but by an entirely different conception of life based on participation, collaboration, understanding, respect, sacredness, and the cyclical and relational fabric of all life. As an organizing principle of society, matriarchy is often attributed to and associated with Indigenous peoples. In feminist thinking, conceptions of matriarchy have ranged from societies with democratic representation of women to radical utopias governed entirely by women, but contemporary applications tend to regard it as framework for calling attention to and subverting patriarchal norms. If patriarchy is about power over others, matriarchy is about empowerment from within. There are multiple ways of knowing, doing, and being within a matriarchy (a notion explored in the dialogue with Ayako Takase and Heather Snyder Quinn in this chapter). Although plurality brings to light uniqueness and difference, it ultimately asks us to consider our shared humanity and interconnectedness.

✳ Feminist design calls for a plurality of open-ended, responsive outcomes that address the complexity of both individual experiences of marginalization as well as the underlying causes of systemic oppression. ✳

Critiques of pluralism in feminism posit that the term is too fuzzy, connoting the friendly coexistence of different things, such as different values, genders, cultures, religions, and sexualities. The transnational feminist scholar Chandra Talpade Mohanty warns against presumptions of "harmony in diversity" and argues that difference seen as benign variation bypasses power and history to suggest an "empty pluralism"[12] (a theory explored in Becky Nasadowski's essay in this chapter). When deployed thoughtfully within an analysis of power, however, the concept of "plurality" reveals something important about what is at stake in contemporary struggles over diversity. Our "differences" must be engaged in terms of their historical origination and meaning, in relation to material and social inequalities, and in light of the possibility of both justice and care between those who are differently situated.[13] Bringing this sort of engagement to design has the potential to generate, if only momentarily and provisionally, the feminist world we seek—a "world in which many worlds fit."[14]

Feminism is often understood as a world-making project. To view design as world making, as opposed to "solutioning," calls on us to recognize that with plurality comes complexity and an opportunity for designers to embrace that complexity rather than avoid it. Plurality complicates solutionism because it exposes the feebleness of a one-size-fits-all approach. In their 2021 essay "Not a

Toolkit," the design educators Maya Ober, Anja Neidhardt, and Griselda Flesler draw a link between designers' need for manuals, tool kits, and answers and the dominant solutionist paradigm of design education. They call instead for a process that prioritizes asking questions, starting from the standpoint of the "other," the one who differs from the dominant norm. "In doing so," they write, "we are constantly unlearning the impulse of making that we acquired through our modern-driven design educations[;] ... we stay uncomfortable, constantly trying to proceed with small steps and small gestures, getting to—as an ongoing process of imagining and realizing transformation."[15]

Without a lens critical of power, solutionism also leads designers to develop individual solutions to systemic problems. Focus is placed on creating interventions and tools to help people navigate problems on a personal level without addressing the political, cultural, and social contexts that contribute to those problems. We target "pain points" and "barriers" rather than the underlying systems that are to blame. As discussed in chapter 1, this is one way that power preserves itself—by obscuring its structures to make individuals think that oppression is a personal experience, not a systemic one. Feminist design calls for a plurality of open-ended, responsive outcomes that address the complexity of both individual experiences of marginalization as well as the underlying causes of systemic oppression, and it reminds us to place the burden of change on institutions and those in power, not on marginalized people.

Plural understandings of people and problems also call for seeing relationships—between the parts of a system, between people and systems, and between designers and people. When we look at systems rather than pain points and at people rather than problems, our task as designers shifts from solving problems to "responding to trouble." Calling in Donna Haraway's notion of "staying with the trouble,"[16] the designer Marie Louise Juul Søndergaard argues for a rejection of the problem–solution dichotomy in favor of a language of trouble and response, which points to the complex adversarial and affective relations between humans and things. "Staying with the trouble" does not imply defining trouble in order to solve it. In her words, "Responding to trouble includes caring for the other, changing attitudes, shifting perspectives and engaging in (re)negotiations. ... It includes not giving answers to open questions but engaging in conflict and conversations."[17] (See Søndergaard's essay in chapter 5, which explores this topic further.) The task for designers is to respond to trouble with trouble—to stir up debate, interrupt what we are doing, disturb thinking patterns, and trouble the story in order to change it.

Authors within this chapter use the lens of plurality to problematize many accepted norms in design, from the violence of design education to the narrow Western canon of design history to the falsehood of the gender binary in aesthetics and artificial intelligence. Their perspectives and practices embody plural ways of designing, teaching, and being. As discussed in the dialogue with the graphic designer Benedetta Crippa, embracing plurality may imply a capacity to hold space for others, but it might also require holding more space for ourselves. Our identities are not fixed, and our ways of knowing and doing can change. The challenge for designers to think and work pluralistically is not necessarily to conceive of existences and experiences beyond our own but rather to find the humility to acknowledge what we *don't* know and what we may never know. We have been trained to assume that we know what is best, to trust that we are right. Holding space for other ways of knowing and doing, for what we do not know, will be an ongoing project of unlearning. Karena Montag, a therapist and activist who leads workshops on antiracism and restorative justice, always opens her sessions with a mantra: "Expect and accept a lack of closure." The work of transformation is an imperfect, ongoing, and unfinished process—a helpful reminder both in our transformation as feminists and designers as well as in our collective transformation as a discipline.

1 Chimamanda Ngozi Adichie, "The Danger of a Single Story," *TED Talks*, July 2009, https://www.ted.com/talks/chimamanda_ngozi_adichie_the_danger_of_a_single_story.
2 See, for instance, Aimi Hamraie, *Building Access: Universal Design and the Politics of Disability* (Minneapolis: University of Minnesota Press, 2017).
3 Shaowen Bardzell, "Feminist HCI: Taking Stock and Outlining an Agenda for Design," in *CHI '10: CHI Conference on Human Factors in Computing Systems* (New York: Association for Computing Machinery, 2010), 1301–1310.
4 bell hooks argues in *Feminism Is for Everybody: Passionate Politics* (New York: Routledge, 2014) that advancing the term *feminisms* has historically served the

conservative and liberal political interests of women seeking status and privileged class power.
5 Bonnie Mann and Jean Keller, "Why a Feminist Volume on Pluralism?," *Philosophical Topics* 41, no. 2 (2013): 1–11.
6 Shulamit Reinharz, with the assistance of Lynn Davidman, *Feminist Methods in Social Research* (New York: Oxford University Press, 1992).
7 Hannah Arendt, *The Human Condition* (Chicago: University of Chicago Press, 1958), 8.
8 Chris Beasley, *What Is Feminism? An Introduction to Feminist Theory* (London: Sage, 1999), 81–82.
9 Donna J. Haraway, "Situated Knowledges: The Science Question in Feminism and the Privilege of Partial

Perspective," *Feminist Studies* 14, no. 3 (1988): 575–599, doi:10.2307/3178066.
10 A violent minority of feminists dubbed TERFs (transexclusionary radical feminists) are known for upholding the gender binary and discriminating against trans, nonbinary, and gender-nonconforming people, which calls into question their identification as feminists.
11 Alok Vaid-Menon, *Beyond the Gender Binary* (New York: Penguin Workshop, 2020).
12 Chandra Talpade Mohanty, *Feminism without Borders: Decolonizing Theory, Practicing Solidarity* (Durham, NC: Duke University Press, 2003).
13 Mann and Keller, "Why a Feminist Volume on Pluralism?"
14 "We want a world in which many worlds fit" is a

slogan coined by Zapatista activists in Latin America.
15 Maya Ober, Anja Neidhardt, and Griselda Flesler, "Not a Toolkit: A Conversation on the Discomfort of Feminist Design Pedagogy," in *Design Struggles: Intersecting Histories, Pedagogies, and Perspectives*, ed. Claudia Mareis and Nina Paim (Amsterdam: Valiz, 2021), 207.
16 Donna J. Haraway, *Staying with the Trouble: Making Kin in the Chthulucene* (Durham, NC: Duke University Press, 2016).
17 Marie Louise Juul Søndergaard, "Staying with the Trouble through Design: Critical-Feminist Design of Intimate Technology," PhD diss., Aarhus University, 2018, 163.

On design pedagogy and empty pluralism

The design educator Becky Nasadowski shares highlights from a studio-seminar course rooted in intersectional feminist concepts.

Becky Nasadowski

This essay provides an overview of "Politics and Ethics of Design," a studio-seminar course that focuses on the sociopolitical contexts in which design is produced, circulated, and consumed. Over the past decade, design educators have increasingly asked students to address complex issues of race, class, and gender under the mantra of "design for good" while overlooking decades of scholarship within such fields as anthropology, Black studies, cultural studies, and gender studies. While a graduate student, I saw firsthand the effects of well-intentioned but superficial lessons when an instructor encouraged an undergraduate designer to perform "ethnographic research" during a community-based assignment. With little support, the student hopped in their luxury SUV and began taking photographs outside of a homeless shelter. Returning to the classroom, the group never discussed these problematic class dynamics. Several projects elsewhere appeared similarly naive, such as the university design class that collaborated with the local police department to rebrand the police's relationship to the community—with no evidence of discussions around *why* that relationship might be contentious.[1]

Community engagement has become an increasingly marketable value on university websites, but any "socially engaged" pedagogy that does not provide historical and political context complies with what the feminist scholar Chandra Talpade Mohanty has called "harmonious, empty pluralism."[2] A feminist pedagogy insists on direct, critical engagement with history and sociopolitical relations. This informed my approach to designing a special-topics course that, due to student demand and evidence of its positive impact on other upper-division coursework, will soon become a requirement within our design curriculum.

Course Structure

Throughout the course, we tackle three design projects: a data-visualization project, an interview-based project, and extension of a previous project. This format encourages a slower production pace, permitting greater engagement with assigned texts and writing that includes responses to a series of in-class prompts and a final paper.

Our reading list is grounded in feminism, and we discuss concepts that may be familiar but often misunderstood. For example, we clarify intersectionality as a political framework coined in 1989 by the legal scholar Kimberlé Crenshaw to elucidate how the legal system draws distinct boundaries around race and sex discrimination, thus compartmentalizing how oppressions are experienced. Crenshaw argued that this partitioning obscures the way Black women are "multiply-burdened," which requires a rethinking of what is deemed the "women's experience" or "the Black experience."[3] The theory explicitly advocates for complexity over single-issue analyses—a productive lens for the class to analyze the failings of visual communication that may critique misogyny but simultaneously ignore the roles of race and class.

A feminist base motivates the students to engage challenging questions around power relations, knowledge production, and systems of violence. We interrogate the positionality of the designer, noting how all knowledge reflects the conditions of its production. We discuss data feminism and countercartography, exploring ways to challenge hierarchical classification systems, resist imposed boundaries, and correct historical omissions. We discover histories of alternative publishing practices that have amplified and continue to amplify counterpublics. We find the limits of design-thinking methods and the magical thinking of *TED Talks*. We collectively ask how we can build our collaborative working relationships in ways that are equitable and mutually beneficial. And we critique the creative industry's neoliberal and ideological entanglement of work and passion.

Situating Our Histories and Ourselves

Our discussions start with Ida B. Wells and the World's Fair of 1893, dubbed by Black newspapers at the time as "the white American's World's Fair" due to its widespread exclusion of Black contributions.[4] In response, Wells edited a pamphlet that speaks to institutionalized racism in multiple contexts, from the mobs to the courts to the media, all supporting white supremacy.[5] This pamphlet contextualizes how and why W. E. B. Du Bois and his team crafted a data-visualization series for the World's Fair of 1900, illustrating that it was the historically constituted afterlives of slavery that subordinated Black Americans to a white-supremacist social and political world.[6] Du Bois's charts have recently resurfaced as exemplary of noncanonical "inclusive" design history, but they often circulate without meaningful contextualization or study. Beginning the semester with Du Bois *and* Wells models a historically informed, socially engaged design practice.

We also study contemporary work, interrogating the relation between design on the one hand and authority, presumed neutrality, and ideology on the other. For example, the artist Ashley Hunt's overwhelmingly intricate diagrams of the prison-industrial complex subvert the visual language of didacticism to call attention to all we do *not* know, inviting a critical engagement with the carceral state.[7] In *Data Feminism*, Catherine D'Ignazio and Lauren F. Klein insist data never speak for themselves and are always a product of ideology.[8] We must identify by whom and for whom data are produced, locating their motivations, limits, and omissions. These critics demonstrate that a feminist design pedagogy privileges inquiry and may render problems complex rather than offer tidy (often marketable) solutions to problems.

Constructing Narratives

Weeks later in the course, we discuss narrative construction, while students prepare for an interview project. To articulate what is at stake in translation, we read the anthropologist Leo R. Chavez on the role images and symbols play in constructing ideas of citizenship. Regarding media representation, Chavez writes: "The virtual lives of immigrants become abstractions and representations that stand in the place of real lives. ... They are no longer flesh and blood immigrants but images."[9] The construction of flattened, threatening social imaginaries communicated through magazines and Twitter feeds creates a racialized hierarchy that comprises the environment in which lawmakers design immigration policies and police enforce them.[10]

Throughout the semester, I share examples of visual communication and ask students to write a response using our readings as a framework, which has proven helpful to give individual students time to collect their thoughts in advance of group conversation. Students are quick to express contempt at the mock immigration sting planned by the Young Conservatives of Texas. Event participants were to earn a gift card for "catching" volunteers wearing shirts labeled "illegal immigrant."[11] More nuanced and surreptitious in its ideology was the Budweiser commercial "Typical American" in 2020. Directed by the Oscar-winning filmmaker Kathryn Bigelow, it conflates nationalism and social justice, framing activism as hip and patriotic. The gravelly, masculine voice-over narrates negative stereotypes of Americans with a tongue-in-cheek visual reframing of them in an admirable light. A couple of these stereotypes, as outlined in Budweiser's press release, include: "Mason Miller from Peoria, Arizona, proves that '*showing up uninvited*' isn't always a bad thing—especially if you're a soldier surprising your family after a tour of duty," and "Ken Nwadike Jr. [...] '*thinking he can save the world*' offers 'free hugs' to a police officer to defuse a tense protest proving there is more that unites us than divides us."[12]

Here, we have a woman director pulling at heartstrings, complicating how students weigh the value of representation. Bigelow deploys nationalism as a marketing tool via sweeping, cinematic music that celebrates military intervention and sentimentalizes the brutality of riot cops through a sleight of hand. Nondescript protest signs and indecipherable messages yelled through a megaphone let viewers know the *image* of saying something overrides the content of what is said. The presence of riot cops communicates an antagonism to the protest; to insert a hug concedes one needs only a saccharine moment for conciliation, never material redress.

Building on these conversations, I pair Sheila de Bretteville's 1974 article "A Reexamination of Some Aspects of the Design Arts from the Perspective of a Woman Designer" with Audre Lorde's 1984 essay "Age, Race, Class, and Sex: Women Redefining Difference." De Bretteville critiques the modernist desire to simplify communication, arguing that the search for one "potent image" is a form of reductive problem solving that lends itself to reinforcing patriarchal stereotypes. She asserts instead that *process* is a feminist praxis able to elevate principles previously "devalued and restricted to women and the home."[13] Lorde's essay similarly resists rigid reductions of identity but furthers de Bretteville's argument by plainly stating, "Some problems we share as women. Some we do not," a point that distinguishes Lorde's writing from much of the (white) feminist scholarship of the 1970s.[14] Lorde insists that both *misnaming* and *refusing to recognize* differences separate us, as opposed to differences themselves. Both authors argue against using the same vessels for new narratives. Reading their texts together offers students historically situated examples of feminist discourse and its relationship to design.

We shape the design, and it shapes us. In this context of framing and representation, I talk students through both logistical and philosophical questions around interviewing. There is power in creating stories, including the potential for perpetuating violence. Who writes the questions, who frames them, and how? Whose voices are chosen, and how are they edited? Critically, I implore them to always ask: Who benefits from this project?

Conclusion

A feminist design pedagogy acts as a response to the neoliberal university's fetishization of shallow community engagement as well as to the continued pressure to submit to capitalist demand. Our students are drowning in the ubiquity of social justice buzzwords that have become hollow signifiers, new forms of empty pluralism. By insisting on a historically informed, critical, and intersectional approach to teaching design, perhaps we can also arrive at a more socially and politically responsive and feminist design culture at large.

Becky Nasadowski is a designer, educator, and researcher exploring design's complicity in various formations of violence within neoliberal landscapes. She is assistant professor in the Department of Art at the University of Tennessee at Chattanooga.

1 Sarasota Police Department, *Sarasota Police News Conference: Launch of Blue + You—April 25, 2014*, video, YouTube, April 25, 2014, 10:45, https://www.youtube.com/watch?v=1528b0lx-h9E&list=UUA-v3lSGs0kF-51HHHRlcUtg.

2 Chandra Talpade Mohanty, *Feminism without Borders: Decolonizing Theory, Practicing Solidarity* (Durham, NC: Duke University Press, 2003), 193.

3 Kimberlé Crenshaw, "Demarginalizing the Intersection of Race and Sex: A Black Feminist Critique of Antidiscrimination Doctrine, Feminist Theory and Antiracist Politics," *University of Chicago Legal Forum* 1989, no. 1 (1989): 140.

4 Elliott M. Rudwick and August Meier, "Black Man in the 'White City': Negroes and the Columbian Exposition, 1893," *Phylon (1960–)* 26, no. 4 (1965): 354–361, doi:10.2307/273699.

5 Ida B. Wells, ed., *The Reason Why the Colored American Is Not in the World's Columbian Exposition* (Chicago, 1893).

6 Whitney Battle-Baptiste and Britt Rusert, eds., *W. E. B. Du Bois's Data Portraits: Visualizing Black America* (Hudson, NY: Princeton Architectural Press, 2018).

7 Ashley Hunt, "A World Map: In Which We See … ," in *An Atlas of Radical Cartography*, ed. Alexis Bhagat and Lize Mogel (Los Angeles: Journal of Aesthetics and Protest Press, 2007), 145–146.

8 Catherine D'Ignazio and Lauren F. Klein, *Data Feminism* (Cambridge, MA: MIT Press, 2020).

9 Leo R. Chavez, "Spectacles of Citizenship and the 2006 Immigrant Marches," in *New World Colors: Ethnicity, Belonging and Difference in the Americas*, ed. Josef Raab (Tempe, AZ: Bilingual Press, 2013), 41.

10 Harsha Walia, *Border and Rule: Global Migration, Capitalism, and the Rise of Racist Nationalism* (Chicago: Haymarket, 2021), 77–92.

11 Julián Aguilar, "Mock Immigration Sting on UT Campus Canceled," *Texas Tribune*, November 19, 2013, https://www.texastribune.org/2013/11/19/conservative-group-hold-mock-immigration-sting-ut/.

12 Budweiser, "This Year, Budweiser's Super Bowl Spot Is an Ode to the American Spirit," news release, January 23, 2020, https://www.anheuser-busch.com/newsroom/2020/01/this-year-budweisers-super-bowl-spot-is-an-ode-to-the-american.html.

13 Sheila de Bretteville, "A Reexamination of Some Aspects of the Design Arts from the Perspective of a Woman Designer," *Arts in Society: Women and the Arts* 11, no. 1 (1974): 115–116.

14 Audre Lorde, "Age, Race, Class, and Sex: Women Redefining Difference," in *Sister Outsider: Essays and Speeches* (Freedom, CA: Crossing Press, 1984), 119.

On challenging power through the visual

The graphic designer Benedetta Crippa discusses design as a dialogue and finding belonging through craft.

Dialogue with Benedetta Crippa

Alison Place In your master's thesis,[1] you write about making work that defies the dominant ideas around "good design." I felt myself in your shoes as a woman in a male-dominated space, bracing myself for disparaging critiques that would write off the work as frivolous, which was a familiar experience from my own design education. Your work seems to anticipate that critique and confront it. What role do fear and courage play in your creative practice?

Benedetta Crippa I think we all share that experience as women. Design education worldwide is embedded with patriarchal ways of defining quality and delivering feedback. When all your life you are looked upon in a certain way because you're female, you learn to anticipate a derogatory perception of your body and your abilities. My fear was internalized and buried under layers of experiences and toxic messages throughout my life. When I arrived to a pedagogical space where I could elaborate upon these questions, I was given words to describe my experiences that built that fear and could find the creative voice to respond to it. When you fully own your fear, you can fully own your courage, too.

AP Design is typically approached as a process of reduction or simplification, which can also be described as a practice of erasure. A term you have used to describe it is *visual silence*. In what ways do the dominant ways of designing perpetuate visual silence?

BC Throughout Western history, "good" design has come to be considered the result of a process of catharsis or purification. The outcome is understood not just as neutral but as evolved to its perfect form, which is typically the design performed by the white, male body. When we frame what is "good" through such a narrow lens, a large portion of people who are trying to express themselves are silenced. Before I found my own creative voice, I was silent creatively. I was designing according to the ideas that someone else established for me, through someone else's voice. Opening up design to include different visual expressions means opening it up to many more voices. To draw a parallel with type design, as Arabic typographer Nadine Chahine says, when we don't have a variety of typefaces to express what we are trying to say, we are voiceless.[2]

AP Can you describe ways in your own practice that you reject the norms of silencing or neutralizing visual form through design?

BC For me, it's about staying very close to what's relevant to me, both in terms of what questions the design answers but also what kind of visual references it builds upon. The first step to finding my own voice, apart from entering a safe space, was to create a visual library of references where I could forget everything I've learned about what is "good" or "visually successful" and go back to the simple question of what *is meaningful* to me, what moves me.

Figure 4.2.1 Ornamental curtain *Everything Has a Name*, 2020. The curtain references the episode from Helen Keller's autobiography when Keller discovers the existence of language. Photograph by Hans-Georg Gaul for A–Z Presents. Courtesy of Benedetta Crippa.

AP You have described that feeling as "visual belonging."

BC When I teach, I encourage students to identify a place of visual belonging made of things they have designed and things others have designed that make them feel at home or emotionally in tune with themselves. This practice of emerging from silence is ultimately about the craft—learning which shade of blue to choose, which stroke of the line, a way in which visual elements interact, in order to create a visual space, not just an intellectual one, where you can truly belong. When I design, I allow myself to bring in colors, shapes, typography, visual elements, and interactions that go beyond what I learned as being "right" or "good" and instead operate on an emotional level—What do I want to

feel and make other people feel? I bring in what excites me, moves me, and leaves me in awe—resulting in something that exists with a certain visual grace, able to wake up the heart. It's like exercising a muscle: it is never easy, but it gets easier with time.

AP Your work embraces aesthetics of ornamentation and decoration, which you describe as an act of care and love. What does that mean to you?

BC Growing up in Italy, I saw some of the most beautiful artwork in the world. But decoration is firstly a humble practice of care for the everyday, the urge to make something more visually cared for than it was before. It is a practice of specificity, stemming from the local and the particular, and looks different depending on time and place. There is no

Figure 4.2.2 Invitations that are part of the visual identity for the cultural program *Artistic Undressings* in Stockholm, 2019. The visual identity was nominated for the prestigious Design S award in Sweden in 2020. Courtesy of Benedetta Crippa.

practical or economic advantage in doing decoration in the current system of capitalism because [decoration's] main goal is creative self-fulfillment and generosity toward others. Those are the most precious and power-disrupting human skills we have.

AP Plurality is a key theme of your work. What is a pluralistic design practice, and what would a design discipline defined by pluralism look like?

BC For me, a pluralistic design field is one where different visual voices and visual cultures are allowed to coexist without judgments of value or creation of hierarchies. A pluralistic design practice appreciates complexity, especially within ourselves. As women or as people belonging to historically oppressed groups, we repeatedly hear a single story that is told about ourselves, such as how design performed by a woman is supposed to look. I don't fit in this single story. Nobody does. We need to acknowledge the plurality in who we are trying to reach and frame the work in a way that welcomes different experiences to be in dialogue with it. If we all did this, we would have a field that is much more welcoming, compassionate, and visually interesting.

AP When we resist complexity and plurality, design tends to devolve into solutionism. Designers may act as though the world's problems are all within their power to conquer because they are equipped with things like design thinking and tool kits. In contrast, your work aims to operate design as a form of dialogue. What does that mean?

BC I do think we are here to solve problems and leave the world better than how we found it, but life is also a place to contemplate and operate carefully within, like a guest that comes for dinner. One of the most important principles of nonviolent communication is that if you enter the conversation already knowing what kind of answer you want to get, you're not there to be in dialogue but to persuade and exploit. That is how advertising operates; it colonizes every space that is available to move the reader to its predecided action. My approach, guided by honest and nonviolent storytelling, is not simply to react but to act and not simply to comment but to transform. For example, in the visual identity *Artistic Undressings* (figure 4.2.2), the frames around the typography are not just in defiance of the graphic design canon. I created an entirely new kind of frame, one that is also not immediately or obviously read as a frame. It becomes a new visual element with its own dignity, it establishes a new "tradition" so that the "norm" it is measured against is no longer on the map. This is an example of how visual work can move from commenting to transforming.

AP One of the primary objectives of your work is "visual sustainability," which you describe as the pursuit of sustainable coexistence. What does sustainability mean to you? And what role does visual form play in the idea of sustainable coexistence?

BC The definition of sustainability that is most important to me is the practice of coexistence that is free of exploitation. That means I am not exploited, and I'm not exploiting others. In graphic design, sustainability has been about materials or supply chains, which are fundamental, but it is necessary to also address how formal qualities of design can be expressions of nonexploitative mindsets and can lead to nonexploitative

outcomes, hence the term *visual sustainability*. We all exist in a cycle where visual literacy affects notions of authority and power and who is exploited by that power. Even so, almost no democratic government in the world right now is intentionally researching the impact of visuality on social equity. I expect this to change in the coming years.

AP You split your time as a practicing designer and an educator. Why are both of those activities important to you?

BC I believe that a sustainable and rich design field begins with pedagogy as most design education is still a destructive process of suppression where students learn to be visually silent. I want to be present in education to create spaces where students are empowered rather than suppressed. Once they are exposed to a nonviolent pedagogical framework grounded in practice where they can find their own visual voice, they will carry all their lives a powerful awareness of their own creative potential. Feminist pedagogical methods are transformative to students, regardless of gender, because they put each of them in the position to shine and transform rather than to conform.

Figure 4.2.3 Ornamental poster for the sustainability-focused agency SALLY in Stockholm, featuring the poem "Lovad vare vreden" (Praised be the rage) by Maria Wine. The poster features an ornamental frame that plays with concepts of past and future. Courtesy of Benedetta Crippa.

AP As we start to wrap up, I want to talk about the future. Envisioning a liberated future is a vital component of feminist consciousness raising and feminist activism. What role does the future play in your work?

BC As a designer, I am deeply aware that I have the very concrete power of imagination. I see the notion of the future as connected to the fundamental mission of designers to imagine otherwise, and the otherwise is always in the future. There are sustainable and feminist ways of visualizing the future, and there are patriarchal and exploitative ways to do it. For example, while the real world becomes increasingly regulated to protect vulnerable groups, companies are working to move life into the metaverse, which is so far unregulated. There are many groups of people, especially women, who have much more to fear from virtual environments because it is today's patriarchal, capitalist, and colonialist ways of thinking that will shape [those environments]. So, imagining and constructing nonexploitative visions of the future is crucial. The more we build those visions, the more those visions become possible, and we will tend toward them.

AP What is your advice to other designers, especially young emerging designers, to develop their own voices?

BC The most important thing is to know that what you believe and who you are *matter*. Design shapes every moment of our lives; therefore, we can only benefit from a design field that centers values and a diversity of unique voices. Unlearn the library of references that we all grew up with and identify an alternative visual vocabulary that mirrors yourself and leads you to your own visual direction. Lastly, find your community. I learned to accept loneliness at first because I was often an exception to the norm. Now, with a community of extraordinary women who are committed to a sustainable, caring design field—in Sweden, in my home country of Italy, as well as internationally—thriving creatively not only is possible but is also the greatest, most rewarding adventure.

This conversation took place over Zoom in October 2021. It has been edited for clarity and length.

Benedetta Crippa is a graphic designer and consultant who works in Stockholm on a wide range of applications of visual communication with a research-based approach. In her practice, aesthetics emerges as a tangible contribution to transformation toward social equity. She is also a recognized educator focusing on the intersections of visuality and power.

1 Benedetta Crippa, "World of Desire," MA thesis, Konstfack University of Arts, Crafts, and Design, 2017.

2 Nadine Chahine, "The Politics of Arabic Design," paper presented at the Konstfack University of Arts, Crafts, and Design, Stockholm, September 30, 2020.

On centering trans voices in design

With and for trans people, the researchers Cami Rincón and Andrew Mallinson created Syb, a voice-activated artificial-intelligence prototype that aims to generate pluralistic outcomes.

Cami Rincón and Andrew Mallinson

Because technology is not neutral, it is open to analysis; because it is not fixed, it is open to intervention.[1] Scholars in the field of feminist technology studies promote the active reshaping of technology[2] toward design that subverts oppressive dynamics.[3] Syb, a collaborative voice-activated artificial intelligence (VAI) prototype that connects trans people with films recommended by their community, puts this theory to practice.

The development of artificial intelligence largely omits recognition and participation of trans people, in turn producing outcomes that expose this community to harm. Broadly speaking, VAIs reflect these practices by treating gender as implicitly cisgender. VAIs serve as socialization tools that evoke emotional bonds with users through conversational interactions. Their accelerating capabilities and intimate uses, paired with a global scale of adoption, give VAIs the ideological power to naturalize trans erasure. Syb, a feminist intervention to this logic, is grounded on design specifications gathered through research into the specific needs and experiences of trans and/or nonbinary users of VAI and was cocreated with a majority-trans team. In this case study, we discuss how Syb exemplifies the ways in which technology can be reconfigured to elevate overridden knowledge, cultures, and communities.

Phase One: Research

Much research has explored how default voice-assistant personas amplify inequalities for cisgender women. The harms of feminine and highly binarized personas, however, extend beyond their impact on cisgender women. Cami Rincón, Os Keyes, and Corinne Cath conducted research exploring the impacts of VAI on trans communities through a series of interviews with trans and/or nonbinary users.[4] Personas also comply with industry standards, which describe "clarity of gender" as a crucial design requirement. This principle contributes to cultures of discrimination by catering to "gender panic" narratives used to justify violence against trans people. Most initiatives mitigating these harms focus on trans representation by incorporating "genderless voices" in design. As well intentioned as this approach may be, it assumes representation as a central requirement and fails to adopt transinclusive constructions of gender.

These practices reflect a lack of awareness of trans experiences. Trans people have significant privacy concerns and increased risks of data harm. Incorporating representation without addressing other needs may serve as a "surveillance trap" that lures trans users into adopting technologies that haven't incorporated appropriate privacy measures. Design specifications from our study were gathered by listening to rather than assuming the needs and experiences of this community. We propose features for trans-specific purposes (such as navigating gender-affirming health care) and basing the development of VAIs within the trans community.

Phase Two: Development

Syb was initially developed as part of "Queering Voice AI: Trans Centered Design," a course we ran at the Creative Computing Institute of the University of the Arts London. Our goal was to develop a prototype grounded in the requirements from the study and introduce participants to trans-competent approaches to design. Considering the design requirements, the final design team almost entirely comprised trans and/or nonbinary individuals (figure 4.3.1).

The course activities were guided by the Trans Competent Design Standards derived from Feminist Internet's and Josie Young's standards for designing feminist chatbots.[5] In determining the device's purpose, the team reflected: How might we create a technology that actively centers trans joy? This question became embedded throughout the process, leading us to create a VAI that connects users to media created by and/or positively representing the community. We aimed to actively counteract dominant narratives of trans people in the media, which are often articulated by cisgender people and focused on trauma.

In addressing trans-specific privacy considerations, we developed a conversation that introduces users to the team and presents the choice to opt in to sharing data. User onboarding begins by Syb disclosing that it can be used without storing data and then asking if the user is willing to share information. Regardless of the

Queering Voice AI: Trans Centered Design was hosted online in September 2020

Figure 4.3.1 Each iteration of Syb creates features and processes built on the knowledge and experiences of previous trans collaborators and their chosen storytellers, amplifying narratives that make space for ways of existing outside cisnormativity. Courtesy of Feminist Internet.

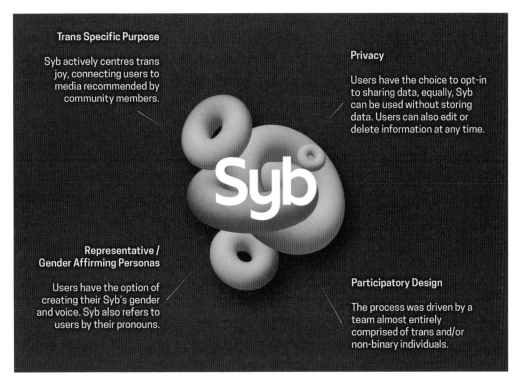

Trans Specific Purpose

Syb actively centres trans joy, connecting users to media recommended by community members.

Privacy

Users have the choice to opt-in to sharing data, equally, Syb can be used without storing data. Users can also edit or delete information at any time.

Representative / Gender Affirming Personas

Users have the option of creating their Syb's gender and voice. Syb also refers to users by their pronouns.

Participatory Design

The process was driven by a team almost entirely comprised of trans and/or non-binary individuals.

Figure 4.3.2 Syb's design reflects and amplifies the knowledge, culture, and joy generated by the trans people and allies who created it. It represents an anomaly within VAI research and development because rarely are trans and nonbinary people afforded the agency to center their experiences in the production of technology. Courtesy of Feminist Internet.

user's initial response, Syb states, "You can always say 'protect my data' to come back and edit or delete your information."

The team felt that it was vital that the device's persona be personable as well as joyful, and we playfully discussed how it should be a friend or trans elder. The name "Syb" is a riff on the word *sibling*, echoing notions of "queer family." This persona would use the team's "queer colloquialisms," such as calling users "hon" instead of referring to them by name.

In addressing requirements around representation and gender affirmation, we were tasked with determining how gender flexibility could be put into practice. Although some of the team felt that gendering Syb was unnecessary, others viewed gender representation as important. We resolved this issue by using a randomized voice for the initial phase of onboarding, after which users have the option of creating a persona by choosing Syb's gender (if any) and a voice from various options, none of which would influence their Syb's personality. This design feature presents an alternative to genderless voice options.

The course resulted in a prototype that walked users through a single-use case, recommending to them movies directed by and featuring trans people. Although Syb was limited in scope and technical performance at this stage, it provided design specifications grounded in research and established foundations for future iterations (figure 4.3.2).

Syb was the recipient of the NewNew Fellowship in 2021, allowing the team to build the prototype into a working product with an expanded database. Moving forward, the team felt it was important for Syb to recommend pieces that are queer-coded or feature trans characters or narratives but aren't necessarily directed by or starring trans people. "Trans media" was therefore redefined as media recommended by the community for the community. The expansion of the database would be equally community driven by enabling users to submit recommendations.

Syb's design reflects and amplifies the knowledge, culture, and joy generated by the trans people and allies who created it. It represents an anomaly within VAI development because rarely are trans and nonbinary people afforded the agency to center themselves in the production of technology. Each iteration of Syb builds on knowledge archived by previous collaborators through chosen features, films, and conversation designs. Together, the archived items form a technology that facilitates and amplifies self-articulated narratives outside cisnormativity.

The Syb design team included Anushka Ansal, Abe Clark, Jo Collier, Maria Demine, Ella Fitzgerald, Maanushi Goel, Tajah Hamilton, Nimco Hussein, Andrew Mallinson, Ama Ogwo, Cami Rincón, Cherub Quist, and Finn Weave.

Cami Rincón is research assistant in public-sector artificial-intelligence ethics and governance at the Alan Turing Institute in London. Cami's research interests explore risks and opportunities for LGBTQ+ people across branches of artificial intelligence.

Andrew Mallinson (they/them) is an artist and writer based in London. They are a cofounder of Feminist Internet and associate lecturer at the University of the Arts London.

1 Wendy Faulkner, "The Technology Question in Feminism: A View from Feminist Technology Studies," *Women's Studies International Forum* 24, no. 1 (2001): 79–95.
2 Maria Lohan, "Constructive Tensions in Feminist Technology Studies," *Social Studies of Science* 30, no. 6 (December 2000): 895–916, doi:10.1177/0306312000 30006003.
3 Judy Wajcman, *Techno-Feminism* (London: Wiley, 2004).
4 Cami Rincón, Os Keyes, and Corinne Cath, "Speaking from Experience: Trans/Non-binary Requirements for Voice-Activated AI," *Proceedings of the ACM on Human–Computer Interaction* 5 (2021): article 132, 1–27, doi:10.1145/3449206.
5 Josie Young and Feminist Internet, "Feminist Design Tool Defensible Decision Making for Interaction Design and AI," Feminist Internet, 2021, https://ugc.futurelearn.com/uploads/files/16/b0/16b088ad-6145-45eb-b5d8-3753a41b4b88/2-10_FeministDesignTool_2.0.pdf.

On feminine exhibition design

The exhibition designer Margaret Middleton confronts the myth of "gender-neutral" aesthetics and reconsiders the feminine in design.

Margaret Middleton

Tracing its origins back 120 years to the progressive education movement, the children's museum field counts many women among its founders and influential thinkers.[1] Today, like the larger museum field, children's museums have a majority-women leadership and workforce.[2] I began my design career in children's museums. As a feminist and queer person, I was drawn to this field built by women that has quietly led inclusive museum practice with its learner-centered, experiential approach. Yet over time I noticed a disconnect between the women-led education department's girl-power messaging and the spaces I designed in the majority-men exhibition department.[3]

As exhibit designers, we aimed for equity through neutrality, avoiding "girly" design choices such as pink, pastels, florals, and anything cute. Later I would come to understand this bias as androcentrism, a norm that positions masculinity as a baseline and femininity as a deviation from that default. Femininity is a socially constructed set of attributes that vary by culture and change over time. Gender, as popularly practiced in the United States, is a "culturally specific, Western bourgeois social construct" based on a set of imperially imported roles and expectations.[4] As a result, dominant feminine and masculine ideals in the contemporary United States are shaped by whiteness, wealth, and heterosexuality. Though people of all genders typically express both feminine and masculine traits, femininity is associated with girls and women. As such, ingrained sexism has aligned the Western cultural understanding of femininity with negative characteristics such as superficiality and frivolity.[5] This systematic devaluing of femininity is femmephobia.[6]

The dominant culture reinforces androcentrism and femmephobia. It requires conscious effort to override the masculine default in design, especially for men, who are significantly more likely to perpetuate androcentrism.[7] When gender neutrality skews masculine, designers must consider who we leave out when we avoid femininity. Intentionally feminine spaces can make girls feel more welcome in museum spaces,[8] and this feeling likely extends to feminine visitors of all genders. Feminine spaces in museums have the potential to be sites where more visitors feel "ambient belonging": the sense of being in a place intended for them.[9]

The nonbinary writer and performer Alok Vaid-Menon asks, "What feminine part of yourself did you have to destroy in order to survive in this world?"[10] What of me has been missing in my work because of my own internalized femmephobia? To become more aware of how I express femininity in my work, I decided to

Figure 4.4.1 Curve: *Patterning Community*, an artwork inspired by the exhibition *Souls Grown Deep: Artists of the American South* in Art Splash at the Philadelphia Museum of Art, 2019. Photograph by Margaret Middleton.

Figure 4.4.2 Softness: *1.8 Renwick* by Janet Echelman in the exhibition *Wonder* at the Renwick Gallery, Washington, DC, 2015–2016. Photograph by Ron Cogswell.

name and notice its presence in the world. I have identified seven feminine design qualities from my perspective as an exhibition designer: curvilinear form, softness, nurturance, sparkle, color, cuteness, and humility.

Curvilinear Form

Familiar and comfortable, the curves of organic shapes evoke nature and the body. Though idealized women's bodies are described as curvaceous, bodies of all genders have curves. The architect Gaston Bachelard considers the curve feminine and describes its hospitality: "The grace of a curve is an invitation to remain. We cannot break away from it without hoping to return. For the beloved curve has nest-like powers; it incites us to possession, it is a curved 'corner,' inhabited geometry."[11] The artist Joy O. Ude's installation *Patterning Community* (figure 4.4.1) invites young visitors and their families to inhabit the geometry of a patchwork dome to read and relax together. This curved corner envelops the visitor like the quilts from Gee's Bend, Alabama, that inspired it.

Softness

Softness is forgiving and accommodating. A soft environment is conducive to comfort and conversation. Texture, form, light, and sound quality together contribute to an overall sense of softness through upholstery, acoustic paneling, and curtains. These components often incorporate textiles, longtime symbols of domesticity and women's work.[12] For *1.8 Renwick,* the artist Janet Echelman used textiles to transform the Renwick Gallery's Grand Salon. In addition to her hammocklike nylon fiber artwork hanging from the ceiling, she also used diffused light, a soft, quiet carpet made from repurposed fishing nets, and bean-bag chairs from which to observe the entire effect (figure 4.4.2).

Nurturance

Associations with motherhood have long aligned nurturance with femininity. The poet and community organizer Cynthia Dewi Oka describes motherhood as a social practice: "The ethos of mothering involves valuing in and of itself a commitment to the survival and thriving of other bodies."[13] A nurturing environment fosters comfort and growth, which designers can express through natural materials such as wood and fiber. The exhibition *The Very Hungry Caterpillar Turns 50* conveyed a sense of warmth and welcome with a palette of greens and natural materials (figure 4.4.3). A thick carpet cut into playful curves ushered visitors into cozy nooks to curl up with books from maple-veneer bins.

Sparkle

The sparkle of glitter and fairy dust is pervasive across toys marketed to girls. Exhibit designers can achieve sparkly effects through glow, refraction, and reflection with lighting and material choices. Sparkle was a key element of the exhibition *Gender Bending Fashion*, referencing camp-aesthetic mainstays such as sequins and disco balls. The glitz began with titles in holographic vinyl lettering and continued throughout the gallery with a dazzling landscape of dichroic acrylic panels reflecting the glow of exhibit spotlights and scattering colorful reflections across the ceiling (figure 4.4.4).

Color

The go-to color for femininity may be pink, but bright colors broadly are associated with femininity. Consumer products intended for women are lighter, brighter, and more colorful, and items for men are darker and confined to a smaller range of colors. In contrast with more somber, muted colors, bright colors communicate playfulness. Vivid color can inject levity and joy into an environment, like the

Figure 4.4.3 Nurturance: *The Very Hungry Caterpillar Turns 50* exhibition at the Eric Carle Museum of Picture Book Art, Amherst, Massachusetts, 2019. Photograph by Margaret Middleton.

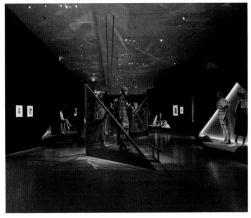

Figure 4.4.4 Sparkle: *Gender Bending Fashion* exhibition at the Museum of Fine Arts, Boston, 2019. Photograph by Margaret Middleton.

Figure 4.4.5 Color: *Colored Shadows* at the Exploratorium, San Francisco. Image courtesy of Amy Snyder, © Exploratorium, www.exploratorium.edu.

Figure 4.4.6 Cuteness: The Teddy Bear Diner at the Discovery Museum, Acton, Massachusetts, 2018. Photograph by Matthew Clowney.

popular Exploratorium exhibit in which visitors interact with their brightly hued shadows (figure 4.4.5).

Cuteness

Linked to femininity through associations with children, cuteness is characterized by qualities that remind us of babies:[14] miniatures, chubby forms, and proportions that emphasize the "head," "feet," or "eyes" of an object. One might assume women are more susceptible to the allure of cuteness, but studies have shown no gender differences in brain responses to cute stimuli.[15] My children's museum colleagues expressed to me, both explicitly and implicitly, that cuteness undermined the rigor of our work. I confronted that bias when creating the Teddy Bear Diner, an even smaller version of a child-size diner exhibit I designed for the Discovery Museum.

Figure 4.4.7 Humility: *Mimi's Family: Photography by Matthew Clowney* at the Boston Children's Museum, 2015. Photograph by Matthew Clowney.

Visitors are delighted to find the secret space tucked under a staircase with a teddy-size diner booth and a family of bears ready to order from mini menus (figure 4.4.6).

Humility

Humility in design resists a patriarchal relationship in which the designer is an expert exerting control over the user's experience and instead favors a less hierarchical approach wherein customization, transparency, and invitation for feedback are central. Shared authority and dialog are essential aspects of feminist facilitation. Honoring visitors' voices and perspectives was an important consideration in *Mimi's Family,* an exhibition I created that tells the story of a family with a transgender grandmother. So as not to portray this one story as representative of a singular trans experience, we included a label affirming that all families are special and provided a talk-back board inviting visitors to "tell us about your family" in their own words (figure 4.4.7).

Of all the museums I have worked for, children's museums are the most invested in addressing sexism and gender bias in learning, yet femmephobia persists. I want to create museum spaces that are welcoming for people of all gender expressions. Identifying feminine design qualities is a way I have found to begin consciously undoing my own bias so I can better appreciate the feminine parts of myself and of the children and adults for whom I design.

An earlier version of this essay was published in the journal Exhibition *in 2019.*

Margaret Middleton is an independent exhibit designer and museum consultant working at the intersection of design and social justice. See their work at margaretmiddleton.com.

1   Jessie Swigger, "The First Four: Origin Stories of the First Children's Museums in the United States," *Hand to Hand* 31 (2017): 2–3.
2   Carrie J. Wieners, "Leadership in the Museum: A Possible Shift in Gender Representation," *Collections* 6, nos. 1–2 (March 2010): 7–24, doi. org/10.1177/15501906100 06001-202; Dana Carlisle Kletchka, "Moralizing Influences: The Feminization of Art Museum Education," in *From Periphery to Center: Art Museum Education in the 21st Century,* ed. Pat Villenueve (Alexandria, VA: National Art Education Association, 2007), 74–79.
3   American Alliance of Museums, *2017 National Museum Salary Survey* (Arlington, VA: American Alliance of Museums, 2017), 21, https://artsandmuseums. utah.gov/wp-content/ uploads/2019/04/2017-AAM-Salary-Survey.pdf.
4   Greg Thomas, *The Sexual Demon of Colonial Power: Pan-African Embodiment and Erotic Schemes of Empire* (Bloomington: Indiana University Press, 2007), 49, 64.
5   Julia Serano, "Reclaiming Femininity," in *Excluded: Making Feminist and Queer Movements More Inclusive* (Berkeley, CA: Seal Press, 2013), 48–69.
6   Rhea Ashley Hoskin, "Femmephobia: The Role of Anti-femininity and Gender Policing in LGBTQ+ People's Experiences of Discrimination," *Sex Roles* 81, nos. 11–12 (February 20, 2019): 686–703, doi.org/10.1007/ s11199-019-01021-3.
7   April H. Bailey and Marianne LaFrance, "Anonymously Male: Social Media Avatar Icons Are Implicitly Male and Resistant to Change," *Cyberpsychology: Journal of Psychosocial Research on Cyberspace* 10, no. 4 (December 1, 2016): 4–8, doi:10.5817/ cp2016-4-8.
8   Maureen Callanan, B. Frazier, and S. Gorchoff, "Closing the Gender Gap: Family Conversations about Science in an 'Alice's Wonderland' Exhibit," unpublished manuscript, University of California, Santa Cruz, 2015.
9   Sapna Cheryan et al., "Ambient Belonging: How Stereotypical Cues Impact Gender Participation in Computer Science," *Journal of Personality and Social Psychology* 97, no. 6 (December 2009): 1045–1060, doi:10.1037/a0016239.
10   Alok Vaid-Menon, *Femme in Public* (New York: Alok Vaid-Menon, 2017), 1.
11   Gaston Bachelard, "Corners," in *The Poetics of Space,* trans. Maria Jolas (Boston: Beacon Press Books, 1994), 146.
12   The art historian Ferren Gipson describes "women's work" as materials and processes that have historic associations with women. She also asserts that "women can and should do whatever-the-hell kinds of work they want" (*Women's Work: From Feminine Arts to Feminist Art* [London: Frances Lincoln, 2022], 9).
13   Cynthia Dewi Oka, "Mothering as Revolutionary Praxis," in *Revolutionary Mothering: Love on the Front Lines,* ed. Alexis Pauline Gumbs, China Martens, and Ma'a Williams (Oakland, CA: PM Press, 2016), 52.
14   Marta Borgi et al., "Baby Schema in Human and Animal Faces Induces Cuteness Perception and Gaze Allocation in Children," *Frontiers in Psychology* 5 (May 7, 2014): 10–11, doi.org/10.3389/ fpsyg.2014.00411.
15   Amanda C. Hahn et al., "Gender Differences in the Incentive Salience of Adult and Infant Faces," *Quarterly Journal of Experimental Psychology* 66, no. 1 (January 2013): 200–208, doi.org/1 0.1080/17470218.2012.7 05860.

On matriarchal design education

The design educators Ayako Takase and Heather Snyder Quinn discuss student-centered pedagogy and redefining how we measure success in higher education.

Dialogue with Ayako Takase and Heather Snyder Quinn

Alison Place How did your collaboration start?

Ayako Takase We met in Rhode Island while we were teaching at the Rhode Island School of Design. We were both having children at the time—Heather's second coincided with my first—so there were many parallels in our lives.

Heather Snyder Quinn We also had studio practices that were very successful in different fields, me in UX [user-experience] design and branding and Ayako in product design, and started full-time academic roles at a similar time. There aren't a lot of women in the design industry who are serious researchers, professors, and have kids, so for us to share all those things was pretty tremendous.

AT We started to share notes on our teaching and the design industry, bouncing ideas around, sharing frustrations, what was working, what was happening in the world as it related to our students. Nobody teaches you how to teach when you enter academia. It was nice to have each other's support while we were figuring it out.

HSQ The way we teach is different from others, but I was afraid to talk about it because it broke traditional rules, and I thought I would "get in trouble." But even though what we were doing was different, it was successful. Not only did our students trust us, engage with us, and want to be in class—they were

getting jobs. So we decided to start sharing it with others, and that's how our collaboration became formalized.

AT A lot of people do what we do, like being vulnerable in the classroom, adapting to students' needs, sharing our lives, bringing our kids to participate in product tests with students. It's nothing new. But it's typically something that caregivers and parents, especially mothers, do because they are already used to carrying the burden of the mental load and caring for others. Educators are not talking enough about nontraditional pedagogy or feminist pedagogy because it's still outside the norms of what is expected.

AP What are the pedagogical methods that make up the framework of matriarchal design futures?

AT At first, we struggled with the binary language of "matriarchal versus patriarchal," but the qualities of our teaching came from our learning as mothers and caregivers. We used to feel like we should hide it [our motherhood] because of how uncool it was to be considered a mom in the classroom or because of how blatantly discriminatory academic culture is toward mothers and caregivers. The matriarchal component of this has a significant parallel to bell hooks's engaged, feminist pedagogy that centers around care and interconnectedness between teachers and students in class.[1] Instead of focusing on individual success in patriarchal, capitalistic, and white societal values, the matriarchal framework focuses on respect, collectiveness, inclusivity, and care.

HSQ [Our method is] nonhierarchical. We are teachers, and the students are also teachers, and we're all learning from each other, which means there are no top students, no patriarchal podium, and the classroom becomes circular. Every student is at a different place in their learning and offers something unique. If you can embrace that as an educator, then they all feel important, and they all feel hopeful about the future.

AT In industrial design, there are many world-renowned star designers, and they're mostly male, white, and European. Students often aspire to be one of them because they're surrounded by so much pressure to be the best. We are antiexceptional because we reject what society sees as exceptional, and we want to redefine that. [That approach] also changes how we manage conflict or challenges with students. If a student is not doing well, we stop to consider the reasons behind it instead of immediately reacting. That's a very matriarchal instinct—to consider the holistic person, not just what's right in front of you.

HSQ What they are getting from this framework is a sense of self-trust and self-awareness. They learn to design, but they learn even more about themselves.

AT Vulnerability is also an important component. We must be vulnerable in order for students to learn to be vulnerable. It takes creating a safe environment and presenting yourself as human first. You have to have heart. I teach heart, agency, and curiosity. Those traits make good designers.

HSQ Just as with mothering, I think about my students and their future. How do I take fear away in the classroom? How do I center students instead of myself, so they're not producing work just for me? For us, it's about small acts in the classroom. Even if [an act] impacts [only] one or two individuals, they go forth and change the field little by little, and then they mentor others. There's beauty in small acts that become hugely radical, especially when they are infiltrating the design industry.

AP There are many parallels between motherhood and teaching, but those can also contribute to stereotypes, like assumptions that schoolteachers are women or that female professors are not as rigorous as male professors. Do you have to be a mother to be a caring teacher? What does this framework mean for people who are not mothers?

AT It's a great question. I absolutely don't think that you must be a mother or female to practice this way. It may come more naturally if you are already a caregiver elsewhere, but anyone can center the needs of a student and commit to their growth. It is less about gender and gender roles and more about values.

HSQ The word *matriarchal* connotes motherhood, but a matriarchy is a framework for culture and power, just like patriarchy. The difference is that [in a matriarchy] power is distributed, and we operate by being attuned to the needs of others. Just as women have adapted to and have been shaped by patriarchy, so too could anyone who is not a mother within a matriarchy.

AP Notions of motherhood in education also contribute to the devaluing of labor when it's associated with caregiving. This framework, by contrast, makes a lot of the invisible work we might already do as educators visible, and it legitimizes [that work] as being central to our pedagogy.

HSQ In design, there's this incredibly pervasive mindset that you're supposed to do it a certain way. Similarly, we assume that in order to enact critical learning or intellectual rigor, we have to teach a specific way, but we don't. My students produce good work, they win awards; the expectations of commitment and output are still high. Meeting the learning outcomes of the class can happen in many ways that have not even been imagined yet. I carry that forth with my students and in my own unlearning to open my mind to what design is and what it can be.

AT Right now, educators are faced with dual burdens of carrying on the traditional way things have always been done while incorporating new and innovative teaching methods. We're all a bit confused, trying to navigate this moment in education.

HSQ These are scary times because we inherit students who are living in a society of metrics, standardized testing, and the cookie-cutter perfection of social media. Individualism is at an all-time high, and we live in societal systems where we don't feel safe. Meanwhile, we're trying to teach them to be adaptable thinkers. They don't only need design skills, but they need to understand humanities and ethics in order to imagine impact, and they need to learn to collaborate not only with technologists but [with] historians, policy makers, climate scientists. Careers are long. They will need to be able to pivot and adapt. It's always going to be impossible for us to teach everything we need to teach. So we have to adapt, too.

AP What else do you find challenging about being a matriarchal design educator?

HSQ It requires that I trust my intuition. I am always unlearning, keeping an open mind, and trying to be better. If I don't engage in active therapy, care, gratitude, and reflec-

tion, I can't move forward in society or in the world. As educators now, particularly as women and caregivers, we're carrying a lot of our students' mental health challenges. It's very tricky to define the lines of what we do as teachers. But if I want my students to succeed, it's not enough to impart some skills. They also must understand themselves and work through their barriers, like perfectionism and fear.

AT Because of the nature of the caregiver mindset, I see a lot of female faculty consumed by taking care of students' needs, which is why we preach self-care, too.

✳ The word *matriarchal* connotes motherhood, but a matriarchy is a framework for culture and power, just like patriarchy. The difference is that in a matriarchy power is distributed, and we operate by being attuned to the needs of others. ✳

AP Your process for developing this framework has been a collective effort with other educators. How has that shaped the outcome?

AT There are multiple perspectives in everything. We're merely the vessels, facilitating dialogues, connecting dots, sharing experiences, and reflecting.

HSQ It's harder to collaborate than to do something by ourselves, but the academy doesn't always value collaboration, even when the world is clearly demanding it. The collective aspect is the focus of the workbook[2] (figure 4.5.1) we developed so that people can self-reflect or workshop their ideas on matriarchal design practice and pedagogy. It's a framework of ideas, but it needs you, the participant, the educator, to engage with it. We're not providing answers.

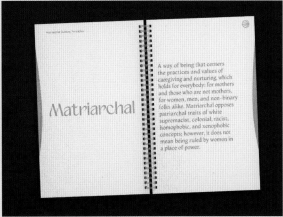

Figure 4.5.1 *Matriarchal Design Futures: Workbook* printed by Binch Press, a volunteer-run print cooperative in Providence, Rhode Island, centering queer and trans artists and artists of color. Courtesy of Ayako Takase and Heather Snyder Quinn.

We call this a work in progress, and I imagine it always will be because I am, and Ayako is, and we acknowledge that we're always trying to become, to unlearn, to evolve.

AT That's a very matriarchal point of view, focusing on the process and not the end results because as a mother your work is never finished. We are not good at this as designers. When we deliver something that is finished and feel like our work is done, that can be really dangerous because it creates a separation of responsibility and accountability.

AP In what ways does the framework address futures?

HSQ People are glommed on to that word right now because many of us feel so much fear and discontent in the present. In our work, we are imagining possibilities in both the present and the future of what education could be through this matriarchal lens. We are sending students into the world who may bring this forward into the future and even bring it back to the academy if they become educators.

AT Education is fundamentally for the future. There's a lot of hope embedded in that word. What we're doing in the present is small scale, but it has a ripple effect, making change gradually.

HSQ Our job in tenure-track or tenured roles is to do research that impacts the field, but through teaching that centers every student we deeply impact the field, maybe even more so than [through] our research. What would it look like to measure and value the impact of our teaching in a way that garners tenure?

AT Teaching is valued by students, but not by the academy. Our measurements for success don't account for it.

HSQ Design educators might be used to rethinking how we teach because our field is always changing, but not so for other disciplines. It would be incredible if this framework could expand in other parts of higher education that are ingrained with rigidity. It'd be such an interesting speculative project to imagine a matriarchal university. How would we evaluate research? How would we measure impact? It's about opening the way for so many new ways of doing and being in design.

AT Our approach to teaching means there's different possibilities, no one solution fits all, and you can't prescribe the outcome. You have to be responsive and adaptive. You're weaving through different pluriverses.

AP In design education, there has traditionally been only one way to show up as a design student—usually white, male, economically secure, ruthlessly competitive, and individualistic. We're finally starting to realize that there are infinite ways to show up as a design student today, and they're all valid, and they all deserve support.

AT Exactly, we are all plural. Not just students but faculty, too. There need to be more flexible mechanisms in place that allow for different ways of being and existing in academia. Institutional leadership can be matriarchal, too, by being adaptive [and] inclusive and encouraging diverse ways of being an educator. For me, it's also about hope. This is a hard world we live in right now, especially for students. We are holding on to the hope of progress.

AP No one knows more about how hard this world is right now than mothers.

HSQ So hard, with so little grace offered.

AP There's something really special about the connection you feel between other mothers and caregivers in academia because it's like a lifeline.

HSQ Absolutely. We need each other. The more of us there are, and the more we can change education, the more space we create for others who have been marginalized in the academy. It's hopeful.

This conversation took place over Zoom in January 2022. It has been edited for clarity and length.

Ayako Takase is a gender-nonconforming Asian mom/parent who is never perfectly here or there, always hybrid. Ayako is associate professor of industrial design at Rhode Island School of Design and coprincipal at Observatory, a multidisciplinary design studio.

Heather Snyder Quinn (she/her) is an interdisciplinary designer, educator, and futurist. She lives in Chicago with her partner and their two daughters.

1 bell hooks, *Teaching to Transgress: Education as the Practice of Freedom* (New York: Routledge, 1994).

2 Heather Snyder Quinn and Ayako Takase, *Matriarchal Design Futures: Workbook* (Providence, RI: Binch Press, 2022), matriar-chalfutures.design. Binch Press is a volunteer-run print cooperative in Providence, Rhode Island, centering queer/trans artists and artists of color (http://binchpress.com).

On design histories woven in patriarchy

The designer and educator Dina Benbrahim calls for unearthing hidden design histories through a case study about Moroccan weavers.

Dina Benbrahim

Life is no longer what it was.
This is the time of knowledge
Even for those who've never been to school
Grab your chance sisters!
It is never too late to learn.
—Fatima Chahou (known as Tabaamrant),
     Amazigh rural poet and singer, untitled oral poem

My identity as a Moroccan woman who moved to the United States at the age of twenty-seven has shaped my feminist intellectual journey. I can access knowledge and reflect from afar on the ultrapatriarchal society in which I grew up. Patriarchy is the product of cultural ideology, laws, policies, and political, legal, and social institutions in which colonized women are the most oppressed sector of society through sexism, racism, and classism. In postcolonial feminist theory, the expression *patriarchal colonialism* examines European policies and laws that are responsible for the institutional gender segregation of the colonized and that impose the Western gender belief of the superior, public man and the inferior, domestic woman.[1]

Morocco has a long history of colonization. The first recorded encounter between the Indigenous population in North Africa, the Amazigh, and another population was with the Greeks. The Phoenicians arrived in the seventh century BCE to establish trade relations and were followed over the centuries by the Romans, the Arabs, and later the French and the Spanish, until 1956, when Morocco obtained its independence. Today, Spain still occupies Sebtah (Ceuta) and Melilla, which it invaded between the fifteenth and sixteenth centuries. Because of these deep roots in colonization, the status of Amazigh women in Morocco became one of a nonelite and underrepresented sociopolitical minority.[2]

Simone de Beauvoir wrote that "representation of the world, like the world itself, is the work of men: they describe it from their own point of view, which they confuse with the absolute truth."[3] As in many design contexts throughout history, this is true of the story of fiber arts in Morocco, which has been narrated by colonial, Orientalist French men and ethnographers. In this essay, I invite you to broaden your understanding of design history through a Moroccan, North African, feminist lens instead by exploring rugs woven by Amazigh women. Although I was not raised as a member of the Amazigh community, I get up every day with a fire in my belly to discover stories that are overlooked in design scholarship and to push back against the hegemonic powers of design history. As a feminist researcher, educator, and designer, I seek a pluralistic experience of design outside our colonized canon of Western, heteronormative, and male-centered narratives. This essay reclaims and validates the erased labor of generations of women designers as a way of rethinking the history and thus the future of design.

A Silent Feminist Revolution

The anthropologist Lewis H. Morgan wrote in the mid–nineteenth century that "the fabrics of a people unlock their social history. They speak a language which is silent, but yet more eloquent than the written page."[4] Amazigh rugs appeared in the second millennium BCE with a unique knot that distinguished them from the others manufactured in Morocco and continues to do so.[5] Design thinking and innovation are at the heart of these rugs, yet Amazigh women have barely been acknowledged for their design contribution, much less for their labor. Wool has been the preferred material for its spiritual association with fertility and the *baraka* (divine blessing).[6] Because of the increased desertification, families kept fewer livestock and had either to purchase wool or to find alternatives, such as unwinding and reusing old wool garments,[7] which increased the variety of colors in the rugs.

Figure 4.6.1 Azilal Rug (11 by 8 feet), made by members of Cooperative Ibilou, Ait Bouli, Morocco. Courtesy of the Anou.

Figure 4.6.2 Close-up of 11-by-8-foot Azilal Rug, made by members of Cooperative Ibilou, Ait Bouli, Morocco. Courtesy of the Anou.

Figure 4.6.3
Kenza Oulaghada dying wool at the Anou's headquarters. Courtesy of the Anou.

The semiotic meaning of the imagery in Amazigh rugs is vast, typically relating to the life cycles in women's environments, such as the process of ripening dates to symbolize women's reproductive power.[8] The triangle is one of the most used symbols weaved onto rugs, representing the body of Tanit, the mother goddess of fertility and the moon. The moon symbolizes change and is associated with womanhood and femininity[9] (figures 4.6.1 and 4.6.2). Although worshiping Tanit has disappeared from the current Amazigh culture, her symbolism lives on, from henna tattoos to jewelry to rugs. In this context, Tanit is a powerful symbol of resistance. Through these rugs, Amazigh women have had a crucial role in leading, weaving, engraving, and narrating feminist concepts in their current conservative society. The act of weaving and the symbology of rugs within the Amazigh women's community are a silent but active feminist revolution. A popular Moroccan proverb says, "A woman who weaves forty carpets is guaranteed a place in heaven." The proverb should say that weaving forty carpets guaranteed a woman's place in the resistance.

Invisible Labor

The process of weaving rugs is complex, time-consuming, and largely invisible. It generally includes three phases: wool preparation, design, and weaving. In an interview, Kenza Oulaghada, the president of Tithrite Organization in the Middle Atlas and a weaver and leader at the Anou, an artisan-owned and artisan-managed e-commerce platform, summarized this process as follows: "First, the wool is washed, sun-dried, and loosened in order to clean it from dirt. Then, it is carded with a wool carder and spun to make it into threads before dyeing it [figure 4.6.3]. This process has become easier with the Anou, [which] enables women weavers to find good-quality wool with different colors and textures and has allowed them more creative freedom."[10] According to Kenza, the visual aspect of Amazigh rugs is always inspired by the surrounding environment and reflects women's feelings—how they navigate their identities and their relationship to the land and water. After the rug design is created, a loom is mounted, and the weaving process begins.[11]

The Amazigh cultural heritage, in particular the pre-Islamic meanings of Amazigh symbols, is at great risk of being lost in oral history. In a conversation, Rebecca Hoyes, a surface-pattern designer who teaches women weavers of the Anou how to think conceptually about their work through online workshops, confirmed that women weavers reproduce symbols without being fully aware of their original meanings.[12] In the case of Kenza Oulaghada, she learned the craft from her mother not only to access revenue but also to preserve the Amazigh identity, culture, and heritage. When I asked her about the meaning of the triangle, she recognized that although this geometric symbol was in multiple Amazigh works, she was not aware of any specific meaning for it. It was the political will of colonizers to fragment the existing Amazigh culture to impose theirs, which makes important the need to preserve the Amazigh design stories and to empower women weavers' activist work.

The conditions of Amazigh women's livelihood are also threatening their individual rights. The craft of weaving is often matrilineal through early exposure as moral education and through marriage as social mobility, but it can also be taught in ministry-run centers and rug-making workshops, solely as a technical and marketable skill with no emphasis on symbology and meaning. These centers and workshops are known for being sweatshops with rough conditions where women weavers earn barely anything for their work. Hamza Cherif D'Ouezzan, the current managing director at the Anou, explained to me how women weavers have been exploited by men in current markets, which are completely unregulated. Women weavers from surrounding villages bring their rugs to markets every week, where they compete with mass-produced rugs, and they are forced to use two middleman: a *dalal* who will sell the rug to a *semsar* in the market, and a *semsar* who will sell the rug to an end customer outside the market. A woman weaver will generally only get 4 percent of the sale, and the remaining 96 percent will be the middlemen's profit.[13] This exploitative system is the result of the women weavers' geographic isolation as well as patriarchal practices that push them out of marketplaces and supply chains. We cannot understand Amazigh women weavers' design contributions without the complexity of their context and the overwhelming *hogra* (a common expression in Darija that means "heartfelt oppression") of postcolonial paternalistic powers.

Toward Pluralistic Futures

This essay highlights the fact that we do not design in a vacuum. The past makes up the present and lays the foundation for the future. Designing more equitable, inclusive, and humane futures starts with making the oppressive systems of the past and the present visible so that we may challenge them and stop replicating them. To do this, we need design histories that are pluralistic and understood through a lens of power.

Amazigh women have played a crucial role in communicating feminist concepts through design—consciously or unconsciously—and preserving the Amazigh culture during periods when it was not legal to teach, write, or publish anything using the Amazigh language. However, because their work has not been validated as "design" by a patriarchal, colonized canon, their knowledge has not been documented. The exploitation of Amazigh women weavers in their local context further contributes to the disappearance of their design stories, like many other stories deemed too threatening to patriarchy to be recorded or valued within the dominant Western discourse. We cannot pretend to design better today when we keep ignoring a constellation of narratives that have always been and are still out there (if we are lucky). The plurality of our design canon depends on our collective effort to look beyond the tyrannical history of the limited Western representations of design and to restore overlooked narratives within their complex context.

Acknowledgments

To the pioneering Amazigh women who are contributing to the design canon for centuries now. I see you in your struggle, and I admire you. I am infinitely grateful to Hamza Cherif D'Ouezzan and Rebecca Hoyes, who generously gave their time to answer my questions and allowed me to meet with the Amazigh weavers of the Anou.

Dina Benbrahim (she/her/ن) is a Moroccan multidisciplinary creative who uses an intersectional feminist lens to investigate design for visibility, civic action, and social justice for marginalized communities to collectively reimagine equitable futures. She is Endowed Assistant Professor of Graphic Design at the University of Arkansas.

1   Suzanne M. Spencer-Wood, "Feminist Theorizing of Patriarchal Colonialism, Power Dynamics, and Social Agency Materialized in Colonial Institutions," *International Journal of Historical Archaeology* 20, no. 3 (July 27, 2016): 477–491.
2   Silvia Gagliardi, *Minority Rights, Feminism and International Law: Voices of Amazigh Women in Morocco* (New York: Routledge, 2020), 136.
3   Simone de Beauvoir, *The Second Sex*, trans. Constance Borde and Sheila Malovany-Chevallier (London: Random House, 2009), 143.
4   Lewis Henry Morgan, *League of the Ho-Dé-No-San-Nee, or Iroquois* (1851; repr., Rochester, NY: Sage, 1964), 3.
5   Bruno Barbatti, *Berber Carpets of Morocco: The Symbols, Origin and Meaning* (Courbevoie, France: ACR édition internationale, 2008), 16.
6   Fatima Sadiqi, *Moroccan Feminist Discourses* (New York: Palgrave Macmillan, 2014), 154.
7   Cynthia J. Becker, *Amazigh Arts in Morocco: Women Shaping Berber Identity* (Austin: University of Texas Press, 2006), 36.
8   Becker, *Amazigh Arts in Morocco*, 36.
9   Sadiqi, *Moroccan Feminist Discourses*, 57.
10   Kenza Oulaghada, conversation with the author, translation by Widade Mohammadi, January 9, 2022, online.
11   Myriem Naji, "Gender and Materiality in-the-Making," *Journal of Material Culture* 14, no. 1 (March 2009): 47–73.
12   Rebecca Hoyes, conversation with the author, February 15, 2022, online.
13   Hamza Cherif D'Ouezzan, conversation with the author, February 15, 2022, online.

☀ Liberation

You have to
act as if it
were possible
to radically
transform the
world. And
you have to do
it all the time.

Angela Davis

SOUTHERN ILLINOIS UNIVERSITY,
CARBONDALE, FEBRUARY 13, 2014

On liberation

Alison Place

Most contemporary feminists would agree that the ultimate objective of feminism is liberation. Where perspectives diverge is when we ask, "For whom?" and "From what?" The term *liberation* itself is fraught with discord, both historically and currently. When people talk about contemporary feminism, there is often an assumption that there has always been an agreed-upon body of principles and beliefs that served as the foundation. That has rarely been true. When the second-wave feminist movement emerged in the United States in the 1960s, there was no clearly defined platform. Initially, especially for white women, feminism was about interrogating and reimagining gender roles. It eventually came to include other forms of sexual oppression, such as violence and abuse. When these women began calling it a movement for "women's liberation," that was an appropriation of the vernacular of Black liberation.[1] And yet white women, especially those from class privilege, were hostile to adopting perspectives that evoked the connection between race and sex. Feminist thinkers who wanted to talk about gender from a race-sex-class perspective were accused of being traitors who were destroying the movement by shifting the focus.[2]

Today, it is commonplace to evoke gender, race, and class as interwoven facets of oppression, but disagreements about the "focus" of the feminist movement still reverberate. Though those involved in the movement share many common threads of what we fight against and resist, a shared vision of feminist politics is still not clearly defined. As previously discussed in the introduction, bell hooks defined the objective of feminism as "freedom from sexism and sexual oppression."[3] I personally return to this definition often for its clarity and simplicity but also because it implies that women are not the only people harmed by sexual oppression. Similarly, if we acknowledge that people are oppressed not just by sexism but also by many other things—classism, homophobia, racism, ageism, ableism, and so on—then it might seem that the goal of feminism is to end all oppression for women or for everyone. Some feminists have adopted this interpretation, but not everyone agrees with such an expansive definition. Although opposing oppression in its many forms may be instrumental to—even a necessary means to—feminism, it is not intrinsic to feminism. According to bell hooks, feminism as a liberation struggle must exist *apart from* and *as a part of* the larger struggle to eradicate domination in all its forms; feminism's singular focus on sexism is what sets it apart from other liberation struggles. hooks wrote, "We must understand that patriarchal domination shares an ideological foundation with racism and other forms of group oppression, and that there is no hope that it can be eradicated while these systems remain intact."[4] Echoing hooks, the feminist scholar Lisa Corrigan offers a blunt reminder: "Feminism is about freedom. It must *free* us. ... Feminism is pointless if it doesn't also dismantle capitalism and anti-Blackness."[5] A dual focus on sexism as a particular form of oppression that is always interlocked with other forms of oppression is the foundational concept of intersectional feminism (see chapter 1).

Beyond general concepts of freedom, the questions of what future we're striving for and whether it is indeed feminist are less clear. There is disagreement among many feminists as to whether feminism has any unchanging features or values at all; many instead conceive of feminism as a critical strategy that is concerned with particular contexts and is short term in its orientation rather than a fully-fledged worldview or doctrine.[6] Indeed, it may be feminism's willingness to change shape and direction over time and not to hold onto outmoded ways of thinking that remains its greatest strength.[7] As discussed in chapter 4, a plurality of views, perspectives, and beliefs is a distinctive characteristic of feminism. It follows, then, that our visions of the future are plural, too. Although bell hooks called for a firm set of beliefs about feminism, she acknowledged that our strategies for feminist change must be varied because "there is no one path to feminism."[8] The question for designers, then, is: How should we do what we do in order to enact the futures we envision?

> ✳ Our commitment to a feminist future is not a path that always leads forward but rather a strategy that leads us to the "otherwise." ✳

Futuring is an exercise in thinking about, picturing possible outcomes in, and planning for the future. Feminism, arguably, is inherently a practice in futuring. Within any critique on power, sexism, or oppression, there is an implied desirable future absent the thing we criticize. Every time we speak out against what we don't want, we are simultaneously outlining a future for what we do want. The feminist theorist Vikki Bell calls feminism an "alternative vision" that entails "a display of an imaginative faculty."[9] Bell warns, however, that feminist visions are not an investment in linearity—in going backward to go forward—but rather ways of recognizing the complex process of iteration and transformation. Our commitment to a feminist future is not a path that always leads forward but rather a strategy that leads us to the "otherwise."

Following the thread of the otherwise, some feminists reject the lens of the future altogether in feminist struggle. Donna Haraway, notably, argues that "staying with the trouble" demands that we inhabit difference in the present rather than directing our focus toward what might be. "In urgent times, many of us are tempted to address trouble in terms of making an imagined future safe, of stopping something from happening that looms in the future, of clearing away the present and the past in order to make futures for coming generations. ... Staying with the trouble requires learning to be truly present, not as a vanishing pivot between awful or edenic pasts and apocalyptic or salvific futures, but as moral critters entwined in myriad unfinished configurations of places, times, matters, meanings."[10] Daniela K. Rosner echoes this argument in her theory of design as "critical fabulations"[11]—ways of storytelling that open different understandings of the past that reconfigure the present and create new opportunities for the future. Instead of orienting our work toward a predetermined result, we should operate it as a process that opens up possibilities.

Traditional ways of doing design focus heavily on predetermined results and practices of futuring. Designers bring artifacts and systems to life that didn't previously exist. We plan. We envision. We evaluate possibilities. But every time we create something, we are not just making a statement about the world we want to live in—we are literally making that world a reality. There is an adage among futurists that "the only thing we know about the future is that it will be different."[12] I would argue that, without a feminist lens to understand design's role in power structures and systemic oppression, the future will not be so different, merely a perpetuation of the status quo. Even when we claim to be designing with the future in mind—speculating, provoking, critiquing—our ability to envision a future that is "different" is only as expansive as our understanding of how oppression operated in the past and operates in the present.

The exercise of futuring is much more complex than simply using our creativity to imagine the world a different way. It is a deeply fraught process shaped by who is in the room, the tools used, and the belief systems that are reinforced. Futuring has been dominated by white, mostly European people. The feminist cultural studies scholar Sarah Kember proposes that futurism is inherently problematic, not so much in its tendency to make predictions that may or may not prove accurate but in its adherence to technology-driven visions that play out a limited dualism of utopias and dystopias.[13] Much more than technology is at stake in thinking about the future.

Many activities in design futuring take place under the guise of "speculative design" and "critical design," frameworks that aim to address big societal problems and challenge narrow assumptions about the role design plays in everyday life.[14] By definition, these approaches aim to reject the status quo, but they, like everything else in design, are fraught with Western, modernist notions of domination and are plagued by bias. In their dialogue in chapter 2, the disability studies scholar and designer Aimi Hamraie called attention to the ways in which critical design centers normate perceptions about bodies because it often aims to produce discomfort and antagonism in a user, as if to reveal to them what has been taken for granted about other forms of design. But, as Hamraie argues, "most disabled people already have the experience of being that type of user, without someone doing some kind of fun, critical project that's trying to produce it." Critical design is founded on the assumption that the user is already normate, and that is why they're having a disorienting experience. If our methods for envisioning the future and advancing our understanding of design in the future simply reify power differentials and reproduce bias, then whose future are we envisioning? Each possible future embodies moral choices, distributes power and resources, and creates winners and losers, insiders and outsiders.[15]

In addition to questioning whose future we're envisioning, we must also question who gets to envision it. People who experience systemic oppression have the most at stake in envisioning a different world, but they may also face the most barriers to doing so. The more visceral your experiences of sexism, racism, ableism, transphobia, and so on, the harder it is to imagine a world without them. Oppression justifies itself by commandeering our logic so that the limits of what *is* constrict our ideas of what *should be*.[16] The activist and designer Lauren Williams calls this constraint a "crisis of imagination," in which the capacity to speculate and to construct futures is the "purview, exclusively, of those who command enough capital to make new worlds appear out of ruins or thin air."[17] Pontificating about the future necessitates an excess of resources, such as time, energy, mental capacity— even hope. In *The Future as Cultural Fact*, Arjun Appadurai writes that "to most ordinary people—and certainly to those who lead lives in conditions of poverty, exclusion, displacement, violence, and repression—the future often presents itself as a luxury, a nightmare, a doubt, or a shrinking possibility."[18]

How, then, can we enlist our collective abilities to both imagine *and* build the worlds people want? An instructive site for exploring this question is feminist uto-pianism. The feminist human–computer interaction researcher Shaowen Bardzell asserts that feminist utopianism is particularly well positioned to engage practices of futuring at scale.[19] Utopian thinking in general has been roundly critiqued as well-intentioned but naive attempts to solve complex social problems with simplis-tic technological solutions.[20] Similarly, Bardzell observes that "in both design and utopia, there is a historical failure to deliver results that meet real human needs."[21] Feminist utopian thinking, however, reconstructs the idea of a radically better future without attempting to define it, viewing utopianism as an activity rather than a completed image. This thinking holds "multiple possible futures-in-process,"[22] is emergent and contingent rather than comprehensive, and embraces conflict as a driver of the process rather than eliminating it. It demands the "continual exploration and re-exploration of the possible and yet the also un-representable."[23] For designers, the path to enacting a more just and equitable society lies not in the creation of more speculative or critical artifacts but in how we build relationships and respond to issues over time.

The designer Alexis Hope, who shares a case study in this chapter about her experience in leading feminist hackathons, writes that imagining future utopias is a process of iteration, not a destination, and "it is important to leave significant time to build relationships with stakeholders, community members and partic-ipants, and between organizing members themselves." She also emphasizes the importance of embracing low- and no-tech solutions. In place of an approach in which the world's problems are solved with design and technology, "it is essential to explore how those domains may play a supporting role in augmenting existing innovations and innovators who are working to challenge and dismantle unjust structures of power."[24]

In both futuring and feminism, we often see the word *radical*. It's worth questioning what this term means and what we mean by using it. As Angela Davis once said, "Radical simply means 'grasping things at the root.'"[25] Radical feminism, which emerged in the 1960s, is based on the idea that sexism is so entrenched that we need to completely dismantle current social structures to eradicate it.[26] Strategies range from abolishing the very idea of gender to establishing separate male and female societies. Interestingly, though, radical feminism's revolutionary model of social change is not sought as a single cataclysmic moment but rather as the consequence of the cumulative effect of many small-scale actions,[27] with an emphasis on small-group organization rather than formalized, centrally administered structures.[28] Although imaginative utopian visions may guide us, they can also include small choices and incremental actions to contribute to radical change.

The importance of small change is echoed in adrienne maree brown's principles of "emergent strategy," which address "how we intentionally change in ways that grow our capacity to embody the just and liberated worlds we long for." brown calls for an emphasis on the personal, the local, and the minute: "Small is good. Small is all. (The large is a reflection of the small.)." She reiterates this by calling in the words of the feminist philosopher Grace Lee Boggs: "Transform yourself to transform your world."[29] Our commitment to designing better, more just, more equitable worlds starts with ourselves, where we are situated. Our vision of alternative futures must be characterized by collaborating, staying in the process, and keeping an open mind. According to brown, "Our entire future may depend on learning to listen, listen without assumptions or defenses."[30]

And—I would argue—on hope. In this chapter, hope undergirds visions of the future that center marginalized voices, reimagine technologies of domination, and enlist designers as community collaborators. Departing from where they are situated, designers and technologists share their stories of "staying with the trouble" in design and their hope for an imagined future. Their work demonstrates that, in design, hope is a form of seeing and making *otherwise*. Hope is an insistence on the possibility for another world. But as the abolitionist Mariame Kaba writes, hope is not optimism—it is an intentional choice: "Hope is a discipline; ... we have to practice it every single day."[31]

1 bell hooks, *Feminist Theory: From Margin to Center* (1984; repr., London: Routledge, 2000).
2 hooks, *Feminist Theory*.
3 hooks, *Feminist Theory*, 26.
4 hooks, *Feminist Theory*, 22.
5 Lisa Corrigan and Laura Weiderhaft, "Joy," *Lean Back: Critical Feminist Conversations*, podcast, January 1, 2021, https://leanbackpodcast.com/post/643190676442513409/joy.
6 Chris Beasley, *What Is Feminism? An Introduction to Feminist Theory* (London: Sage, 1999).
7 bell hooks, *Feminism Is for Everybody: Passionate Politics* (New York: Routledge, 2014).
8 hooks, *Feminism Is for Everybody*, 116.
9 Vikki Bell, *Feminist Imagination: Genealogies in Feminist Theory* (London: Sage, 1999), 5.
10 Donna J. Haraway, *Staying with the Trouble: Making Kin in the Chthulucene* (Durham, NC: Duke University Press, 2016), 31.
11 Daniela K. Rosner, *Critical Fabulations: Reworking the Methods and Margins of Design* (Cambridge, MA: MIT Press, 2020).
12 This quote is attributed to the Australian business strategist Peter Drucker.
13 Sarah Kember, "Notes towards a Feminist Futurist Manifesto," *Ada: A Journal of Gender, New Media, and Technology* 1, no. 1 (November 1, 2012), doi:10.7264/N3057CV3.
14 Anthony Dunne and Fiona Raby, *Speculative Everything: Design, Fiction, and Social Dreaming* (Cambridge, MA: MIT Press, 2014).
15 Shaowen Bardzell, "Utopias of Participation: Feminism, Design, and the Futures," *ACM Transactions on Human–Computer Interactions* 25, no. 1 (2018): art. 6.
16 Alexandra Brodsky and Rachel Kauder-Nalebuff, *The Feminist Utopia Project: Fifty-Seven Visions of a Wildly Better Future* (New York: Feminist Press, City University of New York, 2015).
17 Lauren Williams, "Making Room," *Futuress*, October 12, 2021, https://futuress.org/magazine/making-room/.
18 Arjun Appadurai, *The Future as Cultural Fact: Essays on the Global Condition* (London: Verso, 2013), 289.
19 Bardzell, "Utopias of Participation."
20 Evgeny Morozov, *To Save Everything, Click Here: The Folly of Technological Solutionism* (New York: PublicAffairs, 2014).
21 Bardzell, "Utopias of Participation," 6.
22 Erin McKenna, *The Task of Utopia: A Pragmatist and Feminist Perspective* (Lanham, MD: Rowman & Littlefield, 2001), 9.
23 Drucilla Cornell, *At the Heart of Freedom: Feminism, Sex, and Equality* (Princeton, NJ: Princeton University Press, 1998), 169.
24 Alexis Hope et al., "Hackathons as Participatory Design: Iterating Feminist Utopias," in *CHI '19: Proceedings of the 2019 CHI Conference on Human Factors in Computing Systems, May 2, 2019* (New York: Association for Computing Machinery, 2019), 10, 12, doi:10.1145/3290605.3300291.
25 Angela Y. Davis, "Let Us All Rise Together: Radical Perspectives on Empowerment for Afro-American Women," address, Spelman College, 1987, reprinted in *Women, Culture and Politics* (New York: Random House, 1989), 348–354.
26 Many radical feminists advocated for an agenda of "separatism" from men, ranging from supporting other women to living as much as possible in the exclusive company of women. This approach is inclined to accord lesbianism an "honored place" as a form of "mutual recognition between women" (Beasley, *What Is Feminism?*, 54).
27 Menoukha Robin Case and Allison V. Craig, *Introduction to Feminist Thought and Action: #WTF and How Did We Get Here? #WhosThatFeminist #WhatsThatFeminism* (New York: Routledge, Taylor & Francis, 2020).
28 Beasley, *What Is Feminism?*
29 adrienne maree brown, *Emergent Strategy: Shaping Change, Changing Worlds* (Chico, CA: AK Press, 2017), 41.
30 brown, *Emergent Strategy*, 5.
31 Mariame Kaba, *We Do This 'til We Free Us: Abolitionist Organizing and Transforming Justice* (Chicago: Haymarket, 2021), 26.

On creating spaces for Black women to heal, dream, and innovate

Founder of the Colored Girls Liberation Lab, Jenn Roberts discusses designing spaces for Black women and harnessing intergenerational wisdom.

Dialogue with Jenn Roberts

Alison Place I want to start by reflecting on a quote that you shared recently from Octavia Raheem: "As long as you think the way it is, is the way it has to be, you can't see, perceive or create another way. Rest your eyes to see. Rest your eyes and see."[1] That beautifully describes your work.

Jenn Roberts You're right, it summarizes everything I'm trying to get at. My hope for the Black women I work with is to understand we have the ability to dream up something different for our futures, but we haven't had what we need to create it. We've been robbed of that ability to sit and dream, to play around, to make mistakes, to fail up. After years of being in spaces that meant well for Black folks yet were dominated by white culture, I realized how much my own creativity and dreaming ability have been stifled. With the Colored Girls Liberation Lab, I hope to create a space where we can dream up what we deserve to have in the future and a community that encourages you that your dreams are possible.

AP The tagline of the Colored Girls Liberation Lab describes it as an "intergenerational healing, dreaming and innovation space for Black women." What do each of those words mean to you?

JR The Lab is a place for Black women to dream and to learn how those dreams can be advocated for in the present and in the future. But before that can happen, there's so much unlearning and healing that have to be done. I can't just jump in and tell people about world-building strategies or design-thinking principles because there's so much blocking our ability to access that level of thinking. We have to create a safe space for healing first, a space to just be a Black person and not be questioned about how you show up, to feel understood, and to share stories around the triumphs and the trauma. When we say the word *innovation* these days, you automatically think technology or white—but Black folks have always been innovators since the beginning of time. It's our space. When people dig into a space for dreaming first, what they come up with in an innovation space will be much more expansive because they're able to step outside the box of what's possible right now. And the intergenerational part is about the Black tradition. Everything we do is acknowledging who has been here first, who has wisdom to share, and connecting that to the present and future generations. The spaces where I've grown the most, built the most love, and been able to tell my truth the most are the spaces where we bring Black women together who are not just in my age range but also my elders and young folks, too.

Figure 5.1.1 *Generations of Liberation*. Image created by Arrian Maize for Colored Girls Liberation Lab.

AP What are some of the initiatives that take place through the Lab?

JR A signature space is the Dreams and Schemes space that I hold weekly, which is an accountability and healing space for Black women to check in and reflect on the muck of everyday life that keeps them from being able to dream expansively. As a leader, I'm watching people grow in real time, and it's a reminder that the beauty of being a Black woman is that we are able to simultaneously go through these periods of trauma, pain, and joy all at once and still make something amazing out of it in the end. The Lab is also exploring Dream Retreats that are inter-generational, where we dig into community issues and use design to solve problems but are also exploring who our families are and how we preserve our stories to fuel our visions of what the future should be. The dream of the Lab in the future, and what I hope my daughter will be running someday if she's interested, is a physical Lab space that allows women to collaborate in real time

together and create what they need to live a liberated life, where people see themselves as the designers of their own future both on an individual level but also on a structural level.

AP Creating a space for innovation that centers Black women is a radical thing because most "innovation" spaces center white cis males. When you center marginalized and historically oppressed voices in innovation, how does that word take on new meaning?

JR I think about language and word choice a lot. There are certain terms that I want to reclaim and redefine through my work. I've always felt like we've limited the idea of what *innovation* is supposed to mean. When I hear *innovation*, I think of expansiveness, not just technology. My desire to reclaim the word *innovation* is to show Black women in particular that they belong in that space. I'm aware of how philanthropy moves and how power moves, and folks are being left out. If people are going to be doling out money and assistance to "innovators," there's a whole bunch of them in communities right now. All the things we come up with on a daily basis to make our lives work, that's no accident. Innovation is in us. We've always come up with a way out of no way.

AP In the work you do with communities and organizations, one of your driving principles is the notion that people can solve their own problems. That's a different narrative than what designers are taught, which is to play the role of the hero problem solver. If designers believe that people can solve their own problems, what role, then, do designers play?

JR There's a type of listening technique that we use a lot called "constructive listening," where you're not trying to guide the person to the solution; you're just listening. And in that process, people usually solve their own stuff. Most of the time, people don't need advice; they need the resources, time, and space to work out what is happening and what they want to do about it. But, often, designers don't listen; we jump straight to solutioning. So instead of ... the problem [being solved], the community is left with implementing something you came up with, and the people who are impacted never had a say in it. My work affirms that people are experts in their own lives. They know their own communities and its issues. It is not our job as a designer, a leader, or anybody who is in a position of power to tell them what's best for them. Instead, I think of the designer's role as more of a path clearer. [Designers] should be using their power to find resources, create access, and hold space for people to analyze what their community needs. We need to honor [people's] knowledge by valuing different types of data—not just numbers but people's stories, too. And in order to get that, you've got to go be in the community. Somehow we've decided that the degree gives you expertise instead of the lived experience. I don't have a degree

in design, but I have designed a whole lot of stuff. That's the case for community folks, too. They might not have a degree in policy or education, but they know what's working for their families and what isn't. And we have to trust that their expertise is just as, if not more, valuable than the information we get from places that are deemed to be more valid or more aligned to whiteness. It takes slowing down and getting our egos out of the way and trusting communities.

✳ **When we say the word** *innovation* **these days, you automatically think technology or white—but Black folks have always been innovators since the beginning of time. It's our space.** ✳

AP Your work is grounded in cocreation and participatory processes, often in the form of hackathons, like the Detroit Birth and Breast-feeding Hackathon and the Make the Breast Pump Not Suck Hackathon. How do you utilize hackathons as a space for community-led transformation?

JR Hackathons create space for transformation in communities because they bring people together who are doing similar work but have never worked together before. We make sure those rooms are full of folks from historically excluded groups, particularly Black women, to allow them the space to slow down for a second and think about the problems they face and put their heads together to think about solutions. It's also a reminder of what's possible with the collective. Coming into a space like a hackathon and being introduced to different ways of tackling problems—it changes people. I've heard folks in those spaces say, "I never looked at myself as being a designer or an innovator or a tech

Figure 5.1.2 The Colored Girls Liberation Lab hosted a SistaCircle brunch in Washington, DC, which gave Black women a space to seek fellowship, collectively dream, and just be. Photographs by Jaida Moore of Fiercely Feminine Studios.

person." Those mindset shifts are a critical redistribution of power that reminds folks that their expertise is important and their solutions are valuable.

AP When you are doing work through a feminist lens or an antiracist lens, there's a great deal of unlearning that is required. What are some things you have unlearned or are still unlearning?

JR I've been recognizing my unlearning for a long time, but there's been an extra dose of unlearning this year. One thing I'm still unlearning is perfectionism and understanding how that is connected to white-supremacy culture and how it stifled my creativity. I've also learned to be really unapologetic about my Blackness. I've never been more authen-

tic in my work than I am now. I show up the most myself I ever have, and I realized that gives permission to my daughter and any Black woman who sees me to do the same thing.

AP You've talked about your work as it intersects with the past, the present, and the future. Can you share more about what that means to you?

JR I have a tattoo on my wrist of Sankofa, which is an Adinkra symbol that means "to go back and fetch it." It's a reminder that there are things that were left for me, intentionally or not, from my ancestors that I can bring into the present. And if I'm looking forward, dreaming about the future, there are things in the future that I can bring back into the present, too. I see the connection between all three of those things, and you need all parts to make sense of the world around you and hope for something better. I'm learning to honor my own ancestry while also being cognizant of what I'm leaving for a future generation.

AP Much in the same way, we can't design for today's problems without understanding how they became yesterday's problems or how they will become tomorrow's problems. We have to be constantly looking in both directions to understand.

JR Exactly. And particularly for African Americans, understanding past and future connections is a dream in and of itself because I don't know for sure who I'm looking back at. We can't see all the way back, and we have to go on faith, dreaming of what we believe was wanted or desired for us. I don't think anyone, but particularly Black folks, can design without that ability to suspend themselves in a faith of what was and what could be. It requires you to see yourself as part of this much bigger whole, which goes against white supremacy in so many ways. You are part of an intergenerational community, and your actions have an impact on that community. If we recognized all the ways we are connected, we would make decisions differently.

AP Your work can be labeled as feminist for many reasons, but mainstream feminism has rarely centered the voices of Black women or embraced their needs or aspirations. Do you call yourself a feminist designer? What meaning does that term hold for you?

JR It's a complicated question. Yes, I'm a feminist designer. The world that I dream of is a feminist one; the future I see is a feminist one. I'm sure my definition is different than [that of] most people who call themselves a feminist, but I don't think it's very different from other Black folks who call themselves feminists. Because of that, I'm careful about how I situate my work. It goes back to what I said about language and reclaiming words, and *feminism* is one of those words that has had such a hold on it. I know I practice feminist and womanist principles; wanting Black women to live free is inherently feminist work, but if someone associates feminism with white women and an ivory tower or with the systems that create barriers, then they will feel like this space is not theirs. Everybody has a part to play in reclaiming that word, and for me it's creating spaces that *show* folks what feminism in its true form can look like, not just tell them.

This conversation took place over Zoom in October 2021. It has been edited for clarity and length.

Jenn Roberts is the founder of Colored Girls Liberation Lab. She is a social designer, creative-equity strategist, mother, and artist whose work over the past decade has focused on the intersections of systems change, racial equity, innovation, and design. She is based in Washington, DC.

1   Octavia F. Raheem, *Pause, Rest, Be: Stillness Practices for Courage in Times of Change* (Boulder, CO: Shambhala, 2022), 21.

On feminist hackathons

The designer and researcher Alexis Hope reimagines hackathons to confront feminist issues and generate community-led solutions.

Alexis Hope

Over the past nine years, I have been part of a design collective focused on breast-feeding, birth, and postpartum health. Beginning in 2014, we organized a series of feminist hackathons called "Make the Breast Pump Not Suck" in response to a tech establishment that neglects and fails to innovate technologies such as breast pumps. We believe this failure has occurred because relatively few women and pregnant people shape the agendas of technology design spaces. In these spaces, it is still taboo to design technologies that involve sexualized body parts and the bodily fluids of human reproduction. Although our hackathon in 2014 focused on the breast pump, by the next iteration of the event in 2018, the device had become more of a symbolic starting point to open up a broader design conversation around birth, postpartum health, and family-leave policy.

In the United States, where only 15 percent of workers have access to paid family-leave, 25 percent of women who give birth go back to work within ten days.[1] This is not enough time to heal the body after childbirth, let alone to establish a breastfeeding relationship with an infant. The lack of paid family leave in the United States, along with other factors, contributes to racial and socioeconomic disparities in who gets to breastfeed, and we also see these disparities across other maternal and infant health outcomes. For example, Black and Indigenous women in the United States are two to three times more likely to die from a pregnancy-related cause than are white women.[2]

Our hackathon in 2018, depicted in the photos in this case study, centered around supporting mothers, parents, and their babies and prioritizing low-income women, women of color, and queer and trans parents. Over a weekend, we convened more than 250 parents, technologists, designers, engineers, birth workers, and lactation consultants to create better products, programs, and policies to support breastfeeding and breastpumping parents based on intersectional feminist principles. With the support of mentors and community organizations, hackathon participants worked in teams to design, prototype, and showcase projects that sought to improve the breastfeeding and postpartum experience.

As part of the event, we also organized a multimedia art exhibit, a Baby Village to support the care of young children at the event, and an Innovator's Gallery, to host start-ups and larger companies focused on products and services related to postpartum health. Alongside the hackathon, we also hosted a policy summit called "Make Family Leave Not Suck," which brought 60 advocates, academics, and community organizers together to reimagine and strategize about equitable paid family leave in the United States.

Figure 5.2.1 Scenes like this, where a mother carries her baby on her back as she solders a circuit board, were common throughout the weekend of the "Make the Breast Pump Not Suck" hackathon. We encouraged participants to bring their children with them, and we designed our space to welcome these families by including snacks and meals, play spaces where parents and children could relax, and shared on-site childcare options. Photograph by Mason Marino.

Hackathons can be exciting, creative, playful, and experimental spaces—and spaces like that for adults are incredibly rare. They bring people together around a common cause and create a space for them to learn new skills and ideas while building relationships that persist after the event officially ends. They can also connect attendees with people who have the financial resources to push a project forward and who have an impact on media narratives around an issue.

Historically, hackathons have also had some serious shortcomings. They are not known for being diverse or inclusive spaces and generally have rigid and competitive structures that can exclude potential participants who might be alienated by mainstream technology culture as well as those with childcare responsibilities. Many people also argue that the brief time span of most hackathons, usually one weekend, forces the design of only superficial and purely technological solutions to complex social problems. We believe that the hackathon can be reshaped into a feminist design method that addresses many of these shortcomings, and our work over the past nine years has been to hack the hackathon experience itself. We aim to support community innovation, asserting that anyone can innovate by making choices to change an existing situation into a preferred one. As part of this approach, we partner with community organizations that have on-the-ground knowledge of social issues and ideas for what kinds of projects might help the communities that they are a part of. We make space to talk about policy and history, and we believe that innovation does not have to be technologically advanced to make a difference. Instead, it can work on improving existing resources and amplifying what already works for others to learn from. Community innovation allows us to draw on and amplify all the strengths of our community, not simply to focus on the problems.

Figure 5.2.2 The topics we explore at our hackathons can also bring up emotions of anger and grief. During our hackathons, people have revisited personal traumas, such as the loss of an infant or medical racism. We make space for and honor the full range of human emotion by acknowledging pain and loss instead of asking people to check their feelings at the door. Photograph by Ken Richardson.

Figure 5.2.3 Creating the conditions for joy and play can open up new avenues for thinking and creativity and help people build new relationships and collaborations. When it comes to making people feel respected, creative, and joyful, the details matter. We spent time transforming the sterile technology space to one more welcoming to parents and caregivers. One of our primary design goals was to make people feel as if they matter. This is especially important when people are entering innovation spaces that have historically excluded them. Who is in the room matters for what kinds of ideas will be generated. Photograph by Rebecca Rodriguez.

Figure 5.2.4 We closed our hackathon with a celebratory science fair featuring more than 40 projects, where participants shared what they created with one another and with mentors and judges for feedback. Most hackathons usually end with pitch-style presentations where people present on a stage to sell their idea, but we wanted to create something more participatory, where people could have two-way conversations and make connections. Photograph by Vanessa Simmons.

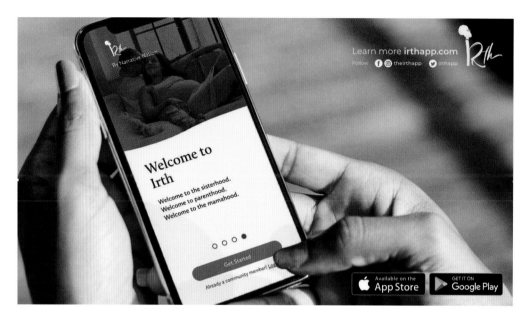

Figure 5.2.5 Irth, created by breastfeeding activist
Kimberly Seals-Allers and her team, is a review and
rating app for hospitals and physicians made by and
for Black women and birthing people of color aimed at
ending racism in maternity care through data collection and storytelling. Irth's slogan is "Birth—without
the B for bias!" Courtesy of Irth.

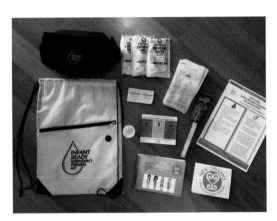

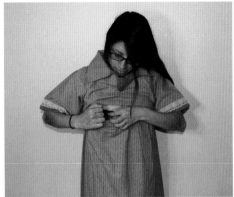

Figure 5.2.6 The New Orleans Breastfeeding Center worked with a team of eight lactation consultants, birth workers, nonprofit leaders, graphic designers, and engineering students to prototype an infant-feeding tool kit for natural disasters. They used their prototype to get a grant, which they used to develop a kit they distributed across New Orleans. Courtesy of New Orleans Breastfeeding Center.

Figure 5.2.7 A team from the community organization Indigenous Women Rising created a retrofit of a traditional Indigenous festival regalia that allows breastfeeding parents to participate in community ceremonial activities while also easily breastfeeding their children. Courtesy of Indigenous Women Rising.

Alexis Hope is an artist and designer based at the MIT Media Lab. She serves as the design director for the "Make the Breast Pump Not Suck" project and is a cofounder of www.focused.space, a company that supports remote and creative workers.

1 Alyssa Pozniak et al., "Family and Medical Leave in 2012: Detailed Results Appendix," Abt Associates, September 6, 2012.

2 Jessica Firger, "Black and White Infant Mortality Rates Show Wide Racial Disparities Still Exist," *Newsweek*, July 3, 2017, http://www. newsweek.com/black-women-infant-mortality-ratec-dc-631178.

On envisioning alternative transfeminist futures

Coding Rights founder Joana Varon shares the story of the Oracle for Transfeminist Technologies, a tool for speculative design and imagining technology otherwise.

Joana Varon
Card design and illustrations by Clarote

For the past few years, inspired by creative exchanges with feminists from different spots around planet Earth and working with the media artist, researcher, and troublemaker Sasha Costanza-Chock and the amazing designer Clarote, I have played with the idea of envisioning speculative transfeminist futures. What would the future look like if the algorithms that command our daily interactions were developed based on feminist values? What if the technologies we cherish were developed to crash instead of maintain the matrix of domination made up of capitalism, heteropatriarchy, white supremacy, ableism, and colonization?[1] This section considers how feminist theories and practices provide lenses to untangle and question power relations that operate within society. The notion of gender itself can be seen as a patriarchal, social construction that operates as a tool for oppression. By using the term *transfeminist*,[2] we reject a binary vision of gender in our definition of feminism. Transfeminist technologies shall recognize a wide variety of experiences and expressions of gender and sexual dissidence as well as the diversity of lived experiences from different bodies and territories.

Throughout history, human beings have used a variety of divination methods to understand the present and to reshape our destinies, including tarot decks. Inspired by these ancient methods, at Coding Rights we developed the Oracle for Transfeminist Technologies in partnership with the Design Justice Network. This virtual and physical card game is a playful tool designed to help us collectively envision, prototype, and share ideas for alternative imaginaries of futuristic technologies. For doing that, we start from a position of transfeminist values, such as agency, autonomy, empathy, embodiment, intuition, pleasure, decolonization—values that emerged from workshops with feminists in Latin America, North America, and Europe.[3]

We like to say that the wisdom of the Oracle, embedded with transfeminist values, can help us foresee a future where technologies are designed by people who are too often excluded from or targeted by technology in today's world—technology designed to maintain the status quo of social inequality and the norms of a consumerist, misogynist, racist, ableist, gender-restricted, and heteropatriarchal

Figure 5.3.1 The Oracle for Transfeminist Technologies. The joker (bottom right card in right image) reads, "Not all tech shall exist. Not everything that is new is better. The future is ancestral. What are you erasing with this idea?" It is a reminder to avoid technosolutionism, to make power checks, and to assess possible unintended harm. Illustrations by Clarote.

society. What would the future look like if we could hack this trend? The Oracle is a hacking tool, focusing on decolonizing our technological imagination.

This is how it works: it is composed of Value cards, Object cards, People and Place cards, and Situation cards (figure 5.3.1). Each Value card represents a transfeminist value that a player may reflect on (figures 5.3.1 and 5.3.2). Object cards represent everyday objects. People and Place cards say the same thing: "Be in your own body. Be in the place you inhabit." So every player gets this reminder: unlike some speculative-design exercises that encourage you to imagine that you are someone else, transfeminism practices highlight the need to recognize the importance of situated and embodied knowledge. Instead of pretending that you

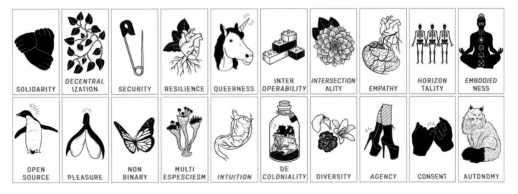

Figure 5.3.2 Some transfeminist values that compose the card deck. Illustrations by Clarote.

are someone else and you know what they need, take a moment to reflect on who you are. What body are you in? Where do you live? What privileges and burdens do your body and place provide? Finally, Situation cards provide players with a situation they need to deal with based on the Feminist Principles of the Internet.[4] There are also two blank versions of each card type for players to add their own Values, Objects, or Situations.

After each player selects their cards, the goal for each is to envision a futuristic technology that is embodied in their Object, is guided by their Value(s), is developed by and for their People in their Place, and helps them solve the Situation presented by the Oracle. Readings can take anywhere from 10 minutes to 45 minutes. After players are finished articulating their vision, they share their ideas with each other and under the hashtag #TransFemTech (figure 5.3.3).

From Imagination to Action

I have always loved technology and how it has played a role in my imagination of futures. Looking back, I remember pretending that my ruler, pencils, and pen were the controls of a spaceship that I was driving while in math class. A few years later, I was amazed that I could visit those other worlds in video games. But all those imaginaries still continued to feel very gender normative, to which I was misfitted. Why did I always need to be Mario or Luigi? Why did we need to save the princess?

When the internet finally arrived, it was like magic—we could suddenly have access to almost any book or song we wanted. I didn't need to wait for ages or

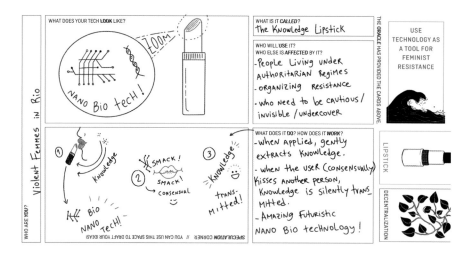

Figure 5.3.3 Sketch of a #TransFemTech envisioned with the help of the Oracle. The "knowledge lipstick" has been imbued with the value of decentralization and envisioned for people who are living under and organizing against authoritarianism and for places where information transmission needs to be decentralized to lower risk. What if we could use nanobiotechnology to build a lipstick that transmits selected knowledge from the person who wears it to another person who is consensually kissed?

bother my aunty in Miami to get that new album from that postpunk queer British rock band. On MySpace or PirateBay, I could listen to tunes peered by online communities. We could use blogs to write things anonymously for unknown people to read and comment on. A positive feeling of autonomy and horizontality was emerging as we transformed from media consumers to media creators, finally able to queer genders and let our imagination fly loose with those new tools.

That was when I came across an invitation to join a platform called Facebook. I didn't know at the time that its origins lay in FaceMash, a sexist "hot or not" game developed by Mark Zuckerberg to compare pictures of two female students side by side and decide who was more "attractive." Facebook's history as a sexist game is directly linked to current legal suits against it regarding privacy violations; complaints about weak content moderation around racism, xenophobia, sexism, and violence; and contributions to the spread of disinformation that puts global democracy at risk. Facebook is living proof that values matter when we design technologies, that people involved in creating them matter, that context matters.

Facebook. Google. Apple. Microsoft. Amazon. As the white male-dominated Big Five in Silicon Valley monopolize most platforms that guide online interactions almost everywhere outside China, any aspiration toward a feminist revolution has become appropriated and monetized. The Big Five flaunt terms such as *community* while turning us into addicted "users" and exploiting our data and our desires.

The past ten years of the internet have seen many threats. Beyond Edward Snowden's revelations on mass surveillance, we have seen coordinated sexist online attacks on Black women, feminists, women journalists, trans women and femmes, nonmale gamers, women politicians, and, really, any vocal women; Google searches that lead to racist results; the Cambridge Analytica Scandal signaling how targeted ads can threaten democracies with misinformation; the Uberization of work that dismantles enforcement of labor rights; governments and private companies engaging in censorship at the Domain Name Service level, such as the mapped blockage of webpages providing information about safe abortion in Brazil or even through automated decision-making processes that end up reproducing inequalities and silencing voices of dissent.

The emergence of what the scholar Shoshana Zuboff calls "surveillance capitalism"[5] has also opened digital space to practices of gendered surveillance: threats by partners who spy on devices; a web full of ads that secretly reinforce gender roles; police infiltrating dating apps; and menstrual period trackers that turn our blood into money (for others) or are funded by the anti-abortion movement to spread misinformation and prevent access to sexual and reproductive rights.

Now, in addition to our devices, our bodies are also becoming data sources.[6] From facial recognition to the internet of things and the collection of DNA information, data sets about our bodies are being linked with data collected from our digital interactions on platforms. Under the narrative of innovation and security, this linkage is taking profiling and discrimination to another level. Most of our interactions with both public and private services will become mediated by biased algorithms carrying over structural inequalities disguised as neutral mathematical operations, a phenomenon that the mathematician Cathy O'Neil has named "weapons of math destruction."[7]

But destruction goes even beyond data extractivism and data colonialism. Developed mostly in the Global North, these technologies are dependent on (conflict) minerals and metals that are sourced in the Global South. Later on, these technologies turn into toxic waste that is also trashed on southern lands. And as databases become bigger and bigger, the processing power of Big Data demands even more energy and water. The sad truth is that technologies developed under a narrative of "innovative solutions" threaten different forms of existence. As the Indigenous leader Ailton Krenak has said, "The future is ancestral."[8] We must consider what future existences might be erased by a particular piece of technology and how technologies could instead praise, recognize, and cherish ancestral knowledge.

Imagination is a tool for revolution. We cannot change unwanted trends if we do not envision alternatives. The feminist science fiction writer Ursula Le Guin exposed how boring and limited is the worldview in which gender is solely a binary concept. She once said, "The thing about science fiction is, it isn't about the future. It's about the present. But the future gives us great freedom of imagination. It's like a mirror. You can see the back of your own head."[9] That is what we are seeking with the Oracle for Transfeminist Technologies. I believe we can turn these imaginative exercises into action: if we can collectively envision a future with transfeminist technologies, we—as designers and hackers of patriarchy—can realize it.

A version of this essay entitled "The Future Is TransFeminist: From Imagination to Action" was previously published by the author for deepdives.in. The revised essay is published under a CC–BY license. The concept of the Oracle was written in collaboration with Sasha Costanza-Chock for transfeministech.org.

Joana Varon is the executive directress and creative-chaos catalyst at Coding Rights, a women-run organization working to expose and redress the power imbalances built into technology and its application, in particular those that reinforce gender and North/South inequalities. She is based in Brazil.

1   For more on the matrix of domination, see Patricia Hill Collins, *Black Feminist Thought: Knowledge, Consciousness, and the Politics of Empowerment* (New York: Routledge, 1990). For a discussion of the relationship between the matrix of domination and sociotechnical design, see Sasha Costanza-Chock, *Design Justice: Community-Led Practices to Build the Worlds We Need* (Cambridge, MA: MIT Press, 2020).

2   For the use of *transfeminism* and *transfeminist*, see Marcos Colon, dir., *Stepping Softly on the Earth*, documentary (Amazônia Latitude Films, 2021).
3   The game was also inspired by a speculative feminist writing workshop with Lucia Egañas, by contemporary design-ideation practices that Sasha writes about in her book *Design Justice*, and by methodologies from a research group at the Internet Engineering Task Force.

4   The Feminist Principles of the Internet can be found at the Feminist Internet website at https://feministinternet.org.
5   Shoshana Zuboff, *The Age of Surveillance Capitalism: The Fight for a Human Future at the New Frontier of Power* (New York: PublicAffairs, 2019).
6   For more information on this shift, see the web series *From Devices to Bodies*, YouTube, https://www.youtube.com/playlist?list=PLD-

Ka5sG19OOP2kIgrs0wD0In-9R0BEaMDA.
7   Cathy O'Neil, *Weapons of Math Destruction: How Big Data Increases Inequality and Threatens Democracy* (London: Penguin, 2018).
8   Interviewed in Colon, *Stepping Softly on the Earth.*
9   Ursula K. Le Guin, *Ursula K. Le Guin: The Last Interview and Other Conversations*, ed. David Streitfeld (New York: Melville House, 2019), 3.

On staying with the trouble of future technologies

The design researcher Marie Louise Juul Søndergaard reflects on feminist critiques of technology and on designing for and with more-than-humans.

Marie Louise Juul Søndergaard

I sometimes ask myself, Why do I design technologies? Does my research reproduce the structural oppression and inequalities that digital technologies reproduce in human and more-than-human life? Although I know that technologies are deeply troubling, they still excite me. They make me curious to understand their materiality and technical workings, to turn them inside out and make them into something else that invites reflections on their potential dangers and (un)intended consequences and creates a portal for dreaming that other worlds are possible. We are already living in a technosphere, a world enmeshed in technologies that cannot be escaped. So what can I do, from the locality and ecology in which I live and work, not to perpetuate techno-scientific-capitalist dreams of escaping Earth for interstellar colonization of other planets? For sustainable and equitable technological futures, what might be needed from us as designers is to reflect on our intrinsic relation with this world in change and to critique and speculate on what this world—and we—could become. This is a task well suited for feminists of all kin(d)s.

On Feminist Critique and Speculation

Although the growing digital transformation of our societies is often praised for bringing solutions to global problems, feminist scholars have critiqued how technologies often reproduce systems of oppression, including sexism, racism, classism, ableism, and transphobia. Critical analysis of technologies can be used to unsettle the dark sides of technologies, including how technologies contribute to the current social-political-environmental crises.[1] However, as designers start to critically analyze technologies and the structural inequalities and systems they uphold and maintain, a sense of exhaustion and hopelessness might creep in. In this way, critique risks becoming a destructive practice that can paralyze action, leaving designers without ideas for where to go next or without hope for radical future change. To move beyond critique, feminist scholars propose to draw on speculation,[2] fabulation,[3] and utopianism[4] as means to build both the capacity for imagining otherwise and the collective action necessary for mobilizing change. When technologies are designed to be feminist, it is crucial both to critique what is and to speculate what could be—to consider how technologies have contributed to current social-political-ecological issues and to imagine ways that technologies might enact change in the worlds we inhabit and care for.

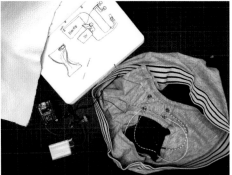

Figure 5.4.1 The image shows "Marcelle," a pair of white underwear that has silicone vibrators sewed into the inner side of the fabric. Courtesy of Marie Louise Juul Søndergaard.

Figure 5.4.2 First prototype of Marcelle where I explored e-textiles with conductive thread, vibrators, and a NodeMCU (an open-source internet-of-things module). Courtesy of Marie Louise Juul Søndergaard.

Staying with the Trouble of Future Technologies

In this essay, I draw on the feminist scholar Donna Haraway's concept of "staying with the trouble" to propose how designers can use critique and speculation to design feminist technologies.[5] The feminist slogan "staying with the trouble" implies that we need to shift away from a utopian belief in technological fixes as well as from a dystopian belief in doomsday. Rather, we must engage with and respond to the complexities that make up and contribute to present-day social-political-environmental crises. Here I share three design projects to speak to how my thinking and doing, practice and theory, are tightly interconnected and shape each other. These projects have been carried out in the Scandinavian context in which I live and are deeply shaped by first-person approaches in design, including my lived experience as a Danish, white ciswoman.

Designing for Joy

As Audre Lorde argued, the erotic has a power—a power that is strongest in humans whose pleasure and joy have been systematically oppressed and left unexpressed.[6] What if we harness the power of the erotic for the design of digital technologies? With inspiration from the pornographic novella *Story of the Eye* written by the surrealist Georges Bataille,[7] I designed a sex technology that embodied both a critique of dominant internet infrastructure and a radical speculation for designing erotic technologies otherwise. "Marcelle" is an internet-connected and wearable sex toy that is activated by surrounding Wi-Fi activity (figures 5.4.1 and 5.4.2). In this way, the rhythms and intensity will be constantly changing as the wearer moves through a landscape. By delegating the control of the vibrators to surrounding Wi-Fi activity, Marcelle plays with ideas of control and access as well as with public/private and submission/dominance tensions. By staying with the trouble of how eroticism is always in relation and movement, Marcelle makes space for the complexities of and the right to expressing and feeling joy.

To design for—and *with*—joy is foundational when constantly grappling with(in) the tension of critique and speculation in a damaged world. When we are finding ourselves in states of exhaustion, without hope, or paralyzed to act, what would it mean to reconnect with ourselves and ask, "What brings me joy?" Designing for joy holds a radical potential for change, for saying "yes" rather than "no," for affirming one another, and for gathering the critical mass, the collective body, needed to keep those excessive joys from being contained. It is by finding joy and meaning in the struggle that we can persist in staying with it.

Designing for Untold Stories

When we speculate on possible futures, many stories are told, but many stories are also not told. In technology design, we often hear only the positive stories of how technologies will solve or has solved *xyz*. This discourse not only fosters a dangerous trust in technologies and their promised good impact on human lives and societal transformation more generally but also fails to acknowledge unintended consequences arising from acclaimed solutions to problems.

With the increased digitization in society, there has been remarkably little technological innovations within the area of menstrual, sexual, and reproductive health due to the underrepresentation of women in technology and business as well as the stigma of women's health. Only recently has there been an increase in digital technologies such as menstrual-cycle trackers and algorithmic contraceptive methods. For instance, the design fiction named "U" is a speculative toilet-based voice assistant that tracks hormone levels in urine and uses these data as a contraceptive method (figure 5.4.3). A short film follows the protagonist Tomoko as she uses a smart toilet to avoid getting pregnant and gets advice on how to live life in symbiosis with her menstrual cycle. The film's plot twists when Tomoko gets pregnant against her will, and it is up to the viewer to reflect on whether the error is in the machine, the data, the user, an algorithmic bias, or a combination of these factors. The story seeks to tell both the hopeful story of a contraceptive

Figure 5.4.3 In the design fiction film *U*, a woman is seen sitting on the toilet while speaking to a voice assistant embedded in the toilet. Photograph by Trieuvy Luu. Courtesy of Marie Louise Juul Søndergaard.

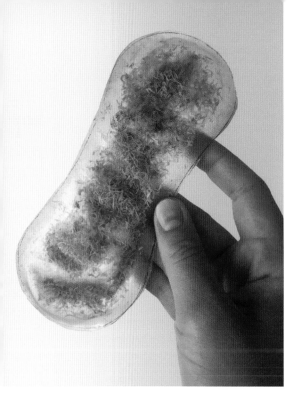

Figure 5.4.4 [left] A hand holding a menstrual pad made out of green sphagnum moss sealed in transparent agar bioplastic, shown on a gradient purple background. Courtesy of Marie Louise Juul Søndergaard and Nadia Campo Woytuk.

Figure 5.4.5 [below] Biomenstrual: Seeds are sprouting out of biodegradable menstrual pads that are slowly composting into soil. Photograph by Nadia Campo Woytuk. Courtesy of Marie Louise Juul Søndergaard and Nadia Campo Woytuk.

method without the negative side effects of artificial hormones but also the story of the possible negative consequences that are inherently part of such a technology. Herein lies the critical potential of speculations, which not only dream about utopian futures but hold these futures open for dystopias to coexist.

Designing for More-Than-Human Flourishing

Although some designs may invite more equitable human flourishing, they tend to neglect the impact that technologies have on more-than-human flourishing and fail to consider other-than-human species as part of technological futures. Faced with extreme weather conditions, dire predictions about climate change, and lockdowns as a result of human attempts to dominate nature, I was left wondering if my feminist design practice was geared only for the human species or if I could find ways of probing intimate care as a more-than-human practice.[8]

In collaboration with the feminist interaction designer Nadia Campo Woytuk, I explored how caring for human menstrual health could also become an environmentally nourishing practice. Current menstrual-hygiene products are both harmful to menstruating bodies (because of toxins and hormonal disruptors in tampons) and to the environment (because of the plastic pollution and material waste that often ends up in sewage systems, landfills, and the ocean). In response to this critique, Biomenstrual explores the use of biodegradable biomaterials (figure 5.4.4) to make one's own menstrual pads, such as gluten, mosses, and agar bioplastic, which can later become part of a composting system where menstrual blood serves as a fertilizer in one's local soil ecology (figure 5.4.5). By relating deeply with our immediate surroundings—cooking pads in our kitchens and gathering moss in the nearby lake—we practice an attention to and humbleness regarding the human dependency on resources and land that ultimately shape design practice, whether that practice involves technologies or not. There is much to be learned and be excited about if we allow ourselves to be surprised and open to the stories and knowledges of other-than-human species and let these approaches influence our design practices.

Intentionally Left Unfinished

By sharing my personal—yet always in relation and still evolving—experience of becoming a feminist designer, I hope to shed a bit of light on how designers can use critique and speculation in designing feminist technologies. Such technologies never act in themselves but are part of an ecology and imaginary of challenging dominant systems of oppression—an imaginary not because it is not real but because it exists as an anchored hope that by continuously advocating for social and environmental justice, we can mobilize and build capacity for radical change. Our collective action and collective dreaming are crucial for change, and so this text, like a dream left unfinished upon waking, is left open as an invitation for a collective readership to evolve into designerly action.

Marie Louise Juul Søndergaard (she/her) is a designer, feminist, and postdoctoral researcher at the Oslo School of Architecture and Design, Norway. She has a PhD in interaction design from Aarhus University, Denmark.

1 James Bridle, *New Dark Age: Technology and the End of the Future*, illus. ed. (London : Verso, 2018).
2 Luiza Prado de O. Martins, "Privilege and Oppression: Towards a Feminist Speculative Design," in *Proceedings of DRS 2014: Design's Big Debates*, ed. Youn-kyung Lim et al. (Umeå, Sweden: Design Research Society, Umeå Institute of Design, Umeå University, 2014).
3 Daniela K. Rosner, *Critical Fabulations: Reworking the Methods and Margins of Design* (Cambridge, MA: MIT Press, 2018).
4 Shaowen Bardzell, "Utopias of Participation: Feminism, Design, and the Futures," *ACM Transactions on Human–Computer Interactions* 25, no. 1 (2018): art. 6.
5 Donna J. Haraway, *Staying with the Trouble: Making Kin in the Chthulucene* (Durham, NC: Duke University Press, 2016).
6 Audre Lorde, "Uses of the Erotic: The Erotic as Power," in *Sister Outsider: Essays and Speeches* (Berkeley, CA: Crossing Press, 1984), 53–59.
7 Georges Bataille, *Story of the Eye*, trans. Joachim Neugroschel (London: Penguin, 1979).
8 María Puig de la Bellacasa, *Matters of Care: Speculative Ethics in More Than Human Worlds* (Minneapolis: University of Minnesota Press, 2017).

On building consentful technology

The Consentful Tech Project raises awareness, develops strategies, and shares skills to help people build and use technology consentfully.

Una Lee

Content warning: Mentions of rape, rape culture, harassment, and state violence.

The Need for Dramatic Changes in Online Consent

Until recently, my design justice practice was focused on facilitating and creating visual identity and print-based projects. However, in the mid-2010s—a time of rampant growth in online abuse and surveillance—I found my work shifting more to websites and digital products and services.

As a survivor of sexual violence, I was stunned by what passed for consent in the tech industry. Whether in the form of incomprehensible terms and conditions, hidden safety settings, "dark patterns," or onerous processes for dealing with harassment, consent on the internet was a disaster. Inherited from rape culture, the idea that consent is about getting someone to agree to what you want in spite of what that other person wants was encoded into the DNA of just about every modern technology product.

Working on tech projects gave me a behind-the-curtain look at the mind-boggling amount and specificity of data being collected. When I saw how easy it was for the projects I was working on to become tools for abusers, repressive state agencies, and predatory companies, I felt compelled to act. The internet needed to see dramatic changes in online consent.

The term *consentful technology* was coined by the engineer Dann Toliver and me in our zine *Building Consentful Tech* in 2017 (figure 5.5.1). It refers to digital applications and spaces that are built with consent at their core and that support the self-determination of people who use and are affected by these technologies. Whereas the term *consensual* implies an agreement between two parties for a specific purpose, the term *consentful* speaks to imbuing technology with a culture of consent. The zine presents consent in technology as

* *An issue that is just as serious as physical consent.* Harm done to our digital selves is just as real as harm done to our physical bodies.
* *An equity issue.* Unconsentful tech has a more profound impact on those who are marginalized by ableism, racism, poverty, patriarchy, transphobia, and heterosexism.
* *Something that affects entire communities.* When organizations unconsentfully collect data about individuals, that act affects not just those particular people but also anyone who shares their characteristics, including what they look like, where they live, and how much money they make.

Figure 5.5.1 *Building Consentful Tech* zine. Courtesy of And Also Too.

∗ *An issue of safety and care rather than of security.* As the data justice activist and Consentful Tech Project collaborator Tawana Petty reminds us, security measures such as digital surveillance do not actually make us safer and in many cases create more harm for marginalized communities. True safety comes not from policing and surveillance but from taking care of one another.

Defining Good Consent

Consentful technology builds on the work of feminist antiviolence activism. Rather than relying on a legal or technical definition of consent, it uses a robust yet accessible framing of good consent adapted from Planned Parenthood's concept that "understanding consent is as easy as FRIES": Freely Given, Reversible, Informed, Enthusiastic, and Specific,[1] which Dann Toliver and I applied to consentful technology (in italics):

"**Freely given.** Doing something with someone is a decision that should be made without pressure, force, manipulation, or while incapacitated." *In technology, if an interface is designed to mislead people into doing something they normally wouldn't do, the application is not consentful.*

"**Reversible.** Anyone can change their mind about what they want to do, at any time." *In technology, you should have the right to limit access or entirely remove your data at any time.*

"**Informed.** Be honest. For example, if someone says they'll use protection and then they don't, that's not consent." *Consentful applications use clear and accessible language to inform people about the risks those applications present and the data they are storing rather than burying these important details in, for example, the fine print of terms and conditions.*

"**Enthusiastic.** If someone isn't excited, or really into it, that's not consent." *If people are giving up their data because they have to in order to access necessary services and not because they want to, that is not consentful.*

"**Specific.** Saying yes to one thing (like going to the bedroom to make out) doesn't mean they've said yes to others (like oral sex)." *A consentful app uses only the data the person has directly provided, not data acquired through other means such as scraping or buying, and uses that data only in ways someone has consented to.*

In Consentful Tech Project workshop settings, participants use FRIES as a lens in analyzing technologies they use, build, or maintain. This activity often reveals that their conception of consent, both digital and physical, might have been more about getting someone to agree to something rather than good consent practices. In a paper I coauthored with the scholar Jane Im, Im expands on FRIES to assert that consent should also be unburdensome: "The costs associated with giving consent should not be so high that a person gives in and says 'yes' when they would rather say 'no.'"[2]

How Might We Build Consentful Tech?

To begin answering the question "How do we actually build consentful tech?," I cowrote a curriculum with Tawana Petty entitled From Protecting Ourselves to Taking Care of Each Other: A Curriculum for Building and Using Technology Consentfully. In it, we put forward the "Making FRIES" framework (figure 5.5.2).

Purpose: What the product/service promises to do and who benefits from this promise. *Some companies might say their purpose is one thing (connecting people to each other) but at the same time are also working toward other, less publicly disclosed purposes (collecting and selling people's data).*

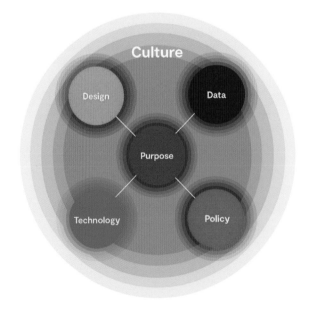

Figure 5.5.2 Applying the FRIES principles to the published curriculum *From Protecting Ourselves to Taking Care of Each Other: A Curriculum for Building and Using Technology Consentfully* by Tawana Petty and Una Lee. Courtesy of And Also Too.

Figure 5.5.3 [top] "Private Browsing" button (bottom right corner) on the 2020 Allied Media Conference website. Developed by Threespot for Allied Media Projects. Website visual design by Una Lee. Courtesy of Threespot.

Figure 5.5.4 [left] Analytics opt-in modal window. Developed by Threespot for Allied Media Projects. Courtesy of Threespot.

Technology: Things the product/service can be programmed to do or not do. *An app might be programmed to require access to your microphone in order to function. It might also be programmed to give you a choice about whether you enable your microphone or not.*

Design: Ways that you interact with the product/service and ways that it presents information and choices. *An app might have location tracking turned on by default, and it might be difficult to figure out how to turn off this feature.*

Policy: Rules and procedures the provider of the service will follow, terms that people must agree to in order to use the service, as well as legislation and regulation that apply to a particular jurisdiction. *A provider might create a rule that it will not sell your location information to third parties.*

Culture: Decisions made about a technology's purpose, design, policy, and features inherit the norms of the culture in which they're made, either intentionally or unintentionally. Multiple cultural forces can be at work—for example, a company's culture, an industry's culture, and the broader social culture of the intended users. *If a provider has a strong culture of antiharassment, the app might prevent a user from being able to message another user who is not already in their friends list.*

For a system to be considered consentful, each of these ingredients must create mechanisms that ensure good consent.

Consentful Tech in Action

Designers are uniquely positioned to make consentful tech a reality. As the design director at Allied Media Projects, I oversaw the creation of a consentful analytics pattern for the organization's website and for the Allied Media Conference (figures 5.5.3 and 5.5.4). Rather than requiring visitors to opt *out* of being tracked—the prevalent pattern, which presumes consent—these sites invite users to opt *in* if they wish.

As a member of the Design Justice Network Steering Committee, I collaborated with Boaz Sender, erika harano, and Grant Chinn to create a set of consentful patterns for people who are becoming signatories of the Design Justice Network Principles. The user-experience copy is written in a way that does not apply pressure to the person using the form. The sign-up flow enables someone to reverse their consent and be forgotten by the system should they change their mind.

I'm currently working with Boaz Sender on the Consentful Tech Standard, an effort to establish shared benchmarks for online consent. The program will include a consentful user-experience/user-interface pattern library that will be available to designers under an open license. It is our hope that consentful tech will become the default on the internet and that services that extract data without good consent will be forced into obsolescence.

Una Lee is a collaborative design facilitator, design practitioner, and design justice organizer. She instigated and facilitated the creation of the Design Justice Network Principles and cofounded the Design Justice Network. She is the founder of the Consentful Tech Project and the creative director of the codesign studio And Also Too.

1   Planned Parenthood, "Understanding Consent Is as Easy as FRIES," Tumblr, April 9, 2017, https://plannedparenthood.tumblr.com/post/148506806862/understanding-consent-is-as-easy-as-fries-consent.
2   Jane Im et al., "Yes: Affirmative Consent as a Theoretical Framework for Understanding and Imagining Social Platforms," in *Proceedings of the 2021 CHI Conference on Human Factors in Computing Systems,* ed. Pernille Bjørn and Steven Drucker (New York: Association for Computing Machinery, 2021), 5.

🌐 Community

No wonder feminism causes fear; together, we are dangerous.

Sara Ahmed

LIVING A FEMINIST LIFE

On community

Alison Place

Feminist design is not just about how we relate to people and the world around us; it is also about how we relate to each other as designers. It requires a critical emphasis on community. In Western, neoliberal, individualistic societies, the word *community* is tossed around like a tetherball, never going anywhere. It is an ideal we strive for, a value we hold, a principle that guides us, but no real meaning is ever assigned to what it is or why we need it. Meanwhile, the word is proliferated by corporations and tech giants to capitalize on our craving for connection and, through artificial attempts to sate us, to monetize it and utilize it for domination.

In design, there are few, if any, ways we use the word *community* that are not problematized by notions of power. It is often dropped casually into design discourse as a more DEI-friendly[1] synonym for *audience* or *users*. It can also be a catchall term for any person, group, or location that exists outside the walls of dominant institutions and governing structures. You'll frequently find it sitting atop lists of principles or webbed within values matrices that are said to guide designers' processes and inform the outcomes they seek to generate. But possibly the most contrived use is mainstream references to designers themselves as a "community," typically while promoting happy hours or networking events that belie the unspoken purpose of self-serving socialization to "get ahead." Forgive me for finding claims of "community" to be disingenuous when they come from a discipline that prizes individualism, competition, and design heroism above all else. If community is a concept that designers are complicit in undermining, artificially espousing, and monetizing—what meaning does it hold?

In political and social activism, community is built into organizing frameworks as a driving force for change. The contemporary feminist movement in particular was founded upon and shaped by an emphasis on the collective. Although there has always been much derision and disagreement about who exactly has been included and excluded in the feminist movement, it is consistently understood as a collective political movement. Collectives can be dynamic, sites for building and forging connection. Sara Ahmed writes about the collective as that which does not stand still but "creates and is created by movement." She writes, "I think of feminist action as ripples in water, a small wave, possibly created by agitation from weather; here, there, each movement making another possible, another ripple, outward, reaching."[2]

The term *collective* is not necessarily synonymous with *community*. If a collective creates movement, perhaps community keeps that collective grounded in its roots. bell hooks wrote that "communities—not nuclear families, or the 'couple,' and certainly not the rugged individualist—sustain life."[3] During the women's liberation movement in the United States in the 1960s, feminists' pursuit of community evolved out of necessity to escape the nuclear family that kept women separated from each other and economically and socially tied to men. Out of the need for connection and sisterhood, consciousness-raising groups emerged.[4] Women came together in small groups to share personal experiences, problems, and feelings, and with sharing publicly came the realization that what was thought to be a personal problem had a social cause and political solution[5]—hence the feminist adage *the personal is political*. Since then, feminist communities have been sites for refuge, solidarity, care, education, and self-actualization. Sara Ahmed says that feminism is about "giving women places to go," which she likens to the release of a pressure valve, where we can reach an account for ourselves with and through others, connecting our experiences with the wider struggle.[6] Striving to find a community where we can discuss ideas and feel validated is a journey that every feminist can relate to. Many voices throughout this book emphasize the essential role community plays in being a feminist designer. As demonstrated by dialogues, case studies, and essays in this chapter, feminist communities around the world have emerged in the design field in recent years as sites for connection, inspiration, and exploration of the otherwise in design.

But, as I asked several people in the dialogues in this chapter, what makes a community feminist, and what makes a group of feminists a community? Many of the struggles, splinters, and divides in feminism throughout history have come about while exploring this question. An espousal of shared feminist virtues is not enough to transform a group of individuals into a community. Notions of feminist community have historically evolved with political contexts over decades, stemming from a range of concerns, such as shared political standing, shared victimhood, or a shared enemy. Rather than placing an emphasis on finding shared experiences, bell hooks called for "sisterhood" in the feminist movement represented by solidarity among women and feminist activists on the basis of their political commitment to end sexist oppression. hooks noted, however, that "solidarity is not the same as support. To experience solidarity, we must have a community of interests, shared beliefs, and goals around which to unite. Support can be occasional. It can be given and withdrawn. Solidarity requires sustained, ongoing commitment."[7]

Today, feminist communities of solidarity take many forms, carving out intentional physical or digital spaces of resilience and mutual aid or emerging out of necessity in patriarchal contexts such as workplaces and academic institutions. They can range from small and local to wide reaching and global. Many are built on structures and actions that center transparency, care, joy, reduced hierarchy, leadership of the marginalized, and the embrace of conflict as a necessary catalyst for progress. In the Feminist Design program at the California Institute for the Arts in the 1970s, Sheila de Bretteville created studio cultures centered around nurturing environments and "the gentle art of mutual aid."[8] One thing many feminist design communities also share, as you'll read throughout this chapter, is a commitment to being in process and "working toward," recognizing that our work is always evolving and never finished.

There are barriers, though, to feminist community in design. Many spaces have fallen prey to corporate feminist "girlboss" culture and the hyperindividualist rallying cry to "lean in," which calls on women to beat the patriarchy simply by working longer and harder (i.e., playing the capitalist, heteropatriarchal game better), while ignoring the systematic disadvantages created by sexism, racism, classism, and ableism. In her podcast with Laura Weiderhaft, the feminist scholar Lisa Corrigan calls for a feminism where we instead "lean back" into community building, solidarity, and an oppositional consciousness that exposes how power works. In contrast to the submission of leaning forward, leaning back resists models of power that are regressive, tokenist, and assimilationist and instead recognizes power in community.[9]

∗ Our challenge is not just to seek feminist ways of collaborating but also to collaborate to transform the discipline itself. ∗

Another barrier is that designers are not typically taught how to collaborate or be in community. Many are trained to work alone, compete with others, center themselves as the expert, and convince others they know best. A design discipline that values community, by contrast, would prioritize access to education for those who have been historically excluded, emphasize transparency in its practices, and, most importantly, structurally incentivize collaboration. Collaboration should not be just a symbolic virtue; our work as feminist designers necessitates it. Intervening in complex social, political, and environmental crises requires us to reach out, build alliances, cooperate and communicate effectively with other designers as well as with historians, politicians, scientists, technologists, and others unlike ourselves. Instead of withholding our knowledge as proprietary, the feminist spirit of collaboration urges us to exchange and share knowledge in order to build on it rather than simply passing it down.[10]

Within design, our challenge is not just to seek feminist ways of collaborating but also to collaborate to transform the discipline itself. Drawing on decades of feminist activism, we understand that change often happens slowly and requires not just community but alliances, strategies, and coalition building. The collective work of feminism has always been to bring others along with us and to navigate the inevitable resistance that comes with it. As every feminist is viscerally aware, feminism in public culture is a site of disturbance at both the broader and personal levels. Sara Ahmed writes about the contradiction of the feminist "killjoy": that when we name a problem, we become the problem. We are made into "containers of incivility and discord" that stop the flow of things and make things tense. We are perceived as in the wrong. But, Ahmed writes, a feminist movement depends on our ability to keep insisting on something, to continue to be killjoys. It requires that we acquire "feminist tendencies, a willingness to keep going despite or even because of what we come up against."[11]

A feminist designer is necessarily a killjoy—one who persistently names the troubles of design and insists on doing it otherwise. In this sense, the feminist designer can be anyone, regardless of gender, race, age, ability, or other quality, but those with privilege have the most responsibility to speak out (but to not speak *for* others) against oppressive and normative thinking in design. We can do this work right where we are by educating ourselves and others. As the designer Silas Munro has said, "It's more important for me to be a better person rather than a better designer, so that's something I'm always working on."[12] This commitment is echoed in this chapter in an essay by the designer and educator Victor Martinez, who writes about his path toward understanding feminism as a cisgender man.

Transforming the discipline requires more than just being a killjoy, however. The transformation must be systemic, radical, from the roots up. Without structural and systemic change, rights granted can easily be taken away. bell hooks asserted that the feminist movement can be successful only if we are committed to *revolution*—the establishment of a new social order, which happens gradually. She insisted that rebellion is not revolution; rebellion disrupts society but does not change it.[13] At present, design is in a stage of rebellion. We are rising up; we are finding common language; we are naming problems and making trouble. I believe our collective revolution is beginning to take shape, as demonstrated by the many and varied acts of resistance described in this book and taking place beyond it. As we continue to strengthen the muscles of our feminist tendencies and work toward revolution, community becomes a matter of survival.

Feminism is often put into action as a response to something we don't want, as in changing policies, resisting norms, speaking out against oppression. We tend to associate it with words such as *fight*, *dismantle*, and *tear down*. But feminism can be a building project, too. With the power of community, we can create something that is feminist by knowing, imagining, and doing otherwise together. Design is still an evolving and yet undefined discipline. It has been presented to us in a certain way, but that does not mean it must stay that way. The inspiring voices in this book are proof that design is more malleable than we might think. Representative Alexandria Ocasio Cortez is known for saying that the world we are fighting for is already here—it exists in small spaces, places, and communities. She argues that many of our biggest problems are the result of isolation from others but that many solutions can be found in creating community. The design discipline we want is already here—in small groups of collaborators, in quiet acts of resistance, in classrooms, in growing online communities, and in the work we continue create.

Our task is to keep learning, keep questioning, keep speaking out, keep staying with the trouble. We must continue to build on the work of those who came before us, laying the groundwork for those who will come after us. Our collective movement will continue to evolve as we do, knowing full well that this *we* is not a foundation, but what we are working toward. As Sara Ahmed writes, by "working out what we are for, we are working out that *we*, that hopeful signifier of a feminist collectivity. Where there is hope, there is difficulty."[14] And—as the growing chorus of feminist voices in design demonstrates—where there is difficulty, there is hope.

1 DEI is corporate and in-stitutional lingo for "diversity, equity, and inclusion." Here it is used to refer not to those principles themselves but to their collective use as an acronym, which oversimplifies and reduces those efforts to insincere maneuvers toward equity within white-supremacist institutions.
2 Sara Ahmed, *Living a Feminist Life* (Durham, NC: Duke University Press, 2017), 3.
3 bell hooks, *All About Love: New Visions* (New York: Harper Perennial, 2018), 51.
4 Consciousness-raising groups were originally practiced as part of the civil rights movement and were later adopted/co-opted by the women's movement.
5 Jo Freeman, *The Politics of Women's Liberation: A Case Study of an Emerging Social Movement and Its Relation to the Policy Process* (New York: Mckay, 1976).
6 Ahmed, *Living a Feminist Life*, 30.

7 bell hooks, *Feminist Theory: From Margin to Center* (1984; repr., London: Routledge, 2000), 67.
8 Sheila de Bretteville, "Feminist Design," *Space and Society* 6, no. 22 (1983): 98.
9 Lisa Corrigan and Laura Weiderhaft, "Manifesto," *Lean Back: Critical Feminist Conversations*, podcast, February 15, 2016, https://leanbackpodcast.com/post/139361165789.
10 Marty Maxwell Lane and Rebecca Tegtmeyer, *Collab-oration in Design Education* (London: Bloomsbury Visual Arts, 2020).
11 Ahmed, *Living a Feminist Life*, 38, 6.
12 Silas Munro, "Designing Public Action With Commu-nities" (keynote address, LA Design Festival, Los Angeles, CA, June 19, 2019).
13 hooks, *Feminist Theory*.
14 Ahmed, *Living a Feminist Life*, 2, emphasis in original.

On community as a process of working toward

Sarah Williams and Mandy Harris Williams of the Feminist Center for Creative Work in Los Angeles discuss continually evolving and unlearning as core values of feminist community.

Dialogue with Sarah Williams and Mandy Harris Williams

Alison Place What was the context when you started the Feminist Center for Creative Work (FCCW)?

Sarah Williams I cofounded the organization with Katie Bachler and Kate Johnston. We saw the exhibition *Doin' It in Public* at Otis College of Art and Design in 2012, which focused on feminist artists and projects at the Los Angeles Woman's Building in downtown LA in the 1970s through the 1990s. We had no idea about the different community practices that were being held in that space, and it was inspiring. We were looking for the 2012 version of that, for an opportunity to talk about feminism and creative practice. We started getting small groups of people together for different kinds of experimental gatherings and events, and the community began forming around that.

Mandy Harris Williams I joined in 2020 as the programming director. I was a part of the FCCW community before that, which is how many people end up being on staff. They interact with us, then just keep coming back and building relationships. Shortly after I started, we had to close the physical space due to the pandemic, so much of my role has been thinking about how to take the previous iterations of FCCW and bring them to an online space.

AP The mission of FCCW focuses on the idea that a creative practice has intellectual, personal, and political value. Why is a creative practice an act of resistance? And how does the center reduce barriers for people to maintain one?

MHW I don't think a creative practice is always an act of resistance, but that's something we're processing. The major feminist premise of what we do is to break down the barriers of an art world that is exclusive and siloed. My goal is to support and create models for practitioners who are making work that is socially engaged. But we consistently process the question of whether we are for artists or for the artists within people.

SW There's a sort of political power in people's perceptions of themselves, especially in how they think about making things in the world. So much of the way the world works is not particularly feminist or equitable. We look for possibilities to foster a community where people feel empowered to make things, to change things, or to develop other ways of existing and doing things, whether or not they think of themselves as artists.

AP In *A Feminist Organization's Handbook*, one of FCCW's earliest publications, an essay by Dori Tunstall discusses the role of design processes and artifacts in making value systems tangible and negotiable among

Figure 6.1.1 Cover of issue number 2 of *SALIMA Magazine.* Designed by Raquel Hazell. Courtesy of Feminist Center for Creative Work.

Figure 6.1.2 *You Can Vibe Me on My Femme Phone* by Kamala Puligandla, published by Co-Conspirator Press at FCCW. Photograph by Salima Allen. Courtesy of Feminist Center for Creative Work.

community members and stakeholders.[1] What are some ways that design shapes the organization, perhaps in tangible or less tangible ways?

SW Much of it is in our internal processes, some of which are less visible to the public, but we are making an effort to make those models of designing equitable systems accessible to other people. The handbook exhibits all of those processes that are negotiated on a team level where everyone's role is identified, and people can advocate for how much time and what resources they need to achieve those different elements. It makes clear the interrelationship of people and activities, with an effort toward a less hierarchical organizational structure.

MHW Our programs and gatherings tend to be ephemeral, but there's an element of curricular design that goes into them. I come from a classroom teaching background, so I think a lot about how to engage multiple modalities of learning or communicating to allow for the greatest number of people to participate. For instance, rather than putting the onus on people to say they need interpretation, just have the interpreter. That's an expensive but also values-based call we made. Our goal is to not have budgetary constraints that keep us from being as accessible as possible, but the reality is that accessibility is currently quite expensive. Accessibility, in the broadest sense, has been a guiding light as far as how we want to communicate via design.

AP One of your core values is that the center is a process, not a product. You value experimentation, failure, process. You also describe it as a practice of "working toward." What does constant evolution and unlearning look like in practice for an organization?

MHW One of the things we're trying to get into is slowness. We can't always anticipate what has to be put in place to make space for those processes, but we can assume it's going to take a lot of time, so we need to make sure we have the time and space to do it and that we feel supported in our physical space, our bodies, and our health.

SW We're often unlearning both the dynamics that we need to rebuild within our organization and the dynamics that predate us coming together in this organization—essentially the capitalist, white-supremacist, antifeminist work culture and ways of existing in the world. One of the most fulfilling aspects of doing this work for me is to unlearn and restructure together and experiment and envision when there aren't a lot of good models for doing it. We're proposing a model and trying it out while learning along the way.

AP The center is built on explicit feminist values such as care, radical transparency, redistribution of power, mutual aid, and joy. But a feminist organization is not a utopia. What are some of the challenges of operating a feminist organization that surprised you?

MHW Feminism is a really big pool at this point, and I think we're all really good, but we're not perfect. There are always going to be difficult group dynamics, and some of us can be assholes at times.

SW Totally. There are also limitations based on resources, and we are often doing the best we can within the constraints we're up against. That's not to say there isn't room for being better, more feminist, more equitable. But operating under the constraints of capitalism and nonprofit funding in the United States leads you to work in ways that are not always aligned with your values. We're always trying to decide together, as a team, where those boundaries are.

AP Even if an organization is 100 percent feminist, if that's even possible, you're still operating within the structures that are decidedly antifeminist, such as capitalism. What are some of the tensions that you encounter when trying to enact feminist ways of being and doing within those structures?

Figure 6.1.3 An image from the Feminist Center for Creative Work's Stock Photo series. Photograph by Salima Allen. Courtesy of Feminist Center for Creative Work.

Figure 6.1.4 Woodworking workshop taught by Michele Liu. Photograph by Salima Allen. Courtesy of Feminist Center for Creative Work.

MHW Honestly, it's the question of my life. It's so broad that I struggle to have an answer. How do you live and not crumble under the cognitive dissonance of what you have to do to get by?

SW That's why we continue to value process. That's not a value that's held widely across our society. How we do things is just as important to us as what we want the outcome to be. When we say we're focusing on slowness and developing ways of working together that are more feminist, there's definitely tension there. It takes a lot of time and process, and it's hard to get funding for that sort of work in a capitalist society that is built around efficiency and productivity. Building out things that are aligned with our values, like care for each other as a community, can be hard to simultaneously fund-raise for.

AP *Community* is a pillar of feminist thought and action, but the word tends to be overused or misconstrued. Do you describe FCCW as a community?

MHW I don't like using the word *community*. It feels manipulative and coercive, and it rarely ends up holding the powerful accountable and keeping the less powerful safe and resourced. Lately we've been asking, Do we have a community? Do we have an audience? Do we have some sort of mix of the two? What is our responsibility toward them? What is the directionality? We have many interwoven, overlapping communities, but we don't lump them together. I don't think we aspire to community as an ideal.

SW *Community* is such a marketing word. It's so hard to define or use in a way that isn't disingenuous. We need new language for this interconnected group of people that have different relationships to each other. It's something we've been struggling with, especially as we move to more digital spaces. When we were in a physical space, there was a physicality you could describe as "community." It was the people who were there together, talking together, deciding to work together. Now it's more dispersed, and, like Mandy said, it goes back and forth in all directions.

AP When the organization is operating beyond a physical site, the idea of a "center" becomes more fluid, shifting across different people and spaces and moments. It's an interesting metaphor for the mission of the organization, which is to empower both individuals and collective action. How has the idea of the "center" evolved?

MHW There's kind of a rhizomatic structure to the center. FCCW is its own thing, but we also function as an umbrella for other smaller communities, like a parents' group and a gender-marginalized electronic musicians' group. Sometimes it's us as a center identifying a space and supporting it, and sometimes it's people coming forward to make space for something, and they're shaping the center. For instance, we decided to change our name [from "Women's Center for Creative Work" to "Feminist Center for Creative Work"] because many people did not feel housed in the identity of "woman" or "women," which became a large part of our evolution. Something I've learned is that we work really hard, but we don't try too hard. We are experimental and don't place too many constraints on how it has to happen.

AP What role does the future play in your process of evolving and becoming?

MHW I am somebody who's always been future oriented, but I find the way that we're told to think about the future, especially from an organizational standpoint, can be very productivity focused, and I'm trying to keep myself from doing that. We are trying to be gentle. It's a scary thing to say about an organization, but I do think we are being gentle in a way that we haven't been before in order to heal from the hyperproductive, hypercapitalist, nonprofit industrial-complex extractive work.

SW Even at all stages of the organization, there's been unexpected things that happen and a need to be responsive to what's going on. The process is much more important to us. That requires embodying a present

moment and doing things as best we can right now. Part of the experiment of it is [to ask], How do we sustain that? There aren't many models for how to do that successfully. We are trying to stay in the process of doing it day to day, week to week, month to month.

AP Do you have any advice for those who might find themselves in a similar space, trying to navigate being present in the process while exploring what's next?

MHW Doing less helps people maintain focus on what is being done. Part of slowing down, for me, has been exploring the question "How do I give my work the credit that it deserves, as opposed to shortchanging it with the desire to do the next thing?" If people are into the thing that you've brought to the world, they'll sit with it for a second, and you should, too.

SW The most helpful thing in navigating times of change and questioning is to sink back into values. Get clear and articulate those values because they're not stagnant things. That's been a fulfilling way of addressing some of these topics. How do we sink back into our values in this process, in this moment of uncertainty around the big existential questioning of what we're trying to do?

This conversation took place over Zoom in November 2021. It has been edited for clarity and length.

Sarah Williams is the executive director of the Feminist Center for Creative Work in Los Angeles. She holds an MA in curatorial practice in the public sphere from the University of Southern California.

Mandy Harris Williams (she/they) is a multidisciplinary vocalization artist and culture worker from New York City, currently living in Los Angeles. She works as programming director of the Feminist Center for Creative Work.

1   Dori Tunstall, "Seven Principles of Designing Conditions for Community Self-Determination," in *A Feminist Organization's* *Handbook* (Los Angeles: Women's Center for Creative Work, 2017), 22–25.

On making code accessible and inclusive

Creator of p5.js, Lauren Lee McCarthy reflects on the collaborative process of building an open-source platform for learning creative expression through code.

Lauren Lee McCarthy

p5.js is a JavaScript library that aims to make creative expression and coding on the web accessible for artists, designers, educators, and beginners. It is free and open source because we believe software and the tools to learn it should be accessible to everyone. Code is a design tool that has long been wielded as a mechanism for exclusion and discrimination in the notoriously exclusive "club" presumed to be only for stereotypical white, male programmers. p5.js rejects this notion in favor of a community-centered approach to making and using code.

Building on its predecessor Processing, p5.js uses a metaphor of a sketchbook to make sketching with code as intuitive as sketching in a notebook. Like making a mark on paper, a single line of code puts a circle on the screen, another changes its color, and a third makes it animate (figure 6.2.1). More than just a library, p5.js is a project that emphasizes inclusivity and access in its community of users and contributors. I initiated the project in 2013, leading the development in collaboration with thousands of contributors around the world. From the beginning, we wanted p5.js to feel welcoming and inclusive. Making p5.js meant starting with deep uncertainty and many questions. It required becoming comfortable with not knowing, with making mistakes, with always being in a process of learning.

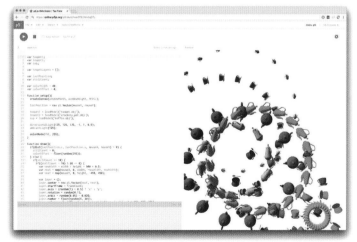

Figure 6.2.1 The p5.js Editor led by Cassie Tarakajian, featuring a sketch by Mathew Kaney. Courtesy of Lauren Lee McCarthy.

199

Figure 6.2.2 Participants at the p5.js Contributors Conference at the Carnegie Mellon Frank-Ratchye STUDIO for Creative Inquiry in 2015. Photograph by Jacquelyn Johnson / shawné michaelain holloway.

Community Statement

At the first p5.js Contributors Conference at Carnegie Mellon Frank-Ratchye STUDIO for Creative Inquiry in 2015, a group of 30 people came together to understand how we could work together with the rest of the growing p5.js community (figure 6.2.2). We drafted the p5.js Community Statement to make our values explicit and to provide a guide for decision-making going forward. No tool is neutral; each is built with the beliefs and biases of its creators. We were making a tool for creative expression, so it felt especially urgent to have a wide diversity of perspectives contributing to its making. We were constantly thinking about community and barriers to entry. How do we welcome someone/everyone? How do we keep updating our understanding of access?

Friendly Error System

Another development that came out of the Contributors Conference was the Friendly Error System (FES), which helps new programmers by providing error messages in simple, friendly language. The FES identifies common errors, suggests code changes, and directs the user to documentation to learn more. This feature pushes back on the idea that technology is only for those with specific backgrounds. Key contributors to this functionality include Chris Hallberg, Alice M. Chung, Luisa Pereira, Akshay Padte, Stalgia Grigg, Shantanu Kaushi, Thales Grilo, and Luis Morales-Navarro.

p5.js Editor

The p5.js Editor, a software project led by Cassie Tarakajian since 2016, has been another place for thinking through the beginner experience. The Editor allows anyone to get started making p5.js sketches online with no setup or cost. In contrast to heavily featured code-editing software, the p5.js Editor is intended to provide an experience that prioritizes people who are learning to code.

p5.js Translation

As the worldwide community for p5.js has expanded, contributors have led translation efforts in Spanish (aarón montoya-moraga and Guillermo Montecinos),

Chinese (Kenneth Lim and Qianqian Ye), Japanese (Katsuya Endoh), Korean (Inhwa Yeom, Seonghyeon Kim, and Yeseul Song), Hindi (Sanjay Singh Rajpoot, Aditya Rana, Manaswini Das, Nancy Chauhan, and Shaharyar Shamshi), and many other languages. At the second Contributors Conference in 2019, an internationalization working group consisting of aarón, Guillermo, Kenneth, Qianqian, Shaharyar, Yasheng She, Soeun Lee, and Dorothy R. Santos developed the p5.js Global Contributors Toolkit, which includes an overview of translation workflow, examples, and resources. It opens with a letter to global contributors: "You don't have to be a software developer or a professional educator to contribute to p5.js. We celebrate contributions of any size and type from anyone who's excited about p5.js. *We believe that contribution is about the process more than the product.*" It concludes with this note: "We want to acknowledge that JavaScript is an English-based programming language, upon which p5.js is developed. With that in mind, we understand the underlying colonialist/(neo)imperialist implications of making p5.js 'globally available.' We believe that English should not be the prerequisite to coding. Expressive coding is a form of creative expression regardless of one's background and language ability. Our translators have employed a variety of means to address this issue, such as rendering programming language into symbols and, in doing so, prioritize its function rather than its linguistic significance."

p5 Access Project

It has been essential to consider how p5.js can be accessible for disabled people. In 2017, Taeyoon Choi facilitated Signing Coders, a series of workshops on creative expression through computer programming, art, and poetry that focuses on reaching out to youth who are deaf or hard of hearing. Similarly, Claire Kearney-Volpe, Luis Morales-Navarro, Mathura Govindarajan, and Cassie Tarakajian worked with assistive-technology experts Chancey Fleet, Sina Bahram, and Josh Miele to introduce functionality that uses sound and description to make p5.js visual outputs accessible to people who are blind or have low vision and/or use screen readers (figure 6.2.3). Building on this work, a decision was made after the 1.0

Figure 6.2.3 Accessible-programming workshop led by Claire Kearney-Volpe and Chancey Fleet. Photograph courtesy of Claire Kearney-Volpe and Chancey Fleet.

release "to only add features to p5.js that increase access."[1] evelyn masso, working with Claire, Sina, Luis, Kate Hollenbach, and Olivia Ross, led the creation of the p5.js Access Statement to provide clear criteria and examples of what the project would prioritize, while also inviting community members into a longer conversation about access.

Leadership Transitions

How do you make decisions with a community that is so large, geographically dispersed, and diverse? How can we create networks of distributed leadership and local organizing? We began rotating the project lead in 2020. We held an open-call process where we asked how this position could support learning for the lead as well as for the community. Moira Turner took over the lead position and then passed it on to evelyn masso and Qianqian Ye. Each lead has brought new questions to p5.js, stewarding it on a path forward from the 1.0 release.

Community

It was clear from the start that our open-source project had many needs beyond code. We needed people to write tutorials and documentation; to answer questions on the forum and respond to issues on GitHub; to create curricula and examples and to teach people how to use the platform; to work with local communities to organize workshops, meetups, exhibitions, community spaces, community days; to share code and ideas through their artwork; to work through conflicts and different opinions. We needed people who could recognize the time this work requires and the importance of pausing sometimes. Making with p5.js is believing you can make things with other people. We are building on decades of learning from teachers in other communities, such as Processing, the School for Poetic Computation, openFrameworks, Design by Numbers, Arduino, Wiring, three.js, POWRPLNT, Afrotectopia, PyLadies, the Design Justice Network, and many others. p5.js is everything we learn from each other when we make ourselves open.

Lauren Lee McCarthy (she/they) is a Los Angeles–based artist examining social relationships in the midst of surveillance, automation, and algorithmic living. She is the creator of p5.js, an open-source platform for learning creative expression through code online.

1   "Our Focus on Access," p5.js, accessed January 27, 2023, https://p5js.org/contributor-docs/#/./access.

On building a flexible and borderless feminist community

Cofounder of the Feminist Design Social Club in Seoul, In-ah Shin considers feminist movements in South Korea and what makes a community feminist.

In-ah Shin
Translated by Donggyo Lee

A sense of stability was what I desperately wanted when I moved back to South Korea after years of living in Australia. But when I returned, somehow it felt so different from what I had expected. I felt as if I were experiencing culture shock in my own country. Shortly after I moved back in 2016, a woman was brutally killed near the Gangnam station by a man who hated women and chose his victim at random. Ewha Women's University students launched a protest, singing a song called "Into the New World." A series of hashtags such as "#sexual_violence_in_XX_industry" spread on Twitter. Millions of people took to the streets, calling for President Park Geun-hye to resign. That year I met a group of feminists and felt that I could finally take root in Seoul.

Two years later, in 2018, I founded the Feminist Designer Social Club (FDSC) with Somi Kim, Meanyoung Yang, and Yuni Ooh. "It just happened" tends to be my answer whenever someone asks how it was formed. We didn't start out with a plan to form a large community. We envisioned a first meeting of ten or so designers; we sent out a call for interest and heard from 204 people. Since then, FDSC has evolved in its scope, size, leadership, and reach. Regional branches were established across the country to connect designers outside Seoul, where the design industry is centered. But, more importantly, our purpose has continued to evolve, too.

To understand this context, one should first understand what "community" means in Korea. The country perceives community as exceptionally important and persistent. From birth, we fall into a strict form of human network called "the family." It is almost impossible to get away from the network. Many women in FDSC seek to escape various forms of oppression—the country, the corset, K-pop, religion, marriage, and family—lurking in the patriarchal society. I, too, had tried to escape by moving abroad. Over time, I came to realize that feminism can save an individual from an oppressing group. From this perspective, I envisioned the FDSC as a sustainable community where no woman sacrifices herself, each member plays a central role, and, most importantly, everyone finds it enjoyable to inhabit.

What FDSC is and does defies a clear summary. We have hosted gatherings, big and small, from two to more than 300 people (figure 6.3.1). We talk, write, sing, and share information. Our gatherings have been documented in books, podcasts,

Figure 6.3.1
Portfolio Review is an opportunity for feminist designers and students to connect. Photograph by Eunjin Gwak.

exhibitions, YouTube clips, and other social media content (figures 6.3.2 and 6.3.3). I often say that each member should be able to explain what the FDSC means to them, even if their answer is totally different from others' answers. The collective meanings expressed by all the members is what makes the FDSC a flexible and free community. To me, the act of explaining ourselves is a way of translating what we experience into language, acting on it, and documenting it to be used as tools for others. The diversity of our community is what makes us ever more brilliant.

However, diverse perspectives can also mean conflict is possible or inevitable among members. Some members expressed concerns and wanted us to establish clear values and beliefs for FDSC, but I was more interested in the possibility of a community where people of different beliefs could gather. We created the community culture team to diagnose any possible inner source of conflict and to prevent it. We conducted experimental workshops to search for an ideal community culture for our club. The deeper we dug into individuals' feelings and perspectives, however, the more we were able to understand our community, and through this

Figure 6.3.2 *Design FM* is a podcast that has been airing since 2019 and features feminist designers working in different fields and methods. Photograph by Eunjin Gwak.

Figure 6.3.3 The first season of the *Design FM* podcast was published as a book. Photograph by Charyung Lee.

Figure 6.3.4 First Design Seodang class. We bow to each other in a traditional way before reading the text about smashing the patriarchal tradition in design. Courtesy of FDSC.

process we learned that the problem we faced was not the possibility of conflict but rather our avoidance of it.

Such a tendency led us to turn a blind eye to any source of discord and to move on without even mentioning it, thus losing a chance to deal with it in real time. Any seed of disharmony not unearthed would lurk in the dark and fester until it finally grew uncontrollably into an unexpected situation. We were too careful. Behind this carefulness, we realized, was a fear for feminism: Perhaps we do not know feminism enough? Perhaps we will ruin our bond by making mistakes? It has taken courage and trust to admit the possibility of confrontation within our community.

The community-culture team activities gave us insight into the launch of a program called Design Seodang (school or place of learning) in 2021, in which participants read design texts based on feminist theory[1] for six weeks to explore their own conceptions of what a "feminist designer" is (figure 6.3.4). Combining what we learned, we came up with the phrase "a community in which the knowledge runs horizontally," and it became our signpost to create a concrete frame for the program. There was no moderator for this program; each member took turns leading a session. The rules were so simple that a participant didn't even have to read or prepare in advance. Each session offered a time to read, and after reading the text, the participants had a conversation. When we talked, we could find others' diverse perspectives due to their status or circumstances, so we encouraged the participants to use these conversations as a chance to get to know each other better. The biggest challenge of this program was the homework, which was to post our thoughts on an Instagram account. We hoped that participants would build up the courage to express their thoughts, no matter how hard or how small they seemed.

The Design Seodang produced more enthusiastic responses from people than we expected. We were surprised by how they expressed genuine joy and sorrow and built a strong bond with one another. We could even discover a delightful change in their perceptions and attitudes. The designer Ha-kyung Lee, who recently joined an FDSC writing program called FDSC.txt, recalled that the Design Seodang changed her concept of social media from a space of censorship into a space for sharing and documenting. She pointed out the importance of revealing and approaching, saying that she came to respect the difference and relationship.

In 2016, a series of sexual abuse exposures flooded social media with despair and horror. In response, a new slogan emerged: "We will be each other's courage!"[2] The phrase reminded us that we were witnessing a moment of solidarity where a courageous victim who has survived an ordeal empowers another. It also expressed a determination that we would give courage to one another. Today, I can better articulate what FDSC is. It's the community I dreamed of when I felt isolated and disconnected. It's a space where diverse people of common goals are connected freely in a creative way. It's a place where we are each other's courage.

In-ah Shin is a graphic designer and organizer based in Seoul. She runs an independent graphic design studio, Scenery of Today, and cofounded the Feminist Designer Social Club.

1   We read both English and Korean texts by Linda Nochlin, Cheryl D. Miller, Martha Scotford, Aggie Toppins, Ece Canli, Anoushka Khandwala, Madeleine Morley, Danah Abdulla, Dennis Grauel, Sarah Fathallah, A. D. Sean Lewis, Terry Wolverton, Kay Jun, Hyun Mee Kim, Heejin Jeong, Hyeeun Jun, Seungyeon Babrielle Jung, Un Jeon Hong, and others. The list continues to expand as the number of participants grows.
2   A tweet by Twitter user Vera (@dooruich) posted in response to a series of sexual abuse exposures under the hashtag #sexual_violence_in_the_XX_industry.

On being a male feminist designer

Victor G. Martinez

The industrial designer and educator Victor G. Martinez reflects on the path he took toward understanding feminist issues in design and how men can be catalysts for change.

Understanding privilege is not complicated, but understanding the systemic nature of privilege and how power works *is* quite complicated. I was taught to understand privilege through an analogy with a staircase, with every step representing a level of power. Generally, if you are a man, you are on a higher step than a woman, but if you are a Black or Brown man and the woman is white, it's usually the other way around. The more money you have, the more steps up the stairs you are. The less education you have, down you go. But when you consider the complexity of individual identities—sexual orientation, skin tone, native language, religion, citizenship, and so on—the staircase begins to twist and turn on itself until it resembles a web more than steps. It wasn't until I began to explore the nature of privilege that I learned this is the basic premise of the concept of intersectionality: discrimination is not experienced at the site of individual characteristics of people's identities but rather at the intersection of their multiple identities. We all have experienced this in one way or the other—even men like me (throughout this essay, "men" refers to cisgender, heterosexual men).

My personal realization of disadvantages within a power hierarchy arrived at an early age, but I also experienced privilege that allowed me to have dreams and to achieve them. Those privileges took me out of my home country, Mexico, to work toward two graduate degrees in Europe. Yet while I was studying and working there, many times I was reminded of my lower position in the hierarchy (I had an accent, I had a precarious work contract, my family name revealed my origin) through nasty stares, passive-aggressive comments, and blatantly racist slurs. Still, those reminders never stopped me from reaching my dream of becoming a car designer working in the first league of the world car industry.

Many years later, I was made aware of the imbalances of power and privilege that I, admittedly, had previously overlooked, and that process is still ongoing (thanks to my wife, many female friends and colleagues who trusted me, and the myriad women who are simply brave enough to tell their stories openly—for whom I am deeply thankful). From stories of sexual assault and *feminicidios* to #MeToo and sexual harassment in the workplace, I was astonished to realize every single woman experienced something like this in her lifetime. The realization spurred in me reactions of shame (of being unaware and complicit in the creation of such disadvantages) and anger (of how widespread and deeply felt the injustices are).

I was equally enraged to learn about rampant discrimination against women in my profession, design, and shocked to learn I was a direct culprit in that discrimination. While working as a car designer in Italy, I translated conceptual sketches into 3D computer models, for which we received a package of dozens of components, including ergonomic and safety factors such as head and hand positions. We could not change these components, so we referred to them as the "black box." I designed dozens of steering wheels, interior door panels, center consoles, and dashboards following these rules. It wasn't until I read Caroline Criado Perez's book *Invisible Women*[1] that I learned that the "black box" of ergonomics I had unquestioningly worked with did not properly represent women's anatomies. Our digital human representation in car design—called "Oscar," fittingly—was clearly male in its proportions, causing women to be treated as smaller versions of men. According to Criado Perez, this lack of representation of women in the data we design with directly contributes to women being more likely than men to be injured or killed in car accidents. I felt deceived and angry with myself for not knowing any better. I knew I had more work to do.

A few years ago in Canada, where I am a professor, academics started to circle the idea of "indigenizing the curricula." Canada has a long history of colonization and genocide of Indigenous peoples, but there has recently been a renewed interest in highlighting the knowledge and experiences of Indigenous groups. I decided to explore with my students the topic of decolonization. Coming from a country that was colonized for 300 years and still struggles with the heavy baggage of colonialism and racism, I could relate to the idea of exploring what decolonization could mean in today's context. I started with a definition that speaks to our present moment rather than to the past: *Colonization is the action of appropriating a place, mind, culture, identity, or domain for one's own use.* Colonization is still alive and thriving today, but it takes place in many different ways, some quite subtle, unconsciously taking over our minds and identities.

On two parallel paths, I delved into literature about feminism and Indigenous cultures. One book stood out for me: in *Women's Ways of Knowing: The Development of Self, Voice, and Mind,*[2] the authors exposed the fact that up to the late 1980s, when the book was published, most social science research was done by studying mainly white male students from top universities because that is the demographic researchers had access to and they did not seek out diversity (sadly, this still happens today). To offer a contrast, the authors studied a large group of diverse women with the intent to understand what most researchers were missing. The results demonstrated that notions of masculinity are more identified with competition, the individual, and stating the consequences of actions, whereas a woman's approach tends to be more about the communal or cooperative and understanding the causes and relationalities of situations to address the root of a problem. I saw connections between these women's ways of knowing and the principles of some Indigenous populations, many of which are matriarchal in structure. Even in systems thinking, an area I have worked in for the past 13 years, the ideas of

Principles for Design

Proposed by students in Victor Martinez's design studio course, based on Indigenous and women's ways of knowing.

Indigenous Principles for Design

* Create systems where everyone's opinion is captured
* Understand context, expectation, and application
* Investigate the intended experience
* Design for cultural inclusiveness
* Take time to make good decisions
* Design to empower all peoples
* Respect the autonomy of environmental bodies (trees, rivers, mountains)
* Recognize Indigenous knowledge as current knowledge
* Recognize the impacts of colonization
* Design to protect our planet
* Teach all sides of a story

Women's Principles for Design

* Center women in opportunities for growth
* Use privilege to advocate for others
* Design to make users feel seen, understood, and cared for
* Include overall context in your designs
* Listen to understand—not to reply
* Consider the emotionality of design
* Recognize that gender disparity is present
* Leave your comfort zone to encourage change
* Consider social values before form
* Create a culture (or space) that embraces emotions to build authentic relationships and connections
* Focus on supporting others rather than competing with them
* Bridge the gap between work and family life
* Ensure power lies with the marginalized and the end user, not with the designer
* Promote and recognize the achievements of others

interdependency, relationalities, or interventions that are rooted in context and the deep origin of the problems are feminist in nature.

In my "Design Studio" course in 2018, I proposed to my second-year students an experiment: What if the focus of our studio was not to design something but to identify some of the things missing in the omnipresent decalogue of "good design"? For example, culturally speaking, I have always known that in Latin America some rules of "good design" do not make sense. If you've ever seen the dashboard or windshield of a taxi or bus in Latin America, it is adorned with objects of importance—figurines of saints, pictures of the family, a favorite football soccer team's mascot, the first child's shoe, and so on. This is a well-known cultural phenomenon called *miedo al vacío*, or "fear of emptiness." It is part of our identity, but it was hammered out of me during my design training when I was pushed toward minimalism as "good design."

To expand our understanding of good design, we invited to the class various experts, teachers, makers, and thinkers who could give us their perspective on women's and Indigenous ways of knowing and making. We had the privilege to host 14 different speakers from four continents, most of them women (some white, some Brown) but also a few men (Indigenous and not). Students captured ideas, insights, and key words from each speaker and later distilled them into a first draft of "design principles" based on Indigenous and women's ways of knowing. Their findings reveal pathways for feminist ways of designing that center empowerment, collaboration, humility, respect, authenticity, and equity. We see these lists as a work in progress—a starting point to continue our path to understanding and to generate dialogues. As the anthropologist Arturo Escobar writes, no single individual or expert holds the key to the future; all solutions should grow from the local and communal.[3]

Keeping in line with my training as a social scientist, I have also listened to some voices against the idea of equality through feminism. What I heard in the opposition was fear—ostensibly, fear that giving space to these ideas will inevitably mean the demise or the conquest of the ideas, culture, identity, or morals of those expressing such opposition, a common fear held by oppressors throughout history. The feminism I support and believe in does not seek revenge but instead seeks a world in which oppressed and marginalized voices as well as alternative views and ideas are heard and can thrive. To be sure, men also experience barriers and difficulties in our society, but such barriers and difficulties are imposed mostly by men themselves or through the construction of patriarchy and gender norms that they willfully uphold. The feminist scholar bell hooks wrote extensively about the ways in which patriarchy oppresses men, too: "Learning to wear a mask (that word already embedded in the term 'masculinity') is the first lesson in patriarchal masculinity that a boy learns. … Asked to give up the true self in order to realize the patriarchal ideal, boys learn self-betrayal early and are rewarded for these acts of soul murder."[4] I seek a feminism that grants men freedom from this nonsense, too.

If you are feminist male designer or a man on the path to understanding feminist design, what can you do? I propose some thoughts:

* Call out men's toxic behaviors as a barrier to us all. Talk about these behaviors with colleagues and friends. Set better examples. Power should not come from others' fear of you but from showing others that you do not need to be feared.

* Recognize systemic barriers and use your position to do something about them. Become aware of your power and privilege and find ways to give them up or hand them over to others. Don't be afraid of being left alone or left out.

* Listen more to women—listen to understand, not to reply. Start asking questions with the intent to build and grow together. Don't make others teach you about the nature of their oppression—do your research and learn on your own.

* Gather robust data from marginalized people to inform how the problem you and they are trying to solve should address the needs of a diversity of users. (Do not shrink it and pink it!)

* Attend conferences and seminars about women in design and feminist design methodologies. Again, listen to understand, not to reply.
* Do not speak for others; instead, create opportunities for others to speak for themselves.
* Accept that you play a part in maintaining the systems of oppression that limit true human potential (we all do). Do not waste time with guilt. Instead, take action.

Victor G. Martinez (he/him) started his professional career as a car designer in Mexico and later in Italy. He is an academic in Canada who explores the sustainability of design linked to systems thinking and complexity theory.

1 Caroline Criado Perez, *Invisible Women: Data Bias in a World Designed for Men* (New York: Abrams, 2019).
2 Mary Field Belenky et al., *Women's Ways of Knowing: The Development of Self, Voice, and Mind* (New York: Basic, 1986).
3 Arturo Escobar, *Designs for the Pluriverse* (Durham, NC: Duke University Press, 2018).
4 bell hooks, *The Will to Change: Men, Masculinity, and Love* (New York: Washington Square Press, 2004), 153.

On the futures(s) of feminist design

The codirectors of *Futuress*, Maya Ober and Nina Paim, discuss feminist publishing and the challenges of collaboration.

Dialogue with Maya Ober and Nina Paim

Alison Place How do you describe what *Futuress* is?

Nina Paim We are a learning community and a publishing platform. We have a double mission, which is to democratize access to design education and to amplify marginalized voices.

AP What are some of *Futuress*'s initiatives and programs?

Maya Ober We're constantly learning and changing because we don't believe there's one model for doing things. One of our primary initiatives has been different iterations of online workshops and fellowships. Our most recent one, "Coding Resistance," brought in designers, researchers, and activists from broadly understood marginalized communities. They propose a research idea, and over several months we help them craft their research into stories that will be later published on *Futuress*. In order to finance the program, we developed a public-lecture series and charged fees on a sliding scale. This allows us to make space for the stories that matter.

NP We also have a monthly agenda of different learning formats, like lecture series, panel discussions, or networking events. We call it a "test kitchen" because we want to experiment. We're building an ecosystem of learning offerings, which generate the content that eventually gets published on our platform.

AP Nina, as one of the cofounders of *Futuress*, you've talked about its inception as something that was not planned or designed from the outset but something that came about through many iterations in response to what you felt was needed in the community. What has the process of constantly "becoming" been like for you?

NP It's been a huge process of self-transformation for me, personally. As a designer, I've been trained to project into the future, but I find it fascinating that this thing called *Futuress* is not something that I project or control but emerges on a daily basis. I allow it to shape me as much as I shape it. The first iteration of *Futuress*, conceived with Eliot Corin Gisel in 2019, started as a small website collecting ideas for books that have yet to exist. It stemmed from the frustration of always being the big mouth in the room complaining about whatever was missing or ignored. It was supposed to be a small project, but it sparked reflection on what is keeping these stories from being told, and it grew from there.

AP Maya, you joined in 2021 as codirector. What has your collaboration been like?

MO I had been running depatriarchise design, a feminist activist platform, alongside Anja Neidhardt since 2017. We saw that the two platforms were very different, but we were going in the same direction, and

Figure 6.5.1 A collection of articles published on *Futuress*.
Courtesy of *Futuress*.

we [figured we] could make a bigger impact by working permanently together.

NP There's a long history of collaboration between us. We are also really good friends, and we wanted to figure out how we can do this and preserve our friendship. That's something we don't get to talk about much because it's not flashy, but it's a challenge to collaborate as friends and learn from each other without risking our relationship together.

MO We are socialized in such a violent society in the ways that patriarchy, racism, colonialism, and capitalism shape us. In design education, we learn competitiveness and individualism, and in turn we're not given tools to collaborate with other people. So, for us, collaboration is a process of unlearning. It's an effort, and it's also a choice. For me, it's

been profoundly transformative, not just as a designer or educator but as a person.

AP Feminism is often seen as a collaborative process, but that can obfuscate how challenging collaboration is and what it requires of us.

MO Feminism is not something that you can just switch off. I think we need to demystify it. It's a lot of hard work. It's much easier to do something on your own when you don't have to discuss things or consider other people. Every day I'm trying to learn how to listen better and to be more empathetic in working together with our whole community.

NP Collaboration comes from a certain openness to change. You have to be willing to change yourself in order to be in a collaborative relationship because, in some ways, collaborating means being transformed by

Figure 6.5.2 *Futuress* curated the *Feminist Findings* exhibit at A-Z in Berlin in 2020, which brought together the collective research of twenty-six womxn and nonbinary people on the history of feminist publishing through the L.i.P. (Liberation in Print) Collective. Courtesy of *Futuress*.

the relationship itself. It also requires an acceptance that your perspective is limited. My field of vision is shaped by who I am and how I was brought up. If I'm trying to expand my field of vision, I can only do that by working with others who are different from me and who see the world differently from me. But the difficulties and the pitfalls are numerous. We are not socially trained to deal with conflict and difference, yet as a transnational feminist platform we are nothing but different as individuals. When we talk about feminism, we are all talking about different things because what feminism is for me, as a Brazilian born and raised, is very different from [what it is for] someone from another part of the world.

AP How does that inform *Futuress*'s collaborative model for authorship and publishing?

NP The model asks, How can our work be better—more rich, more compelling, more nuanced—by doing it together? With the fellowships, we go through a process of sharing ideas and slowly building trust. [It makes one] vulnerable to share an in-process text. We try to build nonviolent sharing spaces to help people formulate their ideas and grow.

The final outcome itself is a web of interlacing influences from everyone who collaborated on it—the writer, those who gave feedback, the copy editor, the designer.

AP As you said, *Futuress* is a transnational feminist community of many different geographic locations, identities, and backgrounds. What are some of the necessary acts of maintenance that sustain such a large and diverse community?

MO There is the daily maintenance of editing and supporting the authors. Because the fellowships are explicitly for people from marginalized communities, oftentimes the fellows find themselves in precarious situations and difficult life circumstances that require additional support. There's also the maintenance of keeping *Futuress* afloat, like writing funding applications, as well as administrative work, like making sure our collaborators are paid on time.

NP It's a lot of responsibility because we're committed to the people that we engage. Long-term active maintenance is something we've been thinking about. There is a rich history of feminist publishing houses that were active in the '70s and '80s, but in the

'90s most of them went bankrupt, and those stories disappeared. With *Futuress*, how can we guarantee these stories will be available not just now but also deep into the future?

AP We tend to throw around the word *community* a lot today, with little clarity around what it means. You both have experience with building communities. What does *community* mean to you? What makes a community feminist?

MO This is a fundamental question we come back to all the time. To me, it's a question of not being *about* but being from *within*. *Futuress* is not about feminism; it's from within feminism. We're not just feminist in the content we cover but also [in] the operational structure. It means paying the invoices and having contracts. It's in how we communicate with people, how we establish spaces, or how we design our code of conduct. It requires us to look at power relations and our positionality within it. It requires transparency.

NP I define *community* from a personal perspective as someone who went through multiple migrations. I left Brazil in 2010, went to Amsterdam, Germany, Switzerland, and now I am in Portugal. For much of it, I was very lonely, craving community and people I could share with, people who read the things I was reading and would discuss books with me. When I was doing my MA in Switzerland, I felt alone in the room when I shared my thoughts, and no one replied. *Futuress* is something that I need because I need others. I don't want to do anything alone. The best joy in life is shared.

MO A feminist community for designers is also about nonviolence. I was trained as an industrial designer in Israel in an environment where violent feedback was normal, and we often cried during critiques. Everything had to be perfectly polished and finished. We want to create a nonviolent space where you can share unfinished work that is valued, and people are generous with their thoughts and kindness. It's amazing

Figure 6.5.3 The *Futuress* community at the Swiss Design Awards show in 2021. Courtesy of *Futuress*.

to be able to counter all of these horrible things that were normalized throughout our education and show there's another way of doing things.

AP In the past, publishing was a way for feminists to find community, whether by making zines or newsletters or by disseminating feminist writings that would not be published in mainstream media. How does the history of feminist publishing influence what *Futuress* does today?

NP There's so much to be learned from the histories of feminist publishing—not just the history of success but also the history of struggle. For example, feminist periodicals can be extremely rich because they often have a less polished and more raw quality to them. In an interview we published recently with Bec Wonders,[1] she talks about how the letters to the editor in feminist magazines and newsletters unfolded like "serialized fiction," where you can follow the discussions and see how disagreements would play out. You can start to see the nitty-gritty issues of how collectives come together and how conflict advances a movement. To me, the past is a living thing, changing what I do in the present.

MO Looking at history has a transgenerational aspect to it. As designers, we are trained always to design from scratch, but feminist histories are a reminder that we can learn from others and build upon it. It's powerful to understand that we are part of the history and present and future of feminist communities or feminist publishing or feminist education. This gives us a lot of strength and hope for our future.

AP You talked about creating something that can live on in the future. How do you see *Futuress* creating possible futures for feminist discourse?

NP One of the things I love about *Futuress* is that everything we publish comes from the community. People come to us with their stories, and whatever they think is relevant is what we eventually will publish. We have over 100 texts that have been published, and now we're starting to see interesting relationships between them and ways that we might bundle them together into a reader. In a way, that original idea of the library of books that don't yet exist comes back into play. But we're not deciding what the books should be and then looking for content to fill them; instead, we're compiling stories about what people have told us matters to them and letting the themes emerge.

MO It also connects to learning. Institutional design education is very much about being molded into a particular type of designer, whereas within our learning community no one is responding to a predefined brief. The writing comes from the authentic stories of the fellows we work with, and those stories deeply resonate with people. It touches us in a different way, and it ultimately expands our understanding of what design research is and could be.

AP As Maya stated, *Futuress* is not about feminism but rather [about] what happens *within* and *through* feminism. The focus of the platform is design. In your perspectives, what is the trajectory of feminist design?

NP There has always been resistance in design, but I think something shifted with the pandemic. People called it the biggest remote-learning experiment in history. There were so many initiatives that emerged, like mushrooms on a devastated planet, such as BIPOC Design History[2] and Design & Opressão[3] in Brazil. The pandemic exacerbated all types of vulnerabilities, but at the same time it also created a global network of resistance, specifically within design. A lot has changed in the last few years, so I think that's really hopeful.

MO There's something powerful about being able to connect with people from another part of the globe that we would not otherwise be able to meet. It's not just academic or intellectual discussions; it's also people connecting on Instagram. There are so many people speaking up, and they're organized, and they're fearless. The more voices, the better. Feminism should not be a unified voice. There should be multiple different ways of doing, and that's the only way we can be in the process of overcoming patriarchy, capitalism, and colonialism. We're doing it together, and it's only growing and growing.

This conversation took place over Zoom in March 2022. It has been edited for clarity and length.

Maya Ober (she/her) is a Polish Israeli activist, designer, researcher, educator, codirector of *Futuress,* and founder of depatriarchise design. She is a PhD candidate at the Institute of Social Anthropology at the University of Bern, researching feminist practices, institutional life, and the intersection of activism and design education. She is temporarily based between Buenos Aires and Basel.

Nina Paim (she/her) is a Brazilian designer, researcher, curator, editor, and cofounder of *Futuress.* She holds an MA in design research from Bern University of the Arts and is a PhD candidate at the Laboratory of Design and Anthropology at the Universidade do Estado do Rio de Janeiro in Brazil. She is based in Porto, Portugal.

1   Bec Wonders, "Please Say More," interview by Nina Paim, *Futuress,* March 8, 2022, https://futuress.org/stories/please-say-more/.

2   BIPOC Design History was started in 2021 by Silas Munro, Pierre Bowins, and Tasheka Arceneaux-Sutton to shed light on moments of oppression and visibility for Black, Indigenous, and people of color in design history.

3   Design & Opressão is a network started in Brazil in 2020 by a small group of educators who wanted to read Paulo Freire. Today it's a network of more than 500 people throughout the country.

Acknowledgments

Sara Ahmed says that even if we can create our path by not following, we still need others before us. To the feminists and feminist designers who came before me, I offer my humble gratitude. This book would not exist without them. The ideas within these pages draw from and expound upon decades of feminist writings and wisdom that line my bookshelves and fill my soul. Each citation in this book is a note of appreciation for their work.

I also wish to extend my gratitude to the designers and writers whose contributions brought this book to life. Their generosity and collaborative spirit made this project a joy to facilitate, and their thoughtful critiques and feedback made it better.

I thank my editor at MIT Press, Victoria Hindley, who believed in this book and pushed me to make it as strong as it could be. And I thank the many peer reviewers, editors, and proofreaders whose feedback throughout the process was critical to this book taking shape.

Three entities importantly provided the funding necessary to make this project possible: the University of Arkansas Humanities Center, the Robert C. and Sandra Connor Endowed Faculty Fellowship, and the University of Arkansas School of Art.

I am grateful to the leaders in the School of Art, especially Marty Maxwell Lane and Christopher Schulte, for embodying heart-centered leadership. And I thank the entire University of Arkansas graphic design family, the kindest group of colleagues and students I've ever worked with. Endless thanks, especially, goes to Ryan Slone for invaluable support and encouragement during the design phase.

This book would have remained nothing more than a bunch of words on my screen without the patience and tireless work of my research assistants, Annie Lefforge and Jen Iseman.

Nothing I have accomplished would have been possible without the warmth and generosity of incredible mentors—especially Marty Maxwell Lane, Robin Landa, and Helen Armstrong—whose advocacy for women and mothers in academia moves mountains. If not for them, I would have remained convinced that having a baby while I was on the tenure track (and writing a book!) was ill advised at best and impossible at worst. Not only did they show me it was possible, but they also had my back the entire time.

I thank the amazing women in academia with whom I have collaborated and written, especially my writing group, Sarah Rutherford, Aggie Toppins, and Kelly Walters, who have been alongside me every step of the way. Thanks also must go to Aaris Sherin and Robin Landa for leading the design writing fellowship program that jump-started this book into existence and introduced me to my writing group.

I thank my family, who have always supported me even when they have no idea what I'm doing or talking about and have believed in me no matter what I set out to do.

Thank you to Sylvia for filling my life with love and light, and for reminding me to be present to joy every day.

Finally, to my partner and love of my life, Ringo Jones, thank you for your unwavering kindness, love, and generosity throughout this process. The thrill of my accomplishments will forever pale in comparison to the joy of being loved by you. Remember when I decided to write a book right after moving across the country and having a baby while we were both on the tenure track in the middle of a pandemic? Yeah, that was wild.

Bibliography

Adichie, Chimamanda Ngozi. "The Danger of a Single Story." *TED Talks*, July 2009. https://www.ted.com/talks/chimamanda_ngozi_adichie_the_danger_of_a_single_story.

Adichie, Chimamanda Ngozi. *We Should All Be Feminists*. New York: Knopf Doubleday, 2014.

Agre, Philip E. *Computation and Human Experience*. Cambridge: Cambridge University Press, 1997.

Aguilar, Julián. "Mock Immigration Sting on UT Campus Canceled." *Texas Tribune*, November 19, 2013. https://www.texastribune.org/2013/11/19/conservative-group-hold-mock-immigration-sting-ut/.

Ahmed, Sara. "Becoming Unsympathetic." *Feministkilljoys*, April 16, 2015. https://feministkilljoys.com/2015/04/16/becoming-unsympathetic/.

Ahmed, Sara. *Living a Feminist Life*. Durham, NC: Duke University Press, 2017.

Ahmed, Sara. *What's the Use? On the Uses of Use*. Durham, NC: Duke University Press, 2019.

Alcoff, Linda Martin. *Visible Identities: Race, Gender, and the Self*. New York: Oxford University Press, 2006.

Allen, Amy. "Feminist Perspectives on Power." In *Stanford Encyclopedia of Philosophy*, edited by Edward N. Zalta. Stanford, CA: Stanford University, 2005. https://plato.stanford.edu/entries/feminist-power/.

Alptraum, Lux. "bell hooks on the State of Feminism and How to Move Forward under Trump: *BUST* Interview." *BUST Magazine*, February–March 2017. https://bust.com/feminism/19119-the-road-ahead-bell-hooks.html.

American Alliance of Museums. *2017 National Museum Salary Survey*. Arlington, VA: American Alliance of Museums, 2017. https://artsandmuseums.utah.gov/wp-content/uploads/2019/04/2017-AAM-Salary-Survey.pdf.

American Institute of Geographic Arts (AIGA). "AIGA Design Census." 2019. https://designcensus.org/data/2019DesignCensus.pdf.

Anderson, Elizabeth. "Feminist Epistemology and Philosophy of Science." In *Stanford Encyclopedia of Philosophy*, edited by Edward N. Zalta. Stanford, CA: Stanford University Press, 2015. https://plato.stanford.edu/entries/feminism-epistemology/.

Appadurai, Arjun. *The Future as Cultural Fact: Essays on the Global Condition*. London: Verso, 2013.

Arendt, Hannah. *The Human Condition*. Chicago: University of Chicago Press, 1958.

Arenyeka, Omayeli. "How to Think Differently about Doing Good as a Creative Person." *Creative Independent*, December 14, 2018. https://thecreativeindependent.com/guides/how-to-think-differently-about-doing-good-as-a-creative-person/.

Arvin, Maile, Eve Tuck, and Angie Morrill. "Decolonizing Feminism: Challenging Connections between Settler Colonialism and Heteropatriarchy." *Feminist Formations* 25, no. 1 (2013): 8–34. doi:10.1353/ff.2013.0006.

Attfield, Judy. *Wild Things: The Material Culture of Everyday Life*. Oxford: Berg, 2000.

Bachelard, Gaston. "Corners." In *The Poetics of Space*. Translated by Maria Jolas. Boston: Beacon Press Books, 1994.

Bailey, April H., and Marianne LaFrance. "Anonymously Male: Social Media Avatar Icons Are Implicitly Male and Resistant to Change." *Cyberpsychology: Journal of Psychosocial Research on Cyberspace* 10, no. 4 (December 1, 2016): 4–8. doi:10.5817/cp2016-4-8.

Bambara, Toni Cade. "Toni Cade Bambara." Interview in *Black Women Writers at Work*, edited by Claudia Tate, 12–38. New York: Continuum, 1983.

Barbatti, Bruno. *Berber Carpets of Morocco: The Symbols, Origin and Meaning*. Courbevoie, France: ACR édition internationale, 2008.

Bardzell, Shaowen. "Feminist HCI: Taking Stock and Outlining an Agenda for Design." In *CHI '10: CHI Conference on Human Factors in Computing Systems*, 1301–1310. New York: Association for Computing Machinery, 2010.

Bardzell, Shaowen. "Utopias of Participation: Feminism, Design, and the Futures." *ACM Transactions on Human–Computer Interactions* 25, no. 1 (2018): article 6.

Bartky, Sandra. *Femininity and Domination: Studies in the Phenomenology of Oppression*. New York: Routledge, 1990.

Bataille, Georges. *Story of the Eye*. Translated by Joachim Neugroschel. New York: Penguin, 1979.

Battle-Baptiste, Whitney, and Britt Rusert, eds. *W. E. B. Du Bois's Data Portraits: Visualizing Black America*. Hudson, NY: Princeton Architectural Press, 2018.

Beasley, Chris. *What Is Feminism? An Introduction to Feminist Theory*. London: Sage, 1999.

Becker, Cynthia J. *Amazigh Arts in Morocco: Women Shaping Berber Identity*. Austin: University of Texas Press, 2006.

Belenky, Mary Field, Blythe McVicker Clinchy, Nancy Rule Goldberger, and Jill Mattuck Tarule. *Women's Ways of Knowing: The Development of Self, Voice, and Mind*. New York: Basic, 1986.

Bell, Vikki. *Feminist Imagination: Genealogies in Feminist Theory*. London: Sage, 1999.

Bennett, Cynthia, and Daniela Rosner. "The Promise of Empathy: Design, Disability, and Knowing the 'Other.'" In *CHI '19: Proceedings of the 2019 CHI Conference on Human Factors in Computing Systems*, 1–13. New York: Association for Computing Machinery, 2019. doi:10.1145/3290605.3300528.

Berne, Patricia, Aurora Levins Morales, David Langstaff, and Sins Invalid. "Ten Principles of Disability Justice." *WSQ: Women's Studies Quarterly* 46, no. 1 (2018): 227–230. doi:10.1353/wsq.2018.0003.

Bhagat, Alexis, and Lize Mogel, eds. *An Atlas of Radical Cartography*. Los Angeles: Journal of Aesthetics & Protest Press, 2007.

Bhasin, Kamla, and Lilinaz Evans. "Women on the Edge of Time." Interview by Hannah Pool. *New Internationalist*, July 2, 2014. https://newint.org/features/2014/07/01/feminism-women-edge-of-time.

Bloom, Paul. *Against Empathy: The Case for Rational Compassion*. New York: HarperCollins, 2016.

Borgi, Marta, Irene Cogliati-Dezza, Victoria Brelsford, Kerstin Meints, and Francesca Cirulli. "Baby Schema in Human and Animal Faces Induces Cuteness Perception and Gaze Allocation in Children." *Frontiers in Psychology* 5 (May 7, 2014): 10–11. doi.org/10.3389/fpsyg.2014.00411.

Brand, David. "NYC's 'Hollowed Out' Enforcement Units Struggle to Keep Pace on Housing Discrimination Cases." *City Limits Housing and Development*, June 1, 2021. https://citylimits.org/2021/06/01/nycs-hollowed-out-enforcement-units-struggle-to-keep-pace-on-housing-discrimination-cases/.

Bridle, James. *New Dark Age: Technology and the End of the Future*. Illus. ed. London: Verso, 2018.

Brodsky, Alexandra, and Rachel Kauder-Nalebuff. *The Feminist Utopia Project: Fifty-Seven Visions of a Wildly Better Future*. New York: Feminist Press, City University of New York, 2015.

brown, adrienne maree. *Emergent Strategy: Shaping Change, Changing Worlds*. Chico, CA: AK Press, 2017.

Buchanan, Richard. "Wicked Problems in Design Thinking." *Design Issues* 8, no. 2 (1992): 5–21.

Buckley, Cheryl. "Made in Patriarchy: Toward a Feminist Analysis of Women and Design." *Design Issues* 3, no. 2 (1986): 3–14. doi:10.2307/1511480.

Buckley, Cheryl. "Made in Patriarchy II: Researching (or Re-searching) Women and Design." *Design Issues* 36, no. 1 (January 1, 2020): 19–29. doi:10.1162/desi_a_00572.

Budweiser. "This Year, Budweiser's Super Bowl Spot Is an Ode to the American Spirit." News release, January 23, 2020. https://www.anheuser-busch.com/newsroom/2020/01/this-year-budweisers-super-bowl-spot-is-an-ode-to-the-american.html.

Butler, Judith. *Gender Trouble: Feminism and the Subversion of Identity*. London: Routledge, 1990.

Butler, Judith. *Undoing Gender*. New York: Routledge, 2004.

Buzon, Darin. "Design Thinking Is a Rebrand for White Supremacy." *Medium*, March 1, 2020. https://dabuzon.medium.com/design-thinking-is-a-rebrand-for-white-supremacy-b3d31aa55831.

Callanan, Maureen, B. Frazier, and S. Gorchoff. "Closing the Gender Gap: Family Conversations about Science in an 'Alice's Wonderland' Exhibit." Unpublished manuscript, University of California, Santa Cruz, 2015.

Care Collective, Andreas Chatzidakis, Jamie Hakim, Jo Litter, and Catherine Rottenberg. *The Care Manifesto: The Politics of Interdependence*. London: Verso, 2020.

Case, Menoukha Robin, and Allison V. Craig. *Introduction to Feminist Thought and Action: #WTF and How Did We Get Here? #WhosThatFeminist #WhatsThatFeminism*. New York: Routledge, Taylor & Francis, 2020.

Centre for Heritage, Arts and Textile (CHAT). *Interweaving Poetic Code*. Exhibition catalog. Hong Kong: CHAT, 2021.

Chahine, Nadine. "The Politics of Arabic Design." Paper presented at the Konstfack University of Arts, Crafts and Design, Stockholm, September 30, 2018.

Chavez, Leo R. "Spectacles of Citizenship and the 2006 Immigrant Marches." In *New World Colors: Ethnicity, Belonging and Difference in the Americas*, edited by Josef Raab, 37–49. Tempe, AZ: Bilingual Press, 2013.

Cheryan, Sapna, Victoria C. Plaut, Paul G. Davies, and Claude M. Steele. "Ambient Belonging: How Stereotypical Cues Impact Gender Participation in Computer Science." *Journal of Personality and Social Psychology* 97, no. 6 (December 2009): 1045–1060. doi:10.1037/a0016239.

Chu, Aaron. "'Inclusive Design' Has Become so Widely Used That It's Meaningless. That Has to Change." *Fast Company*, November 29, 2021. https://www.fastcompany.com/90697288/inclusive-design-has-become-so-widely-used-that-its-meaningless-that-has-to-change.

Collins, Patricia Hill. *Black Feminist Thought: Knowledge, Consciousness, and the Politics of Empowerment*. New York: Routledge, 2000.

Colon, Marcos, dir. *Stepping Softly on the Earth*. Documentary. Amazônia Latitude Films, 2021.

Combahee River Collective. *The Combahee River Collective Statement*. April 1977. https://www.blackpast.org/african-american-history/combahee-river-collective-statement-1977/.

Cornell, Drucilla. *At the Heart of Freedom: Feminism, Sex, and Equality*. Princeton, NJ: Princeton University Press, 1998.

Corrigan, Lisa, and Laura Weiderhaft. "Joy." *Lean Back: Critical Feminist Conversations*, podcast, January 1, 2021. https://leanbackpodcast.com/post/643190676442513409/joy.

Corrigan, Lisa, and Laura Weiderhaft. "Manifesto." *Lean Back: Critical Feminist Conversations*, podcast, February 15, 2016. https://leanbackpodcast.com/post/139361165789.

Costanza-Chock, Sasha. *Design Justice: Community-Led Practices to Build the Worlds We Need*. Cambridge, MA: MIT Press, 2020.

Crenshaw, Kimberlé. "Demarginalizing the Intersection of Race and Sex: A Black Feminist Critique of Antidiscrimination Doctrine, Feminist Theory and Antiracist Politics." *University of Chicago Legal Forum* 1989, no. 1 (1989): 139–167.

Criado Perez, Caroline. *Invisible Women: Data Bias in a World Designed for Men*. New York: Abrams Press, 2019.

Crippa, Benedetta. "World of Desire." MA thesis, Konstfack University of Arts, Crafts, and Design, Stockholm, 2017.

Cyril, Malkia A. "Motherhood, Media, and Building a 21st Century Movement." In *Revolutionary Mothering: Love on the Front Lines*, edited by Alexis Pauline Gumbs, China Martens, and Ma'a Williams, 30–44. Oakland, CA: PM Press, 2016.

Design Justice Network. *Design Justice Zine #2: Design Justice: An Exhibit of Emerging Design Practices*. Detroit: Design Justice Network, 2016.

D'Ignazio, Catherine, and Lauren F. Klein. *Data Feminism*. Cambridge, MA: MIT Press, 2020.

Davis, Angela Y. "Let Us All Rise Together: Radical Perspectives on Empowerment for Afro-American Women." Address, Spelman College, 1987. Reprinted in *Women, Culture and Politics*, 348–354. New York: Random House, 1989.

Davis, Angela Y. *Women, Race & Class*. New York: Penguin, 1981.

Davis, Cherry-Ann, and Nina Paim. "Does Design Care?" *Futuress*, September 10, 2021. https://futuress.org/magazine/does-design-care/.

De Beauvoir, Simone. *The Second Sex*. Translated by Constance Borde and Sheila Malovany-Chevallier. London: Random House, 2009.

De Bretteville, Sheila. "Feminist Design." *Space and Society* 6, no. 22 (1983): 98–103.

De Bretteville, Sheila. "A Reexamination of Some Aspects of the Design Arts from the Perspective of a Woman Designer." *Arts in Society: Women and the Arts* 11, no. 1 (1974): 113–124.

Di Prima, Diane. *Revolutionary Letters, Etc.* San Francisco: City Lights Books, 1979.

Dunne, Anthony, and Fiona Raby. *Speculative Everything: Design, Fiction, and Social Dreaming*. Cambridge, MA: MIT Press, 2014.

Dzodan, Flavia. "My Feminism Will Be Intersectional or It Will Be Bullshit!" *Tiger Beatdown*, October 10, 2011. http://tigerbeatdown.com/2011/10/10/my-feminism-will-be-intersectional-or-it-will-be-bullshit/.

Economic Policy Institute. "Child Care Costs in the United States." Last updated October 2020. https://www.epi.org/child-care-costs-in-the-united-states.

Escobar, Arturo. *Designs for the Pluriverse*. Durham, NC: Duke University Press, 2018.

Faulkner, Wendy. "The Technology Question in Feminism: A View from Feminist Technology Studies." *Women's Studies International Forum* 24, no. 1 (2001): 79–95.

Financial Inclusion Insights. "Pakistan Wave 5 Report: Fifth Annual FII Tracker Survey." 2018. http://finclusion.org/uploads/file/pakistan-wave-5-quicksites_final.pdf.

Firger, Jessica. "Black and White Infant Mortality Rates Show Wide Racial Disparities Still Exist." *Newsweek*, July 3, 2017. http://www.newsweek.com/black-women-infant-mortality-ratecdc-631178.

Fisher, Michelle Millar, Amber Winick, and Alexandra Lange. *Designing Motherhood: Things That Make and Break Our Births*. Cambridge, MA: MIT Press, 2021.

Foster, Shannon, Joanne Paterson Kinniburgh, and Wann Country. "There's No Place like (without) Country." In *Placemaking Fundamentals for the Built Environment*, edited by Cristina Hernandez-Santin, 63–82. Singapore: Palgrave Macmillan, 2020.

Freeman, Jo. *The Politics of Women's Liberation: A Case Study of an Emerging Social Movement and Its Relation to the Policy Process*. New York: Mckay, 1976.

Friedan, Betty. *The Feminine Mystique*. New York: Norton, 1963.

Gagliardi, Silvia. *Minority Rights, Feminism and International Law: Voices of Amazigh Women in Morocco.* New York: Routledge, 2022.

Gipson, Ferren. *Women's Work: From Feminine Arts to Feminist Art*. London: Frances Lincoln, 2022.

Goldberg, Michelle. "The Future Isn't Female Anymore." *New York Times*, June 17, 2022. https://www.nytimes.com/2022/06/17/opinion/roe-dobbs-abortion-feminism.html.

Gordon, Sarah A. *"Make It Yourself": Home Sewing, Gender, and Culture, 1890–1930*. New York: Columbia University Press, 2009.

Gram, Maggie. "On Design Thinking." *N plus One Magazine* 35 (Fall 2019). https://www.nplusonemag.com/issue-35/reviews/on-design-thinking/.

Grosz, Elizabeth. *Volatile Bodies: Toward a Corporeal Feminism*. Bloomington: Indiana University Press, 1994.

Hahn, Amanda C., Dengke Xiao, Reiner Sprengelmeyer, and David I. Perrett. "Gender Differences in the Incentive Salience of Adult and Infant Faces." *Quarterly Journal of Experimental Psychology* 66, no. 1 (January 2013): 200–208. doi:10.1080/17470218.2012.705860.

Hamraie, Aimi. *Building Access: Universal Design and the Politics of Disability*. Minneapolis: University of Minnesota Press, 2017.

Haraway, Donna J. "Situated Knowledges: The Science Question in Feminism and the Privilege of Partial Perspective." *Feminist Studies* 14, no. 3 (1988): 575–599. doi:10.2307/3178066.

Haraway, Donna J. *Staying with the Trouble: Making Kin in the Chthulucene*. Durham, NC: Duke University Press, 2016.

Harding, Sandra G., ed. *The Feminist Standpoint Theory Reader: Intellectual and Political Controversies*. New York: Routledge, 2004.

Harrington, Christina, Sheena Erete, and Anne Marie Piper. "Deconstructing Community-Based Collaborative Design." *Proceedings of the ACM on Human–Computer Interaction* 3, no. CSCW (November 7, 2019): article 216, 1–25. doi.org/10.1145/3359318.

Harris, Cheryl I. "Whiteness as Property." *Harvard Law Review* 106, no. 8 (June 1993): 1707–1791. doi:10.2307/1341787.

Hartman, Saidiya V. *Scenes of Subjection: Terror, Slavery, and Self-Making in Nineteenth-Century America*. Oxford: Oxford University Press, 1997.

Hartsock, Nancy. *Money, Sex, and Power: Toward a Feminist Historical Materialism*. Boston: Northeastern University Press, 1983.

Hedva, Johanna. "Sick Woman Theory." 2020. https://johannahedva.com/SickWomanTheory_Hedva_2020.pdf.

Hollant, Rich. "Rh_sharing_w/My Peeps." Paper presented at the Design + Diversity Conference, Columbia College, Chicago, August 1–3, 2019. https://www.youtube.com/watch?v=6_OSXeYdrH4.

hooks, bell. *All about Love: New Visions*. New York: Harper Perennial, 2018.

hooks, bell. "Beyoncé's *Lemonade* Is Capitalist Money-Making at Its Best." *Guardian*, May 11, 2016. https://www.theguardian.com/music/2016/may/11/capitalism-of-beyonce-lemonade-album.

hooks, bell. "Choosing the Margin as a Space of Radical Openness." *Journal of Cinema and Media* 36 (1989): 15–23.

hooks, bell. "Eros, Eroticism and the Pedagogical Process." *Cultural Studies* 7, no. 1 (January 1993): 58–63. doi:10.1080/09502389300490051.

hooks, bell. *Feminism Is for Everybody: Passionate Politics*. New York: Routledge, 2014.

hooks, bell. *Feminist Theory: From Margin to Center*. 1984. Reprint, London: Routledge, 2000.

hooks, bell. "Homeplace (a Site of Resistance)." In *Yearning: Race, Gender, and Cultural Politics*, 41–49. Boston: South End Press, 1990.

hooks, bell. *Teaching to Transgress: Education as the Practice of Freedom*. New York: Routledge, 1994.

hooks, bell. *The Will to Change: Men, Masculinity, and Love*. New York: Washington Square Press, 2004.

Hope, Alexis, Catherine D'Ignazio, Josephine Hoy, Rebecca Michelson, Jennifer Roberts, Kate Krontiris, and Ethan Zuckerman. "Hackathons as Participatory Design: Iterating Feminist Utopias." In *CHI '19: Proceedings of the 2019 CHI Conference on Human Factors in Computing Systems, May 2, 2019*, 1–14. New York: Association for Computing Machinery, 2019. doi:10.1145/3290605.3300291.

Hoskin, Rhea Ashley. "Femmephobia: The Role of Anti-femininity and Gender Policing in LGBTQ+ People's Experiences of Discrimination." *Sex Roles* 81, nos. 11–12 (February 20, 2019): 686–703. doi:10.1007/s11199-019-01021-3.

Hunt, Ashley. "A World Map: In Which We See...." In *An Atlas of Radical Cartography*, edited by Alexis Bhagat and Lize Mogel, 145–146. Los Angeles: Journal of Aesthetics and Protest Press, 2007.

Ilmonen, Kaisa. "Feminist Storytelling and Narratives of Intersectionality." *Signs: Journal of Women in Culture and Society* 45, no. 2 (December 2019): 347–371. doi:10.1086/704989.

Im, Jane, Jill Dimond, Melody Berton, Una Lee, Katherine Mustelier, Mark S. Ackerman, and Eric Gilbert. "Yes: Affirmative Consent as a Theoretical Framework for Understanding and Imagining Social Platforms." In *Proceedings of the 2021 CHI Conference on Human Factors in Computing Systems,* edited by Pernille Bjørn and Steven Drucker, 1–18. New York: Association for Computing Machinery, 2021.

Juvenal. "La mujer costarricense: Su fisonomía moral y la influencia en la evolución de nuestra sociedad" [The Costa Rican woman: Her moral physiognomy and its influence on our society's evolution]. In *Estudios de la mujer: Conocimiento y cambio* [Women's studies: Knowledge and change], 27. San José, Mexico: EDUCA, 1988.

Kaba, Mariame. *We Do This 'til We Free Us: Abolitionist Organizing and Transforming Justice*. Chicago: Haymarket, 2021.

Kabeer, Naila. *Gender Mainstreaming in Poverty Eradication and the Millennium Development Goals: A Handbook for Policy-Makers and Other Stakeholders*. London: Commonwealth Secretariat, 2003.

Kabeer, Naila. "Resources, Agency, Achievements: Reflections on the Measurement of Women's Empowerment." *Development and Change* 30, no. 3 (July 1999): 435–464. doi:10.1111/1467-7660.00125.

Kember, Sarah. "Notes towards a Feminist Futurist Manifesto." *Ada: A Journal of Gender, New Media, and Technology* 1, no. 1 (November 1, 2012). doi:10.7264/N3057CV3.

Khandwala, Anoushka. "What Does It Mean to Decolonize Design?" *Eye on Design*, June 5, 2019. https://eyeondesign.aiga.org/what-does-it-mean-to-decolonize-design/.

Klatt, Mary Beth. "Samplers Trace the History of Women and Their Families." *Chicago Tribune*, February 15, 1998. https://www.chicagotribune.com/news/ct-xpm-1998-02-15-9802150435-story.html.

Kletchka, Dana Carlisle. "Moralizing Influence: The Feminization of Art Museum Education." In *From Periphery to Center: Art Museum Education in the 21st Century*, edited by Pat Villenueve, 74–79. Alexandria, VA: National Art Education Association, 2007.

Knight, Linda. "Playing: Inefficiently Mapping Human and Inhuman Play in Urban Commonplaces." In *Feminist Research for 21st-Century Childhoods*, edited by B. Denise Hodgins, 139–148. London: Bloomsbury Academic, 2019.

Kumar, Neha, Naveena Karusala, Azra Ismail, Marisol Wong-Villacres, and Aditya Vishwanath. "Engaging Feminist Solidarity for Comparative Research, Design, and Practice." *Proceedings of the ACM on Human–Computer Interaction* 3, no. CSCW (November 7, 2019): article 167, 1–24. doi:10.1145/3359269.

Lane, Marty Maxwell, and Rebecca Tegtmeyer. *Collaboration in Design Education*. London: Bloomsbury Visual Arts, 2020.

Le Guin, Ursula K. *Ursula K. Le Guin: The Last Interview and Other Conversations*. Edited by David Streitfeld. New York: Melville House, 2019.

Lennon, Kathleen. "Feminist Perspectives on the Body." In *Stanford Encyclopedia of Philosophy*, edited by Edward N. Zalta. Stanford, CA: Stanford University, 2019. https://plato.stanford.edu/entries/feminist-body/.

Lisy, Brandon. "Steve Wozniak on Apple, the Computer Revolution, and Working with Steve Jobs." *Bloomberg Businessweek*, December 4, 2014. https://www.bloomberg.com/news/articles/2014-12-04/apple-steve-wozniak-on-the-early-years-with-steve-jobs.

Lohan, Maria. "Constructive Tensions in Feminist Technology Studies." *Social Studies of Science* 30, no. 6 (December 2000): 895–916. doi:10.1177/030631200030006003.

Lorde, Audre. "Age, Race, Class, and Sex: Women Redefining Difference." In *Sister Outsider: Essays and Speeches*, 114–123. Berkeley, CA: Crossing Press, 1984.

Lorde, Audre. "The Master's Tools Will Never Dismantle the Master's House." In *Feminist Postcolonial Theory: A Reader*, edited by Reina Lewis and Sara Mills, 25–28. Edinburgh: Edinburgh University Press, 2003.

Lorde, Audre. "Poetry Is Not a Luxury." In *The Master's Tools Will Never Dismantle the Master's House*, 5. 1984; reprint London: Penguin, 2018.

Lorde, Audre. "Uses of the Erotic: The Erotic as Power." In *Sister Outsider: Essays and Speeches*, 53–59. Berkeley, CA: Crossing Press, 1984.

Lu-Culligan, Alice, and Randi Hutter Epstein. "No, We Don't Know If Vaccines Change Your Period." *New York Times*, April 20, 2021. https://www.nytimes.com/2021/04/20/opinion/coronavirus-vaccines-menstruation-periods.html.

Lupton, Ellen. "Graphic Design in the Urban Landscape." In *Design and Feminism: Re-visioning Spaces, Places, and Everyday Things*, edited by Joan Rothschild, 57–65. New Brunswick, NJ: Rutgers University Press, 1999.

Maines, Rachel P. *Hedonizing Technologies: Paths to Pleasure in Hobbies and Leisure*. Baltimore: Johns Hopkins University Press, 2009.

Mann, Bonnie, and Jean Keller. "Why a Feminist Volume on Pluralism?" *Philosophical Topics* 41, no. 2 (2013): 1–11.

Manzini, Ezio. *Design, When Everybody Designs: An Introduction to Design for Social Innovation*. Translated by Rachel Coad. Cambridge, MA: MIT Press, 2015.

Mareis, Claudia, and Nina Paim. "Design Struggles: An Attempt to Imagine Design Otherwise." In *Design Struggles: Intersecting Histories, Pedagogies, and Perspectives*, edited by Claudia Mareis and Nina Paim, 11–22. Amsterdam: Valiz, 2021.

Mareis, Claudia, and Nina Paim, eds. *Design Struggles: Intersecting Histories, Pedagogies, and Perspectives*. Amsterdam: Valiz, 2021.

Martin, Nina. "Black Mothers Keep Dying after Giving Birth. Shalon Irving's Story Explains Why." NPR, December 7, 2017. https://www.npr.org/2017/12/07/568948782/black-mothers-keep-dying-after-giving-birth-shalon-irvings-story-explains-why.

Martins, Luiza Prado de O. "Privilege and Oppression: Towards a Feminist Speculative Design." In *Proceedings of DRS 2014: Design's Big Debates*, edited by Youn-kyung Lim, Kristina Niedderer, Johan Redström, Erik Stolterman, and Anna Valtonen. Umeå, Sweden: Design Research Society, Umeå Institute of Design, Umeå University, 2014.

McDowell, Ceasar. "Design for the Margins." TEDx Indiana University, June 9, 2016.

McKenna, Erin. *The Task of Utopia: A Pragmatist and Feminist Perspective*. Lanham, MD: Rowman & Littlefield, 2001.

Miller, Cheryl D. "Black Designers: Missing in Action." *Print*, September–October 1987, 58–65, 136–138.

Miller, Jean Baker. "Women and Power." In *Rethinking Power*, edited by Thomas E. Wartenberg, 240–267. Albany: State University of New York Press, 1992.

Mohanty, Chandra Talpade. *Feminism without Borders: Decolonizing Theory, Practicing Solidarity*. Durham, NC: Duke University Press, 2003.

Morgan, Lewis Henry. *League of the Ho-Dé-No San-Nee or Iroquois*. 1851. Reprint, Rochester, NY: Sage, 1964.

Morgan, Robin. "Planetary Feminism: Politics of the 21st Century." In *Sisterhood Is Global: The International Women's Movement Anthology*, edited by Robin Morgan, 1–37. New York: Feminist Press, 1996.

Morozov, Evgeny. *To Save Everything, Click Here: The Folly of Technological Solutionism*. New York: PublicAffairs, 2014.

Munro, Silas. "Designing Public Action With Communities." Keynote address, LA Design Festival, Los Angeles, CA, 2019.

Murphy, Michele. *Seizing the Means of Reproduction: Entanglements of Feminism, Health and Technoscience*. Durham, NC: Duke University Press, 2012.

Mushtaq, Sehrish, and Fawad Baig. "Reclaiming Public and Digital Spaces: The Conundrum of Acceptance for the Feminist Movement in Pakistan." In *The Routledge Handbook of Religion, Gender and Society*, edited by Emma Tomalin and Caroline Starkey, 103–118. New York: Routledge, 2022.

Naji, Myriem. "Gender and Materiality in the Making." *Journal of Material Culture* 14, no. 1 (March 2009): 47–73.

New York City Department of Homeless Services. "NYC Department of Homeless Services Brings Women of Color Faith and Community Leaders Together for New, Targeted Homelessness Prevention Event." Press release, June 24, 2016. https://www1. nyc.gov/site/dhs/about/press-releases/ prevention-breakfast-press-release.page.

New York University. "Health Literacy." 2020. https://www.nyu.edu/life/safety-health-wellness/live-well-nyu/priority-areas/health-literacy.html.

Noddings, Nel. *Caring: A Feminine Approach to Ethics & Moral Education*. Berkeley: University of California Press, 2013.

Ober, Maya, Anja Neidhardt, and Griselda Flesler. "Not a Toolkit: A Conversation on the Discomfort of Feminist Design Pedagogy." In *Design Struggles: Intersecting Histories, Pedagogies, and Perspectives*, edited by Claudia Mareis and Nina Paim, 205–225. Amsterdam: Valiz, 2021.

Oka, Cynthia Dewi. "Mothering as Revolutionary Praxis." In *Revolutionary Mothering: Love on the Front Lines*, edited by Alexis Pauline Gumbs, China Martens, and Ma'a Williams, 50–64. Oakland, CA: PM Press, 2016.

O'Neil, Cathy. *Weapons of Math Destruction: How Big Data Increases Inequality and Threatens Democracy*. London: Penguin, 2018.

Owermohle, Sarah. "Why Louisiana's Maternal Mortality Rates Are so High." *Politico*, May 19, 2022. https://www.politico.com/ news/2022/05/19/why-louisianas-maternal-mortality-rates-are-so-high-00033832.

Papanek, Victor. *Design for the Real World: Human Ecology and Social Change*. New York: Pantheon, 1971.

Pedwell, Carolyn. *Affective Relations: The Transnational Politics of Empathy*. London: Palgrave Macmillan, 2014.

Peluso, Nancy Lee. "Whose Woods Are These? Counter-Mapping Forest Territories in Kalimantan, Indonesia." *Antipode* 27, no. 4 (October 1995): 383–406. doi:10.1111/j.1467-8330.1995.tb00286.x.

Phadke, Shilpa, Sameera Khan, and Shilpa Ranade. *Why Loiter? Women and Risk on Mumbai Streets*. New Delhi: Penguin, 2011.

Planned Parenthood. "Understanding Consent Is as Easy as FRIES." Tumblr, April 9, 2017. https://plannedparenthood.tumblr.com/post/148506806862/understanding-consent-is-as-easy-as-fries-consent.

Pozniak, Alyssa, Katherine Wen, Krista Olson, Kelly Daley, and Jacob Klerman. "Family and Medical Leave in 2012: Detailed Results Appendix." Abt Associates, September 6, 2012.

Puig de la Bellacasa, María. *Matters of Care: Speculative Ethics in More Than Human Worlds*. Minneapolis: University of Minnesota Press, 2017.

Quinn, Heather Snyder, and Ayako Takase. *Matriarchal Design Futures: Workbook*. Providence, RI: Binch Press, 2022. matriarchalfutures.design.

Raheem, Octavia F. *Pause, Rest, Be: Stillness Practices for Courage in Times of Change*. Boulder, CO: Shambhala, 2022.

Reinharz, Shulamit, with the assistance of Lynn Davidman. *Feminist Methods in Social Research*. New York: Oxford University Press, 1992.

Retallack, Joan. *The Poethical Wager*. Berkeley: University of California Press, 2003.

Right to Counsel Coalition, JustFix.nyc. "NYC's Top 20 Worst Evictors in 2019." N.d. https://www.worstevictorsnyc.org/evictors-list/citywide/.

Rincón, Cami, Os Keyes, and Corinne Cath. "Speaking from Experience: Trans/Non-binary Requirements for Voice-Activated AI." *Proceedings of the ACM on Human–Computer Interaction* 5 (2021): article 132, 1–27. doi:10.1145/3449206.

Rosner, Daniela K. *Critical Fabulations: Reworking the Methods and Margins of Design*. Cambridge, MA: MIT Press, 2020.

Rothschild, Joan, ed. *Design and Feminism: Re-visioning Spaces, Places, and Everyday Things*. New Brunswick, NJ: Rutgers University Press, 1999.

Rothwell, Jonathan, and Lydia Saad. "How Have US Working Women Fared during the Pandemic?" Gallup, March 8, 2021. https://news.gallup.com/poll/330533/working-women-fared-during-pandemic.aspx.

Rudwick, Elliott M., and August Meier. "Black Man in the 'White City': Negroes and the Columbian Exposition, 1893." *Phylon (1960–)* 26, no. 4 (1965): 354–361. doi:10.2307/273699.

Sadiqi, Fatima. *Moroccan Feminist Discourses*. New York: Palgrave Macmillan, 2014.

Sarasota Police Department. *Sarasota Police News Conference: Launch of Blue + You—April 25, 2014*. Video, YouTube, April 25, 2014, 10:45. https://www.youtube.com/watch?v=1528b0Ixh9E&list=UUA-v3ISGsOkF51HHHRIcUtg.

Sarikakis, Katharine, Romona R. Rush, Autumn Grubb-Swetnam, and Christina Lane. "Feminist Theory and Research." In *An Integrated Approach to Communication Theory and Research*, edited by Don W. Stacks and Michael B. Salwen, 504–523. New York: Taylor & Francis, 2008.

Schalk, Meike, Thérèse Kristiansson, and Ramia Mazé, eds. *Feminist Futures of Spatial Practice: Materialisms, Activisms, Dialogues, Pedagogies, Projections*. Bamberg, Germany: Spurbuchverlag, 2017.

Scotford, Martha. "Messy History vs. Neat History: Toward an Expanded View of Women in Graphic Design." *Visible Language* 28, no. 4 (October 1994): 367–387.

Sengers, Phoebe, Kreisten Boehner, Shay David, and Joseph Kaye. "Reflective Design." In *Proceedings of the 4th Decennial Conference on Critical Computing: Between Sense and Sensibility*, 49–58. New York: Association for Computing Machinery, 2005. doi.org/10.1145/1094562.1094569.

Serano, Julia. "Reclaiming Femininity." In *Excluded: Making Feminist and Queer Movements More Inclusive*, 48–69. Berkeley, CA: Seal Press, 2013.

Smith, Dorothy E. "From the Margins: Women's Standpoint as a Method of Inquiry in the Social Sciences." *Gender, Technology and Development* 1, no. 1 (March 1997): 113–135. doi:10.1080/09718524.1997.11909845.

Solano Arias, Marta E. "A 90 años de la fundación de la Liga Feminista Costarricense: Los derechos políticos" [Ninety years after the foundation of the Costa Rican Feminist League: The political rights]. *Revista derecho electoral del Tribunal Supremo de Elecciones de la República de Costa Rica*, no. 17 (2014): 358–375.

Søndergaard, Marie Louise Juul. "Staying with the Trouble through Design: Critical-Feminist Design of Intimate Technology." PhD diss., Aarhus University, 2018.

Spencer-Wood, Suzanne M. "Feminist Theorizing of Patriarchal Colonialism, Power Dynamics, and Social Agency Materialized in Colonial Institutions." *International Journal of Historical Archaeology* 20, no. 3 (July 27, 2016): 477–491.

Sprague, Joey. *Feminist Methodologies for Critical Researchers: Bridging Differences*. Lanham, MD: Rowman & Littlefield, 2016.

Springgay, Stephanie, and Sarah E. Truman. *Walking Methodologies in a More-Than-Human World: Walking Lab*. London: Routledge, 2018.

Stinson, Liz. "Terry Irwin on Navigating a Mid-career Crisis and Solving Big Problems through Design." *Eye on Design*, August 16, 2021. https://eyeondesign.aiga.org/terry-irwin-on-navigating-a-mid-career-crisis-and-solving-big-problems-through-design/.

Swigger, Jessie. "The First Four: Origin Stories of the First Children's Museums in the United States." *Hand to Hand* 31 (2017): 2–3.

Taylor, Keeanga-Yamahtta. *How We Get Free: Black Feminism and the Combahee River Collective*. Chicago: Haymarket, 2017.

Thomas, Greg. *The Sexual Demon of Colonial Power: Pan-African Embodiment and Erotic Schemes of Empire*. Bloomington: Indiana University Press, 2007.

Treisman, Karen. *A Treasure Box for Creating Trauma-Informed Organizations: A Ready-to-Use Resource for Trauma, Adversity, and Culturally Informed, Infused and Responsive Systems*. London: Jessica Kingsley, 2021.

Tronto, Joan C. *Moral Boundaries: A Political Argument for an Ethics of Care*. London: Routledge, 1993.

Tunstall, Dori. "Seven Principles of Designing Conditions for Community Self-Determination." In *A Feminist Organization's Handbook*, 22–25. Los Angeles: Women's Center for Creative Work, 2017.

Tyson, Lois. *Using Critical Theory: How to Read and Write about Literature*. Milton Park, UK: Taylor & Francis, 2011.

US Center for Preparedness and Response. "Infographic: 6 Guiding Principles to a Trauma Informed Approach." Last reviewed September 17, 2020. https://www.cdc.gov/cpr/infographics/6_principles_trauma_info.htm.

US Centers for Disease Control and Prevention (CDC). "Access to Health Care." *CDC Vital Signs*, January 6, 2020. https://www.cdc.gov/vitalsigns/healthcareaccess/index.html.

US Centers for Disease Control and Prevention (CDC). "Healthy People 2020: Legal and Policy Resources Related to Access to Health Services." 2016. https://www.cdc.gov/phlp/publications/topic/hp2020/access.html.

Vaid-Menon, Alok. *Beyond the Gender Binary*. New York: Penguin Workshop, 2020.

Vaid-Menon, Alok. *Femme in Public*. New York: Alok Vaid-Menon, 2017.

Valdes, Francisco. "Unpacking Hetero-patriarchy: Tracing the Conflation of Sex, Gender & Sexual Orientation to Its Origins." *Yale Journal of Law and the Humanities* 8, no. 1 (1996): 161–211.

Vedantam, Shanker. "Remembering Anarcha, Lucy, and Betsey: The Mothers of Modern Gynecology." NPR, February 7, 2017. https://www.npr.org/2017/02/07/513764158/remembering-anarcha-lucy-and-betsey-the-mothers-of-modern-gynecology.

Vostral, Sharra, and Deana McDonagh. "How to Add Feminist Approaches into Design Courses." *Design Principles and Practices* 4, no. 4 (2010): 113–128. doi:10.18848/1833-1874/cgp/v04i04/37928.

Wachter-Boettcher, Sara. *Technically Wrong: Sexist Apps, Biased Algorithms, and Other Threats of Toxic Tech*. New York: Norton, 2018.

Wajcman, Judy. *TechnoFeminism*. London: Wiley, 2004.

Walia, Harsha. *Border and Rule: Global Migration, Capitalism, and the Rise of Racist Nationalism.* Chicago: Haymarket, 2021.

Wang, Jen. "Now You See It: Helvetica, Modernism and the Status Quo of Design." *Medium*, December 8, 2016. https://medium.com/@earth.terminal/now-you-see-it-110b77fd13db.

Wang, Tricia. "The Most Popular Design Thinking Strategy Is BS." *Fast Company*, June 28, 2021. https://www.fastcompany.com/90649969/the-most-popular-design-thinking-strategy-is-bs.

Warren, Virginia Lee. "Woman Who Led an Office Revolution Rules an Empire of Modern Design." *New York Times*, September 1, 1964.

Wells, Ida B., ed. *The Reason Why the Colored American Is Not in the World's Columbian Exposition*. Chicago, 1893.

Westmarland, Nicole. "The Quantitative/Qualitative Debate and Feminist Research: A Subjective View of Objectivity." *Forum: Qualitative Social Research* 2, no. 1 (2001): article 13.

Wieners, Carrie J. "Leadership in the Museum: A Possible Shift in Gender Representation." *Collections* 6, nos. 1–2 (March 2010): 7–24. doi:10.1177/1550190610006001-202.

Williams, Lauren. "Making Room." *Futuress*, October 12, 2021. https://futuress.org/magazine/making-room/.

Winslow, Barbara, and Raymond Lifchez. *Design for Independent Living: The Environment and Physically Disabled People*. New York: Whitney Library of Design, 1979.

Withers, A. J. *Disability Politics and Theory*. Winnipeg, Canada: Fernwood, 2019.

Wonders, Bec. "Please Say More." Interview by Nina Paim. *Futuress*, March 8, 2022. https://futuress.org/stories/please-say-more/.

Wood, Ellen Meiksins. *The Origin of Capitalism: A Longer View*. London: Verso, 2017.

Woodly, Deva. "Black Feminist Visions and the Politics of Healing in the Movement for Black Lives." In *Women Mobilizing Memory*, edited by Ayşe Gül Altınay, María José Contreras, Marianne Hirsch, Jean Howard, Banu Karaca, and Alisa Solomon, 219–238. New York: Columbia University Press, 2019.

World Economic Forum. *Global Gender Gap Report 2020*. Geneva: World Economic Forum, 2020.

Wright, Erik Olin. *How to Be an Anticapitalist in the 21st Century*. London: Verso Books, 2019.

Young, Iris Marion. *Justice and the Politics of Difference*. Princeton, NJ: Princeton University Press, 1990.

Young, Josie, and Feminist Internet. "Feminist Design Tool Defensible Decision Making for Interaction Design and AI." Feminist Internet, 2021. https://ugc.futurelearn.com/uploads/files/16/b0/16b088ad-6145-45eb-b5d8-3753a41b4b88/2-10_FeministDesignTool_2.0.pdf.

Zuboff, Shoshana. *The Age of Surveillance Capitalism: The Fight for a Human Future at the New Frontier of Power*. New York: PublicAffairs, 2019.

Recommended Reading

The following texts are recommended for further exploration of the topics within each chapter. The lists were compiled with input from all contributing authors.

Feminism and Feminist Design

Adichie, Chimamanda Ngozi. *We Should All Be Feminists*. New York: Knopf Doubleday, 2014.

Ahmed, Sara. *Living a Feminist Life*. Durham, NC: Duke University Press, 2017.

Beasley, Chris. *What Is Feminism? An Introduction to Feminist Theory*. London: Sage, 1999.

Buckley, Cheryl. "Made in Patriarchy: Toward a Feminist Analysis of Women and Design." *Design Issues* 3, no. 2 (1986): 3–14. doi:10.2307/1511480.

Buckley, Cheryl. "Made in Patriarchy II: Researching (or Re-searching) Women and Design." *Design Issues* 36, no. 1 (January 1, 2020): 19–29. doi:10.1162/desi_a_00572.

Case, Menoukha Robin, and Allison V. Craig. *Introduction to Feminist Thought and Action*. New York: Routledge, Taylor & Francis, 2020.

De Beauvoir, Simone. *The Second Sex*. London: Random House, 2009.

De Bretteville, Sheila. "Feminist Design." *Space and Society* 6, no. 22 (1983): 98–103.

De Bretteville, Sheila. "A Reexamination of Some Aspects of the Design Arts from the Perspective of a Woman Designer." *Arts in Society: Women and the Arts* 11, no. 1 (1974): 113–124.

Freedman, Estelle B., ed. *The Essential Feminist Reader*. New York: Random House, 2007.

Mohanty, Chandra Talpade. *Feminism without Borders: Decolonizing Theory, Practicing Solidarity*. Durham, NC: Duke University Press, 2003.

Morgan, Robin, ed. *Sisterhood Is Global: The International Women's Movement Anthology*. New York: Feminist Press, 1996.

Morgan, Robin, ed. *Sisterhood Is Powerful: An Anthology of Writings from the Women's Liberation Movement*. New York: Random House, 1970.

Rothchild, Joan, ed. *Design and Feminism: Re-visioning Spaces, Places and Everyday Things*. New Brunswick, NJ: Rutgers University Press, 1999.

Power

Ahmed, Sara. *Complaint!* Durham: Duke University Press, 2021.

Armbrust, Jennifer. *Proposals for the Feminine Economy*. Topanga, CA: The Fourth Wave, 2018.

Attfield, Judy. *Wild Things: The Material Culture of Everyday Life*. Oxford: Berg, 2000.

Beck, Koa. *White Feminism: From the Suffragettes to Influencers and Who They Left Behind*. New York: Simon & Schuster, 2021.

Butler, Judith. *Gender Trouble: Feminism and the Subversion of Identity*. London: Routledge, 1990.

Collins, Patricia Hill. *Black Feminist Thought: Knowledge, Consciousness, and the Politics of Empowerment*. New York: Routledge, 2000.

Collins, Patricia Hill, and Sirma Bilge. *Intersectionality*. Cambridge, UK: Polity Press, 2016.

Costanza-Chock, Sasha. *Design Justice: Community-Led Practices to Build the Worlds We Need*. Cambridge, MA: MIT Press, 2020.

Crenshaw, Kimberlé. "Mapping the Margins: Intersectionality, Identity Politics, and Violence against Women of Color." *Stanford Law Review* 43, no. 6 (1991): 1241–1299. https://doi.org/10.2307/1229039.

Davis, Angela Y. *Women, Race & Class*. New York: Random House, 1981.

hooks, bell. *Feminist Theory: From Margin to Center*. 1984. Reprint, London: Routledge, 2000.

Noble, Safiya Umoja. *Algorithms of Oppression: How Search Engines Reinforce Racism*. New York: NYU Press, 2018.

Olufemi, Lola. *Feminism, Interrupted: Disrupting Power*. London: Pluto Press, 2020.

Taylor, Keeanga-Yamahtta. *How We Get Free: Black Feminism and the Combahee River Collective*. Chicago: Haymarket, 2017.

Walters, Kelly, Jennifer Rittner, Lesley-Ann Noel, Kareem Collie, Penina Acayo Laker, and Anne H. Berry, eds. *The Black Experience in Design: Identity, Expression & Reflection*. New York: Skyhorse, 2022.

Wizinsky, Matthew. *Design after Capitalism: Transforming Design Today for an Equitable Tomorrow*. Cambridge, MA: MIT Press, 2022.

Wright, Erik Olin. *How to Be an Anticapitalist in the 21st Century*. London: Verso, 2019.

Knowledge

Alcoff, Linda Martín. *Visible Identities: Race, Gender, and the Self*. New York: Oxford University Press, 2006.

Alcoff, Linda, and Elizabeth Potter, eds. *Feminist Epistemologies*. New York: Routledge, 1993.

Belenky, Mary Field, Blythe McVicker Clinchy, Nancy Rule Goldberger, and Jill Mattuck Tarule. *Women's Ways of Knowing: The Development of Self, Voice, and Mind*. New York: Basic, 1986.

Criado Perez, Caroline. *Invisible Women: Data Bias in a World Designed for Men*. New York: Abrams Press, 2019.

D'Ignazio, Catherine, and Lauren F. Klein. *Data Feminism*. Cambridge, MA: MIT Press, 2020.

Guffey, Elizabeth. *Designing Disability: Symbols, Space, and Society*. London: Bloomsbury, 2018.

Hamraie, Aimi. *Building Access: Universal Design and the Politics of Disability*. Minneapolis: University of Minnesota Press, 2017.

Haraway, Donna J. "Situated Knowledges: The Science Question in Feminism and the Privilege of Partial Perspective." *Feminist Studies* 14, no. 3 (1988): 575–599. doi:10.2307/3178066.

Harding, Sandra, ed. *Feminist Standpoint Theory Reader: Intellectual and Political Controversies*. New York: Routledge, 2004.

hooks, bell. "Homeplace (a Site of Resistance)." In *Yearning: Race, Gender, and Cultural Politics*, 41–49. Boston: South End Press, 1990.

Kafer, Alison. *Feminist, Queer, Crip*. Bloomington: University of Indiana Press, 2013.

Nivedita, Menon. *Seeing Like a Feminist*. New York: Penguin, 2012.

Reinharz, Shulamit, with the assistance of Lynn Davidman. *Feminist Methods in Social Research*. New York: Oxford University Press, 1992.

Resnick, Elizabeth, ed. *Developing Citizen Designers*. New York: Bloomsbury, 2016.

Sprague, Joey. *Feminist Methodologies for Critical Researchers*. London: Rowman & Littlefield, 2016.

Wong, Alice, ed. *Disability Visibility: First-Person Stories from the Twenty-First Century*. New York: Random House, 2020.

Care

brown, adrienne maree. *Pleasure Activism: The Politics of Feeling Good*. Chico, CA: AK Press, 2019.

Care Collective, Andreas Chatzidakis, Jamie Hakim, Jo Litter, and Catherine Rottenberg. *The Care Manifesto: The Politics of Interdependence*. London: Verso, 2020.

Fisher, Michelle Millar, and Amber Winick. *Designing Motherhood: Things That Make and Break Our Births*. Cambridge, MA: MIT Press, 2021.

Garbes, Angela. *Essential Labor: Mothering as Social Change*. New York: HarperCollins, 2022.

Hendren, Sara. *What Can a Body Do? How We Meet the Built World*. New York: Random House, 2020.

Holmes, Kay. *Mismatch: How Inclusion Shapes Design*. Cambridge, MA: MIT Press, 2018.

Kern, Leslie. *Feminist City: Claiming Space in a Man-Made World.* Toronto: Between Lines, 2019.

Lorde, Audre. *The Master's Tools Will Never Dismantle the Master's House*. New York: Random House, 2018.

Massey, Doreen. *Space, Place and Gender*. Cambridge, UK: Polity Press, 2013.

Meenadchi. *Decolonizing Non-violent Communication*. Los Angeles: Co-Conspirator Press, 2019.

Nelson, Maggie. *The Argonauts*. Minneapolis, MN: Graywolf Press, 2015.

Pauline, Alexis, China Martens, and Mai'a Williams, eds. *Revolutionary Mothering: Love on the Front Lines*. Oakland, CA: PA Press, 2016.

Puig de la Bellacasa, María. *Matters of Care: Speculative Ethics in More Than Human Worlds*. Minneapolis: University of Minnesota Press, 2017.

Ross, Loretta, and Rickie Solinger. *Reproductive Justice: An Introduction*. Oakland: University of California Press, 2017.

Tronto, Joan. *Moral Boundaries: A Political Argument for an Ethics of Care*. London: Routledge, 1993.

Tsing, Anna Lowenhaupt. *The Mushroom at the End of the World: On the Possibility of Life in Capitalist Ruins*. Princeton, NJ: Princeton University Press, 2021.

Plurality

Escobar, Arturo. *Designs for the Pluriverse*. Durham, NC: Duke University Press, 2017.

Halberstam, Judith [Jack]. *The Queer Art of Failure*. Durham, NC: Duke University Press, 2011.

Hester, Helen. *Xenofeminism*. Cambridge, UK: Polity Press, 2018.

hooks, bell. *Teaching to Transgress: Education as the Practice of Freedom*. New York: Routledge, 1994.

Mareis, Claudia, and Nina Paim, eds. *Design Struggles: Intersecting Histories, Pedagogies, and Perspectives*. Amsterdam: Valiz, 2021.

McCann, Hannah. *Queering Femininity*. New York: Routledge, 2019.

Vaid-Menon, Alok. *Beyond the Gender Binary*. New York: Random House, 2020.

Liberation

Boggs, Grace Lee. *The Next American Revolution: Sustainable Activism for the Twenty-First Century*. Berkley: University of California Press, 2011.

Brodsky, Alexandra, and Rachel Kauder Nalebuff. *The Feminist Utopia Project*. New York: Feminist Press, 2015.

brown, adrienne maree. *Emergent Strategy: Shaping Change, Changing Worlds*. Chico, CA: AK Press, 2017.

Crabb, Cindy, ed. *Learning Good Consent: On Healthy Relationships and Survivor Support*. Chico, CA: AK Press, 2016.

Davis, Angela Y., Gina Dent, Erica R. Meiners, and Beth E. Richie. *Abolition. Feminism. Now*. Chicago: Haymarket, 2022.

Drew, Kimberly, and Jenna Wortham. *Black Futures*. New York: Random House, 2020.

Haraway, Donna. "A Cyborg Manifesto: Science, Technology, and Socialist-Feminism in the Late Twentieth Century." *Simians, Cyborgs and Women: The Reinvention of Nature*. New York: Routledge, 1991.

Haraway, Donna J. *Staying with the Trouble: Making Kin in the Chthulucene*. Durham, NC: Duke University Press, 2016.

Rosner, Daniela K. *Critical Fabulations: Reworking the Methods and Margins of Design*. Cambridge, MA: MIT Press, 2020.

Russell, Legacy. *Glitch Feminism: A Manifesto*. London: Verso, 2020.

Saba, Mariella, Tamika Lewis, Tawana Petty, Seeta Peña Gangadharan, and Virginia Eubanks. *From Paranoia to Power: Our Data Bodies Project 2016 Report*. May 2017. https://www.odbproject.org/wp-content/uploads/2016/12/ODB-Community-Report-7-24.pdf.

Community

Ahmed, Sara. *Willful Subjects*. Durham, NC: Duke University Press, 2014.

Beins, Agatha. *Liberation in Print: Feminist Periodicals and Social Movement Identity*. Athens, GA: University of Georgia Press, 2017.

Frichot, Héléne. *How to Make Yourself a Feminist Design Power Tool*. Baunach, Germany: Spurbuchverlag, 2016.

hooks, bell. *All about Love: New Visions*. New York: HarperCollins, 2001.

hooks, bell. *Feminism Is for Everybody: Passionate Politics*. New York: Routledge, 2015.

hooks, bell. *Teaching Community: A Pedagogy of Hope*. New York: Routledge, 2003.

Kaba, Mariame. *We Do This 'til We Free Us: Abolitionist Organizing and Transforming Justice*. Chicago: Haymarket, 2021.

Kim Hyun Mee. *Feminist Lifestyle*. 2021.

Lee Min-kyeong. *Reclaim the Language: How to Deal with a Sexist*. 2017.

Lorde, Audre. *Sister Outsider: Essays and Speeches*. New York: Random House, 1984.

Lupton, Ellen, and Jennifer Tobias. *Extra Bold: A Feminist, Inclusive, Anti-racist, Nonbinary Field Guide for Graphic Designers*. New York: Princeton Architectural Press, 2021.

Index

Disability design
  barriers, 61, 62
  design frameworks, 49, 59–63, 79, 155
  open-source programming, 201–202
Disciplinary power, 15–16, 18n20
Discrimination, ix, 69–72, 81, 117, 121n10,
    122–123, 131, 140, 173, 199, 207, 208
Dominant knowledge, 46

Ecological mapping, 109–110, 112–113
Editorial/publication design, 105–108, 195,
    212–216
Educational institutions, 23–27, 140–144
Embodiment, 91, 93, 95, 170
Empathy, 78–79, 81, 98–99, 170
Empowerment, 53–54, 119, 129, 210
Empty pluralism, 119, 122–125
Entrepreneurship, 64, 66–68
Epistemologies, feminist, 45–50
Equality, 2–4, 24, 36, 64, 66, 118, 210
Equity. *See also* Social inequity
  branding identities, 30
  care-related practices, 77, 99, 164
  collaborative practices, 123, 156
  community engagement, 194–196
  consentful technologies, 180
  design frameworks, 1–2, 6–7, 28, 49, 51, 178,
    210
  futurism/futuring practices, 156–157, 175
  gender constructs, 64
  museum exhibition design, 135
  patriarchal societies, 64
  pluralism, 148
  power structures, 13, 17
  visual literacy, 129
Erotic technologies, 176
Exhibition design, 135–139
Exoskeletons, 101–103
Exploitation
  capitalism, 14–15
  care-related practices, 78, 98
  design frameworks, 6
  patriarchal societies, 119
  power structures, 1–2
  social media platforms, 173
  visual literacy, 126–130

women weavers, 148–149
Expressive typefaces, 36–38

Fabulation, 109, 112–113, 175. *See also*
  Storytelling
Facebook, 173
Family-leave policies, 164–165
Feminine design qualities, 135–139
Feminist branding, 28–32
Feminist Center for Creative Work (FCCW),
  194–198
Feminist Designer Social Club (FDSC),
  203–206
Feminist epistemologies, 45–50
Feminist movement, 2–4, 56, 59, 153–157,
  163–164, 189–193
Feminist research methodologies, 46–50
Femmephobia, 135, 139
Femvertising, 30
Fiber artwork, 136, 145–149
Financial inclusion, 51–53
Fluid typefaces, 37–38
Fonts, 31, 34–38
Freedom, 153–154
Futurism/futuring practices, 153–157,
  162–163, 170–179, 212–217

Gender constructs
  binary individuals, 14, 118, 121, 121n10
  design frameworks, 2, 14, 17, 20–21, 23–26,
    122–123
  discriminatory practices, 69–72, 135,
    207–208
  feminist movement, 3
  financial inclusion, 51–53
  intersectionality, 16, 28
  museum exhibition design, 135–139
  patriarchal societies, 64, 66, 145, 148–149,
    153, 170, 210
  pluralism, 118
  privacy norms, 53, 173
  social inequities, 27, 64, 66, 170
  stereotypes, 23, 37, 141
  surveillance platforms, 173
  transgender individuals, 131–134, 139
  trauma-related experiences, 81